THE TRIAL OF MARSHAL PÉTAIN

Other books by Jules Roy

JOURNEY THROUGH CHINA

THE BATTLE OF DIENBIENPHU

THE TRIAL OF
Marshal Pétain

✤ ────────────────────────────────

JULES ROY

Translated from the French by Robert Baldick
with an introduction by Douglas Johnson
Professor of Modern History, University of Birmingham

FABER AND FABER
24 Russell Square London

First published in England in mcmlxviii
by Faber and Faber Limited
24 Russell Square London WC1
Printed in Great Britain by
Latimer Trend & Co Whitstable
All rights reserved

This book was originally published in France under the title
Le Grand Naufrage. © 1966 by René Julliard.

To Sublieutenant Michel Revault d'Allonnes,
lost at sea on November 8, 1942, on board the
submarine *Argonaute,* and to all those who
believed they were serving their country by
serving Marshal Pétain, this book is dedicated.

Contents

Acknowledgments

The author has been able to evoke the atmosphere of the trial in detail thanks to the reports of Georges Bonyx, Francine Bonitzer and Jean Dutourd, Germaine Picard-Moch, Georges Altschuler, Maurice Clavel, Jean Schlumberger, Paul Turpaud, Pierre Bénard and Joseph Kessel, Madeleine Jacob, Angèle Veyre and Jacques Debû-Bridel, René L'Hermitte and Paul Vienney, Fernand Pouey, André Chassaignon, Rémy Roure, Claire Gonon, Pierre Scize, Georges Salvago, Alex Ancel, Pierre Demartre, J. Luciani and J. P. Daras, Jacques Vico, Léon Werth, Georges Lesur (Géo London), Paul Regage, published in Paris newspapers of the time: *L'Aube, L'Aurore, Cité-Soir, Combat, L'Époque, Le Figaro, France-Libre, France-Soir, Franc-Tireur, Front-National, L'Humanité, Libération, Libé-Soir, Le Monde, La Nation, Les Nouvelles du matin, L'Ordre, Le Parisien libéré, Paris-Presse, Le Pays, Le Populaire, Résistance, Ce Soir, La Voix de Paris.*

The author wishes to thank these writers for helping him to relive those three historic weeks, and would also like to acknowledge his debt to *Pétain et de Gaulle* by J. R. Tournoux and *Le Maréchal aux liens* by Jean Tracou.

Introduction

The war in the West came alive on May 10, 1940, when German armies invaded Holland, Belgium and Luxembourg. In France, the government was headed by Paul Reynaud, who had replaced Édouard Daladier in March, and who had gained parliamentary approval by a majority of one. Politically speaking, therefore, it was a weak government which witnessed the rapid overthrow of the Belgian defense system, the capitulation of the Dutch Army, and the successful German advance through the Ardennes and across the Meuse. Paul Reynaud found it necessary both to change the men who were directing the war and to strengthen his government. On May 17 Marshal Pétain, French Ambassador to Madrid, was made Vice-President of the Council and Georges Mandel became Minister of the Interior. On May 19 General Weygand replaced General Gamelin as the Commander in Chief. And at the beginning of June these appointments, which recalled the heroic days of 1914 and revived memories of Foch and Clemenceau, were followed by the appointment of a young and junior general, Charles de Gaulle, to the Undersecretaryship of State at the War Ministry. It was the first and the last of these appointments which were to be the most notable.

At this time, Marshal Pétain was eighty-four years old. He was the most famous of living French soldiers, his name being associated with the victory of Verdun, the long and agonizing battle of attrition which seemed to symbolize everything that was most terrible and heroic in the First World War. In this war, Pétain had not only appeared as one of the senior officers who had the clearest understanding of the nature of warfare, but he had also gained the reputation of being the general most concerned with the lives and welfare of his men. Even the anti-militarist Left esteemed him and there was rejoicing that he had returned to France and to office. Reynaud promised that Pétain would stay by his side until victory was won (although de Gaulle reported him as saying that he had only appointed Pétain because he thought him less dangerous inside the government than outside). It was forgotten that the defeat of the French Army and the failure of French strategic planning were in certain ways Pétain's defeats, since between the wars he had exercised a considerable influence over military thinking and over most senior appointments.

In spite of what was to be alleged later, it is not clear that the Marshal had shown much political ambition. He had been Minister for War in the government formed by Gaston Doumergue after the disturbance of February 6, 1934, but he had given little encouragement to those who subsequently urged him to take some more positive and important political action. Although he showed himself completely out of sympathy with the political system of the Third Republic and was reputed to be favorable to certain Right-wing groups, he did not allow his name to be put forward for the Presidential elections and he refused to join Daladier's government. He had accepted, in March 1939, the appointment as French Ambassador to Madrid, when it was thought that someone with Pétain's reputation was most likely to better French relations with General Franco. One can hardly argue that he saw this as a steppingstone to higher power. It seems impossible that anyone of Pétain's age had any expectations of supreme office, and his acceptance of Reynaud's invitation was a patriotic reaction rather than a calculated maneuver.

But once in office, he quickly made his influence felt. Whereas soldiers were supposedly confined to the purely military sphere, Pétain was both a soldier and the Vice-President of the Council, and certain generals, including Weygand, had a tendency to report to him. Possibly from the time of his appointment, certainly from the beginning of June, Pétain seems to have been pessimistic about the outcome of the war. He did not think that there was much chance of halting the German advance and he was suspicious of British policies. He did not believe that Great Britain was putting all her strength into the war, and he speculated on the possibility of the British Government making peace with Germany after France had been defeated. Events could only confirm his misgivings, with the evacuation of Paris and the government's flight to Bordeaux, the Italian declaration of war, and the failure of Weygand's plan to stop the Germans on the Somme. It was on June 11 that Reynaud told Churchill that Pétain was in favor of an armistice, and after General Weygand had, the next day, insisted on the need for an armistice, Pétain became the leader, both inside and outside the government, of those who were pressing for this. On June 16 Pétain threatened to resign if this policy was not pursued. Instead, it was Reynaud who offered his resignation and the President of the Republic, Lebrun, pursued the normal course in asking Pétain to form a government. On June 17 General de Gaulle arrived in London.

The main events of Pétain's government are easily described. The armistice was signed on June 22, 1940, and France was divided into two zones: the Occupied Zone was north of a line which ran from the Swiss frontier at Geneva, passing through Bourges to Saint-Jean Pied de Port, to the southeast of Bayonne; the Unoccupied, or free, Zone, had Vichy as its capital and seat of the French Government. By a law of July 10, 1940, the constitution of the Third Republic was abolished and full powers were conferred on Marshal Pétain. This marks the end of the Republic, and the beginning of the État Français, the abolition of Republican symbols and the Republican slogan of "Liberty, Equality, Fraternity," and their replacement by the cult of the

Marshal and the slogan of *"Travail, Patrie, Famille"* ("Work, Country, Family"). On October 24, 1940, occurred what was the most dramatic incident in the history of the Vichy Government, the interview between Pétain and Hitler at Montoire, after which Pétain stressed the need for a "collaboration" between France and Germany. But Montoire was followed, on December 13, 1940, by Pétain's dismissal of Pierre Laval, his Foreign Secretary, who had been the most persistent advocate of this collaboration. After this, the principal personality of the government was Admiral Darlan, until the Germans insisted on the return of Laval in April 1942. The Allied landings in French North Africa, beginning on November 8, 1942, led to the German abolition of the Unoccupied Zone, although the Vichy Government theoretically continued to exist. In June 1944 when the Allies landed on the Normandy coast, Marshal Pétain urged the French to remain inactive; in August the Germans insisted that he leave France, installing him in the Hohenzollern Château of Sigmaringen.

But as easy as these dates are to enumerate, in fact the politics of the Vichy period were of extreme complexity. On the one hand, there was the conception of the National Revolution, the belief that a new era had begun in France; on the other hand, there was the conviction that France had been defeated and that it was necessary to bargain with the victors and to try to gain whatever advantages one could from the situation as it evolved. Between these two positions there were an infinity of possible courses of action. It is striking to see how Pétain himself is representative of so many different attitudes. His room in the Hôtel du Parc at Vichy became the center of a whole series of varied and even contradictory initiatives, evolving within an atmosphere of secrecy and mistrust, with many misunderstandings and deceptions. During the 1914 war one of Pétain's friends had reproached him with thinking too much about the French and not enough about France. Between 1940 and 1944 he succeeded in bewildering the French, while maintaining his own conviction that he was protecting and serving France.

It was on August 26, 1944, that General de Gaulle walked down the Champs Élysées and a provisional government was established under his direction. The liberation of France was everywhere accompanied by insurrection and by accusation and recrimination against those who had supported Pétain and collaborated with the Germans. In all the territories which the Germans had occupied and which were liberated, the same situation held. Perhaps in the case of France there was a deeper reason which impelled Frenchmen to denounce certain of their compatriots and to try them for treason. Perhaps the desire for a scapegoat was an expression of social and ideological disunity. Just as Pétain had acquiesced in the bringing to judgment of Reynaud, Gamelin and the former Socialist Premier Léon Blum, at Riom in 1942, so an important movement of opinion insisted that the leaders of Vichy should also be tried. The trial and execution in Algiers of Pierre Pucheu, a former Vichy Minister of the Interior, was a harbinger of this. It was inevitable that the demand for Pétain's trial should be particularly strong. That the man who could be held responsible for the state of the French Army in 1940, who had arranged for the armistice, and who had worked with the Germans, should be branded a traitor seemed essential. That it could be shown that he had always planned to overthrow Republican democracy and establish a Fascist régime seemed desirable. The need to find Pétain guilty was as great as the need to find Dreyfus guilty.

It does not seem that General de Gaulle was anxious to see the trial of Marshal Pétain. He would have preferred Pétain to have lived in exile. But from October 1944 Pétain had been preparing his defense, probably for a trial. An ordinance of November 18, 1944, had instituted a High Court of Justice which was to be presided over by three judges and where the accused were to appear before a twenty-four-member jury. The normal method of instituting legal proceedings was to open what was called an *instruction,* that is, to collect evidence. One of the magistrates appointed to the High Court, Béteille, began collecting evidence concerning Pétain. With the appearance before the High Court of Admiral Esteva, formerly Resi-

dent-General in Tunisia, and General Dentz, formerly commanding in
Syria, it became certain that Pétain would be tried, although it seemed
likely that his trial would take place in his absence. But on April 5,
1945, Pétain wrote to Hitler and requested permission to return to
France in order to defend himself. Hitler did not reply, and had
preparations made to have Pétain sent further east, but a local German
commander allowed Pétain to go to Switzerland. Pétain entered
Switzerland on April 24 and crossed into France on the twenty-sixth.
Accompanied by hostile demonstrations, the Marshal's train took him
to Igny, and from there to the fort of Montrouge. Together with his
lawyers he underwent some cross-examination from the *juge d'instruction,* Bouchardon, handed over a number of documents and
studied his defense.

On Saturday July 20, 1945, in the presence of the defense lawyers,
a special jury of twenty-four was drawn by lot from two lists which
had been drawn up by the commissions of the Assembly. The one
consisted of men who had been members of Parliament, the other
was made up of citizens who were considered to have shown "a national and resistant attitude toward the enemy." Twelve were chosen
from each list, and the defense lawyers exercised their right of object-
ing to a number of jurors. The presiding judge, Mongibeaux, was the
first President of the Court of Cassation. He was assisted by two other
judges, Donat-Guigue, President of the Criminal Court, and Picard,
first President of the Appeal Court. According to French custom, the
judges conferred and voted with the jury. According to French custom
too, the judge outlined the case against the accused before any witnesses were called.

It was a time of great bitterness. During 1944 some forty thousand
French people had been killed by their fellow countrymen and more
than four hundred thousand had been imprisoned. "One in a thousand
massacred, one in a hundred deprived of liberty."* The bitterness was
not confined to France. In Belgium there was intense controversy over
the conduct of King Leopold and his attitude toward the Germans;

* *Histoire de l'Épuration* by Robert Aron, Paris, Fayard, 1967, p. 433.

in Norway the trial of Quisling was about to begin. There were important events taking place in the world: the summit meeting at Potsdam, the dropping of atomic bombs at Hiroshima and Nagasaki, and the ending of the war with Japan. It was perhaps only for a moment that the eyes of the world were fixed on the Palais de Justice in Paris. But the trial of Marshal Pétain presented the gravest moral issues as well as the most complicated historical problems, and it has remained unforgettable.

DOUGLAS JOHNSON

Preface

The time seems to have come to find out whether Marshal Pétain was a traitor or not, and whether those Frenchmen who trusted the word of the victor of Verdun and made him their king in 1940 were deceived by him.

As I never wallowed in the quagmires of Vichy, London and Algiers, I shall confine myself to what was said under the lofty gilded ceilings of the First Chamber of the Palais de Justice. I have listened to the witnesses, the judges, the Attorney General and the defense lawyers, examined their words and their silences, and closely scrutinized the features of the accused. Why shouldn't I too offer my own testimony as a soldier who, for over two years, loved Marshal Pétain and obeyed him?

His trial unfolded like an an agonizing drama. For my part, I raise my right hand and swear to tell the whole truth, even when it is embarrassing, and nothing but the truth. If the truth exists, it must be found in a cry from the depths of the soul.

EDMUND: Sir, I thought it fit
To send the old and miserable King
To some retention and appointed guard;
Whose age has charms in it, whose title more,
To pluck the common bosom on his side
And turn our impress'd lances in our eyes
Which do command them. With him I sent the Queen,
My reason all the same; and they are ready
To-morrow, or at further space, t' appear
Where you shall hold your session. At this time
We sweat and bleed: the friend hath lost his friend;
And the best quarrels, in the heat, are curs'd
By those that feel their sharpness.

—SHAKESPEARE: *King Lear,* Act V, Scene 3

THE DOGE: I asked no remedy but from the law—
I sought no vengeance but redress by law—
I called no judges but those named by law—
As sovereign, I appealed unto my subjects,
The very subjects who had made me sovereign,
And gave me thus a double right to be so.
The rights of place and choice, of birth and service,
Honours and years, these scars, these hoary hairs,
The travel, toil, the perils, the fatigues,
The blood and sweat of almost eighty years,
Were weighed i' the balance, 'gainst the foulest stain,
The grossest insult, most contemptuous crime
Of a rank, rash patrician—and found wanting!
And this is to be borne!

BYRON: *Marino Faliero,* Act I, Scene 2

THE TRIAL OF MARSHAL PÉTAIN

I

❋

My greatest surprise, rummaging through my notes of that period twenty years later, was to find nothing in them recalling the event. And yet all the mingled intoxication, hope and fear which filled our hearts at that time had left their trace on those pages. I was thirty-eight and I had come back from the war with my hair sprinkled with salt as if I had been through sea spray in a storm, my face furrowed with wrinkles, my belly hollow, my pockets empty and my eyes uneasy. A few months earlier, clouds had still been shaking the tin can from which we unloaded bombs on Germany, but sometimes on France as well; the joys of victory had not lasted, and they bore little resemblance to what we had imagined.

The recollection of May on the Champs Élysées, the swords of light crossing above the Arc de Triomphe, the sky echoing with exploding flares, and the starry rain of the fireworks displays could not banish from our memory the great festivals of death held above burning Dortmund or Coblenz, with hundreds of searchlights dancing in the night. Survivors of that adventure, lost in a peace which offended us and searching for new loves, members of a scattered army which was trying to come together again, we embraced when we met and talked about comrades who had left their bones in the bonfires. We asked ourselves questions too.

In the spring, joining my family at Sétif, I had landed right in the middle of a repressive operation. A revolt was being drowned in blood. The Algerian drama was beginning. Back in Paris I met Camus, who was burning himself out on *Combat* and took us at night around the bars of Saint-Germain-des-Prés. The city was coming to life again. The girls went barelegged and rode about on bicycles. We took our meals in dismal eating houses where the food was meager and poor. The black market was rampant and my pay was barely enough to live on. Through the thin wall of the room in which I was billeted, I could hear the voice of Edith Piaf, who was leading a wild life in which the entire hotel shared. The future cast a gloom over us.

All that is recorded in my notebooks. But of the trial which crucified before the judges of the High Court a Marshal of France whom we had obeyed and then disobeyed during the war, nothing remains. Not a single line. Not a single word. Not even the name of a man we had saluted and loved and to whom we had remained loyal as long as possible. Had Pétain really been driven to the Palais de Justice in a prison van, accused of treason and sentenced to death, without my feeling anything? Had the newspapers really published pictures of that deaf old man, so weak that a nudge from the gendarmes flanking him would have felled him to the ground, soiled with the spittle of a sentence which tried to dishonor him, without Jules Roy, ex-officer of the armistice army, batting an eyelid?

It must be admitted that we remained silent, as if we were standing before a grave. Most of us had served under Pétain. We had belonged to the formations he had saved from disaster until we decided to go over to the Allies. At that time, just as the Navy had more admirals than ships, we had more generals than fighter aircraft. In 1943 we all joined the British, American or Soviet air forces, under the Cross of Lorraine whose first adherents gave a cool welcome to us laborers of the eleventh hour. General de Gaulle never deigned to come and see us, as if he were pretending he didn't even know of our existence. Yet we didn't consider we had committed a crime in not rallying to Great Britain after Mers-el-Kebir. Some of us even imagined that de Gaulle and Pétain were working together to trick the Germans.

Suddenly, in 1945, with all the cards on the table, it became clear that this had not been so. We had been taken in. Wounded in our loyalty to one man, and deceived by his senility, how could we have given our support to another? We knew the price of believing in big words and supreme sacrifices, we refused to be tricked by the slogans which have led soldiers to the slaughter ever since Hannibal, and we kept quiet. At the slightest reminder of that deception, we would fall silent. After the Pétain trial, we witnessed a shipwreck in which a part of ourselves was lost. I cannot remember a single discussion on this subject in any officers' mess. The Army was hiding its shame just as a family conceals a bastard. But like a good many officers, I ordered at the time a copy of the transcript of the trial printed by the *Journal officiel*. Twenty years later I found the parcel which contained it, intact, with my name, rank and the address where I was living. I had never dared to open it. The paper had turned yellow and the edges were worn.

At twenty years' remove, that restraint resembles the restraint shown by the French Army today with regard to the Algerian war. It astonishes only the uninitiate. There are wounds a man is not proud of, wounds that scar the soul more than the body. Yet it seems as if the Army no sooner recovers from a shock which has shaken it to the core than it tries to console itself by throwing itself into another adventure, like those human hearts which never lose their eternal youth. At the slightest appeal for help it rushes off in search of a myth; it is utterly incorrigible.

Take some innocent young men, eager to believe and impatient to fight. Teach them unselfishness, the history of the great deeds of their country, and the art of handling weapons. Inculcate hero worship into them. Accustom them to sleeping rough, rising early to the sound of a bugle, living together, wearing out their bodies, bolting down coarse food, and braving danger and hardship. Encourage their desire to command while training them to obey every order they receive. All you need then are some carefully organized meetings, a good military band, and a few harangues delivered with gusto, to turn them into knights or foot soldiers, capable of going to their baptism of fire wearing a plumed shako and white gloves, or of continuing a hopeless fight.

Since the country needs such men in its tragic hours, it manufactures them in peacetime in isolated seminaries, just as it manufactures nuclear weapons. But while it is possible to stockpile atom bombs in well-guarded depots, men of that sort cannot be kept in chains; they long to be put to use, if only to prove to themselves that they count for something. The dynamite with which they have been loaded asks for nothing better than to explode. Ill-prepared to live a humdrum life, and rightly inclined to regard themselves as the salt of the earth, they suffer, in their every contact with society, from a condition which condemns them to give up most ordinary ambitions. Their own ambitions are stern taskmasters. Soldiers serve without counting their time or trouble. They dedicate themselves to their country like monks to their God, and while their devotion varies according to character, taking every form from contemplation to fanaticism, the faith joining their souls together is sealed in the same sacrament. As in all religions, you find lukewarm and fervent believers, camp followers and saints, renegades and martyrs, and it sometimes happens that these churches are rent by schism. Then the result is catastrophe.

Although I wore no shako, I was one of those idiots, and I must be one still. I now go and dine at Lipp's among the flower of the French intelligentsia, who indulge only in games of the mind, usually without risk to life or limb, but I can still get involved for no good reason in lost causes, the only ones it is worth supporting. In June 1940, General de Gaulle's cause was an example, and no one could possibly deny the merit of the man who initiated it or of the men who followed him. Besides, who wouldn't have imitated him if it had been in their power to do so? In notebooks saved from those disastrous days, I wrote in pencil under the date June 20:

Ready to drop on Algiers, we are waiting for the favorable wind we need on account of our low stocks of gasoline. General de Gaulle has asked all French officers and N.C.O.'s to join him in England. He has been disowned by the government. What's the meaning of all this? If they try to hand us over, we shall all take our planes to England or Egypt.

Two days later we landed at Algiers. All hopes of carrying on the war were shattered. "We are not short of good planes, good pilots and good officers. We are not short of colonels or generals either. We are simply short of leaders." That is the explanation I find I gave for our attitude, and I still think it was valid. De Gaulle himself had not dared to go to Algiers, where any attempt at rebellion would have been suppressed by the institutions of the regime still in power and the touchy jealousy of the men in control. No one there understood the extent of the disaster or thought that the system had collapsed onto the hierarchy. We ourselves, accustomed to obeying orders without noticing we were being led by oxen, ended up by finding ourselves in a bull pen whose gates closed behind us.

On July 5, after the British had crushed the French fleet at Mers-el-Kebir, we had to choose, without knowing the facts, between Pétain and Churchill, Weygand and Sir Samuel Hoare. We believed that France, which had remained for so long the first dominion in the British Empire, was becoming herself again. We thought that she was no longer led by petty politicians but by an old Marshal who had "given his person to his country." A letter from Tunis told me that my friend Jean Amrouche, who had previously shown a deep-rooted and infectious admiration for the British, now actually longed for their annihilation. Our change of heart was not an isolated phenomenon.

The Pétain trial was all that to us. We remained silent because it was a part of ourselves that was on trial. Probably the most innocent part. The most stupid part without a doubt. The purest part. The part of which we were ashamed at the time, when we were made to feel like bastards, and after two years streaked with lightning, scattered with flames and splashed with blood, we were afraid that our shame might not have been washed away. Marshal Pétain had agreed to be soiled on our behalf. Why, then, should I now stir up this mud again? Because the time has come to decide whether we must hold in contempt a man who, like de Gaulle, personified France's honor and our own, or whether he deserves to return to his own, like a king who has died in exile, to the sound of fanfares and the thunder of guns.

The complete record of the Pétain trial as issued by the High Court covers 386 pages, divided into twenty sections, of the *Journal officiel* printed at No. 31 Quai Voltaire in 1945. Every page is set up in special eight-point type. Reading it is tiring for the eyes and depressing for the spirit. It takes two weeks to read through those twelve hundred columns of closely printed text, in which there are very few gaps. To save expense, parliamentary shorthand writers were not used, and certain phrases or exclamations which were undoubtedly uttered have been omitted. However, with the books already written on the subject, the newspapers of that year and a hundred photographs of the courtroom and its approaches, of the accused, the judges, the members of the jury, the witnesses for the defense and the Attorney General, it is possible to reconstruct that moment of history.

I should also have consulted the record of the preliminary investigation, but the High Court hides its secrets behind the argument that if they were revealed, they might assist certain persons sentenced *in absentia*. On the day when none of the accused remain alive and the court is dissolved, some pretext will be found to bury its records in the dungeons of the archives of France. With prohibition after prohibition, every attempt will be made to protect authority and the judges from any errors they may have committed. For the moment, the Attorney General doesn't even answer the letters addressed to him.

Calm and dry-eyed, his heart beating at its normal rhythm and a magnifying glass at hand to scrutinize things and faces, Jules Roy, sometime pupil of the Saint-Maixent School of Infantry and Tank Warfare, has tried, with the help of those who were present, to relive the drama of the Pétain trial.

II

❖

Monday, July 23, 1945

Paris was enjoying a glorious summer. The first clouds of the day were gathering in the south and rising into the sky. A burning hand seemed to be resting on the city roofs. The stones of the houses were warm to the touch. In front of the news stands, at the entrance to the Métro stations, the papers announced the opening of the trial with huge headlines. The storm which had been prowling around Paris for a week drew nearer and then broke up. The suffocating heat gradually spread to the suburbs, immobilizing the woods flanking the city to the east and west, and appearing to hold back the gray waters of the winding river. The tar spread out under the tires of the few cars driving through the streets. The Prix Goncourt had just been given to Elsa Triolet. At the Vieux Colombier, Jean Vilar was playing in T. S. Eliot's *Murder in the Cathedral*, and the courts had sentenced to death Paul Chopine, the leader of the Seine-et-Oise militia, and the writer Abel Bonnard. In spite of all the petitions for a reprieve, the poet Robert Brasillach had been shot on February 6. Every day fresh charnel houses were discovered, and the newspapers kept publishing long lists of missing persons.

To get through the gates of the Palais de Justice, where eagles and Napoleonic symbols dominated the black walls bristling with pointed turrets, you had to show cards or letters authorizing admission to the trial at several barriers. A few days earlier, *Franc-Tireur* had published a cartoon of the Marshal in civilian clothes, sitting in an armchair under the eyes of the Republic. The Republic was saying: "He has given me his person." To which the *Franc-Tireur* retorted: "The time has come to take custody." On the walls opposite the Palais de Justice, a poster caught the eye: the Marshal's hand was grasping Adolf Hitler's over a heap of French corpses.

Through the windows of the First Chamber of the Court of Appeal where the High Court was due to sit, a harsh light fell from a sun which was almost at its zenith. By the gilt sun of the clock, it was nearly one in the afternoon. To increase the number of seats in the crowded chamber, a few crude wooden tiers had been erected over the gallery which dominates the courtroom on the left, separated from it by four square columns with Louis Quinze capitals. They are still there, for the First Chamber has been used a great deal since, and will be used again.

The heat was stifling. Behind the empty seats of the court, distinguished guests and members of the diplomatic corps and the judiciary were crowded together. The jury were sitting in the boxes on either side of the floor of the court, which was occupied by about a hundred journalists and photographers. Between them, at the end of a narrow corridor up which the witnesses would advance, in front of the defense bench and almost directly below the first of two bronze, wheel-shaped chandeliers hanging from chains, a heavy oak table had just been installed, together with an armchair like those of the judges, in the Directoire style, upholstered in blue with a curved light-oak back.

Under the lofty paneled ceiling, Napoleon sat enthroned among the clouds, crowned with glory like a god, protecting the weak and striking down the wicked. Everyone was suffocating, in spite of the little Gothic window which the army doctor detailed to attend the accused had ordered opened, and of which I have been unable to find any trace. It had been difficult to open, so it seems, since a magistrate who was afraid of drafts had had it sealed during the reign of Louis XIV.

Like the dull rumbling of a busy capital in the middle of the day, a murmur of voices rose from the public, the lawyers and the witnesses, who were nearly all notables of the Third Republic. Those who recognized each other exchanged brief nods and winks, or else turned their backs disdainfully. It seemed impossible for anyone else to find a seat in the crowded courtroom, yet more people kept arriving who slipped between the politicians and the robed lawyers, moved forward, leaned against the paneling, or sat down on one of the deal steps of the gallery ladder. In the spectators' gallery, women were chatting together, weighed down under fragile and complicated coiffures. Every time the leather-lined doors into the merchants' gallery opened, the noise rose abruptly and then subsided, as if the whole city were surrounding the courtroom with its murmuring, its footsteps and the throbbing of its pulse.

To reach the chamber where the High Court was sitting, the Marshal had only a little way to walk. The day before, at the same time, a police van had brought him to the Palais de Justice, through the gateway at No. 34 Quai des Orfèvres. He had got out with just a small suitcase as his only luggage. He was lodged in the gloomy judges' cloakroom, where the prison service had installed two hospital beds for himself and his wife, between a table and some chairs. There were bars on the window, which was partly walled up. The washroom served as a lavatory. His jailers occupied the vestibule of the record office. The adjoining rooms were used as sleeping quarters by two nursing sisters, Captain Racine of the Medical Corps and Monsieur Joseph Simon, the governor of the Fort of Montrouge, a burly man with a bald head and a debonair mustache, who would keep a careful record of every incident of the Marshal's detention.

Everyone was wondering whether the accused would dare to appear in the uniform of a Marshal of France or whether he would wear an unobtrusive civilian suit. At one o'clock, preceded by a guard, he appeared at the witnesses' entrance. Silence fell abruptly, and with a few exceptions everyone stood up and looked at the old man with mute uneasiness. He came down the four steps, which creaked under his weight, then walked forward, followed by his three lawyers. He had put on the khaki gabardine uniform of a French officer: a tunic with gusseted pockets and straight facings with four buttons, trousers with a double red stripe, and a silk belt with a gilt buckle. ". . . A sort of abstract sorrow not addressed to mankind, and bound up with glory, fate and country, the great symbols whose weight this old man bears," wrote Joseph Kessel in *France-Soir*. A single decoration hung on his breast, the highest that could be conferred on a general: the Médaille Militaire. In his right hand, as if he were afraid of dropping it, he gripped his kepi with its triple wreath of golden oak leaves on a black ribbon with a red ground, and in his left hand, a pair of chamois leather gloves and a roll of white paper which some people mistook for a moment for his marshal's baton. Seven stars glittered on his sleeves. He held himself erect, walking with the stiff dignity of a wounded prince, in an impressive silence in which you could hear the tap of his heels, the rustle of the three lawyers' robes and the whirring of the cameras. Here and there, under the blue carpet, the floor boards creaked.

Everyone recognized the man whose picture had appeared in the papers for thirty years and on the walls of France during the Occupation—that pink skin, those sky-blue eyes, that kindly patriarchal face carved in marble, that noble forehead, that crown of snowy hair and that white mustache which had gradually been cut shorter since Verdun. "We, Philippe Pétain . . ." French chief of state or King of France? The difference was minimal. Expecting to see a decrepit old man, everyone was astonished at the vitality of this upright octogenarian. But the cheeks hung in tragic folds. Sadness had given a hard glint to the eyes, which were blinking in the light of the flashbulbs, and drawn furrows across the forehead. From the collar, which was so tight that it pushed out the tie, there emerged a pale, withered neck.

The guard moved the table in front of the empty armchair. The

Marshal sat down and carefully arranged before him his kepi, his gloves and the roll of paper, which came undone and spread out. It was then seen to consist of several sheets covered with a text in large royal type. Everyone else then sat down and started chattering. For ten minutes the photographers shot the accused from every possible angle without his flinching, but then, in sudden exasperation, he turned a ravaged face toward his lawyers.

"Is this going on much longer?"

"That's enough!" someone called out.

The photographers fell back.

His arms resting on the arms of the chair, his thumbs tucked into the belt on which every medallion bore a Medusa head, the Marshal seemed to be far away.

At ten past one, through one of the doors at the back, surmounted by angels holding a lilied shield, the court entered with a heavy tread. Monsieur Mongibeaux took his place in the elevated seat of the presiding judge. Under his cloak decorated with squirrel-fur trimmings, the richest cloak any judge could dream of, which was worth twice as much as an academician's coat and placed the President of the High Court of Justice on the same footing as a king, Monsieur Mongibeaux was suffocating. He was a good-natured man of imposing height, who with his little pointed beard looked like an aged, respectable D'Artagnan, torn between his indolence and the ambition to wear the sash of the Legion of Honor. It was said that he had applied the laws of the Vichy regime with an easy conscience. Rumor had it that he had said before the hearing, "Pétain wallowed in degradation to the point of treason."

On his right sat Monsieur Donat-Guigue, the President of the Criminal Chamber of the Appeal Court, smooth-faced and surly, a friend of the Pétain family who had not dared ask to be dispensed from judging this case, and on his left the inscrutable Monsieur Picard.

A strange figure passed them, pushing his way between the rows of journalists and in front of the accused, who did him the courtesy of pulling aside the table on which he had placed his kepi and his gloves. A red-feathered bird of prey, with the collar of the Legion of Honor on top of his imitation-ermine cloak, clutching his heavy leather briefcase to his chest, his eyes lowered, his beak pointed, his face bristling with gray hairs, Attorney General Mornet climbed up to his seat and installed himself in it, like a vulture settling in his nest with a great fluttering of fleshless wings.."When I look into his eyes, I see his teeth," Anatole de Monzie said of him.

The presiding judge drew himself up, placed his forearms on the long table in front of him, and with the gray shaving brush of his beard lathering his collar, which was decorated only by a rosette of the Legion of Honor and a Croix de Guerre, started lecturing the court:

". . . The accused appearing before us today has for many years aroused the most varied feelings: on the one hand an enthusiasm you will all recall, a sort of love, and on the other hand extremely violent feelings of hatred and hostility. . . . I must ask the public to remember that if, here and now, we are judging the accused, history will one day judge the judges and will most certainly judge the atmosphere in which the trial will have been conducted. . . ."

His voice was clear and unaffected, spiced with scarcely a hint of Gascon garlic. Then the presiding judge declared the hearing open and, looking down at the Marshal, uttered the terrible words:

"Accused, stand up."

The Marshal rose. His face suddenly lost its pink color and turned pale. The light falling on his left shoulder glinted on his Médaille Militaire. "You see me here, you gods, a poor old man, as full of grief as age; wretched in both. . . ." He was King Lear driven out of his own palace.

"State your surname, Christian name, age and occupation."

The Marshal tried to swallow. His mouth was parched. The silence suddenly became more profound. The journalists' pens stopped in mid-air. The emotion filling that tired old heart spread to the public. Judge Donat-Guigue seemed to shrink into his cloak.

"Pétain, Philippe, Marshal of France."

Bâtonnier* Payen, who was leading the defense, immediately stood up. He was a distinguished figure with a gaunt, uneasy face, whose forehead, bald at the temples, seemed to be continually ravaged by squalls. He asked for and was granted permission to put forward certain arguments. The Marshal sat down again. In an attempt to persuade the High Court to declare itself unqualified, Bâtonnier Payen, taking his stand on the legitimacy of Marshal Pétain's assumption of power, argued that it was the Senate which should be trying the former chief of state. The Marshal had always refused to leave the country, and when his German escort had taken him into Switzerland he had promptly returned to France, to the intense disappointment, so it was said, of General de Gaulle. According to Bâtonnier Payen, the 1875 Constitution which was still in force despite a recent decree, the fact that the entire Convention sat in judgment on Louis XVI, and the declared hostility of certain members of the jury toward the accused, all suggested that this High Court was unqualified to try this case, especially as some of the judges had formerly taken an oath of loyalty to the accused himself.

President Mongibeaux leaned across to Monsieur Picard. "Here we go," he said.

It was hard to hear what Bâtonnier Payen was saying. A reedy voice came from the lips of this man of seventy-three, racked with violent twitches, who seemed to be hanging onto life by a thread. Already the Marshal was cupping his left hand around his ear.

The Bâtonnier had scarcely sat down on the defense bench before the Attorney General sprang up, his beak in the air. A loud snarling voice came from his mouth. He had not taken the oath mentioned by the Bâtonnier, for he had been in retirement at the time. Would he have taken it if he had been forced to? Possibly. In any case, that oath had no moral or judicial validity and was only a parody of an oath. As for Pétain, in 1940 the National Assembly had not made him the President but the administrator of a Republic which he had strangled.

* The Bâtonnier is the President of the French Bar. (Tr.)

The *Journal officiel* mentions shuffling and murmurs among the public during this speech. The presiding judge announced that the court would retire to consult together.

That oath was one which I took too, like every officer who served with the French forces after the Armistice. It must still be in my file, unless the joker who was my group captain at the end of 1942 destroyed it while covering his own tracks, for fear that his promotion might be affected. We would have been very surprised at the time if we had been told that an attorney general would later poke fun at that oath. The Attorney General had never known our anguish. Besides, why was it necessary to force officers to take an oath of loyalty? By the nature of his profession a soldier must obey or resign. If he remains with the colors, that means he will carry out all the orders he is given, except for those directed against discipline and the law. The trouble was that we didn't know where the Republic was, and that every side claimed to be the only one serving it. Who among us was sufficiently conversant with affairs of state to know where honor lay? Attorney General Mornet maintained that if he had sworn that oath he would not have considered himself bound by it in the slightest degree. The art of the jurist consists of giving the force of law to something which lacks it, or of taking it from something which claims to possess it. Our profession consisted of living and dying decently under arms.

The court rejected the Bâtonnier's arguments, and the clerk of the court, in his corner near the witnesses' entrance, read out the indictment. Pétain (Henri-Philippe-Bénoni-Omer) was accused of having "committed crimes against the internal security of the state" and of having "dealings with the enemy with a view to promoting their enterprises in conjunction with his own."

Is it true that an armistice with Germany was signed on June 22, 1940? Yes. Is it true that that armistice handed over to Germany three-fifths of the territory of France and all her war material? Yes. Is it true that France had lost a battle and had to pay the penalty? Is it true that that armistice saved everything that could still be saved?

How could I honestly fail to answer yes? Yet the accusation of treason was built on a quagmire. It reached far back into the past, pointing to the support given to Pétain by certain notorious Fascists, and to the sympathy he showed the Franco regime when he was Ambassador in Madrid; it named him as the standard-bearer of the Cagoule; and it reproached him with having shaken hands with Hitler at Montoire, and having urged his officers to resign themselves to defeat. Nothing, in fact; bagatelles, mere trifles. After Marshal Pétain, another chief of state addressed his officers in equally Machiavellian terms, yet now, a few years later, no one is plotting to bring him before the High Court.

Everything points to the Marshal's guilt, you may say. Yes, but if you prefer, everything he did was trickery. When he told the fleet to scuttle, he knew he would not be obeyed, and when he asked to share in the defense of France against the British, what was that but an attempt to deceive the enemy and obtain weapons for the French? Besides, if the sailors had wanted to leave port, no one could have forced them to remain at anchor. The sailors, who were not traitors, were more royalist than King Philippe VII, placed on the throne by the will of the people under the name of Philippe Pétain.

Read out at such length by the clerk of the court, the indictment may have sounded impressive at the time. Today those eight columns in the *Journal officiel* make us shrug our shoulders. We would even smile, if we dared, at the sight of a waste basket being emptied over the head of a Marshal of France, in a public courtroom with gilded ceilings and sky-blue walls. But, after all, this was a political trial of an old man with no means of defense except the eloquence of his lawyers. His age prevented him from standing up for himself. The witnesses for the prosecution nudged each other on their benches; the old man was done for. They would be able to keep their privileges and perquisites. Besides, the old man hadn't even tried to catch the faraway, expressionless voice of Monsieur Jean Lot, the clerk to the High Court. What did it matter, after all? His lawyers had told him the accusations leveled against him.

Now and then, with a brief, almost furtive gesture, he touched the sheets of paper under the heavy embroidered kepi in front of him. There lay his salvation, where it had always lain before. Who had ever resisted a statement from his lips? Still a Marshal of France, he looked at the seven five-pointed stars spaced along his sleeve from the elbow to the wrist, in the shape of a double Southern Cross. These people couldn't be expected to know. But all of a sudden the truth was going to burst forth, unless one of his former disciples, who had become head of the government in his turn, after being his rival, had decided to pursue him with deadly hatred. He shook his head, then shrugged his shoulders, unconcerned.

"Usher, call the roll of the witnesses."

The Marshal woke up abruptly at Monsieur Mongibeaux's clarion call. There was no reply from the usher, who had disappeared.

"Somebody go and find him! Apprehend him!" added Monsieur Mongibeaux in a loud voice. "Then he'll know what it feels like."

And he gave a chuckle which found no echo. People looked at each other in astonishment. This southern witticism, at the beginning of such a solemn trial, seemed in bad taste.

The usher eventually returned and called the witnesses, who withdrew from the courtroom.

"Monsieur le Bâtonnier, gentlemen," said the presiding judge, "I am about to begin questioning the accused. In view of his great age, do you consider it necessary to have an adjournment, or does he wish to be questioned immediately?"

"He wishes the questioning to begin," replied the Bâtonnier, going down to join the Marshal.

"He can of course remain seated, for you may be sure that everything will be done for him that is consistent with both humanity and justice."

"First of all he has a declaration to make, with your permission, Monsieur le Président."

"We are ready to hear his declaration."

Bâtonnier Payen placed his hand on the Marshal's shoulder and whispered in his ear. The accused got to his feet and picked up his sheets of paper. Then, without putting on his spectacles, and speaking in a clear, firm voice which suddenly broke the silence, he began reading out his text.

"It was the French people who, through their representatives gathered in the National Assembly, entrusted power to me on the tenth of July, 1940. It is to the French people that I have come to give an account of my stewardship. . . ."

The old man was holding his head high. He was squaring up with all the spirit left in him. He was standing firm. Where had he found this new strength of his? He had prepared himself for the occasion. He had read his text over a score of times because he was afraid of stumbling over a word or of losing his voice, as often happened. He knew it all off by heart. He wanted to reach the farthest corners of France. To do that, he had to speak clearly, hold himself erect, appeal to the people who had cheered him wherever he went. The court scarcely recognized the voice of 1940 which still quavered in our memories, saying, "It is with a heavy heart that I tell you we must lay down our arms. I approached the enemy last night. . . ." In that voice endowed with what François Mauriac called an "almost unearthly quality" there were no more tearful tremolos. He spoke quietly, hammering out the syllables of his crisp little phrases, in a style so simple it was almost naïve, a style intended to strike ordinary men with irrefutable arguments like the blows of an ax on a tree. "It was the abominable voice of disaster, the voice of our humilation, the voice which spread both poison and confusion. . . ." This comment, as cutting as a sword, came from the *Franc-Tireur* correspondent, Madeleine Jacob, who was to prove the harshest of all the journalists covering the trial.

Even today, Pétain's royal declaration has an air about it. Although it was his attorney Isorni who had the idea of writing it, and who put it down on paper, it was his own work. He had copied it out in his own careful, childish handwriting, and had corrected and polished every phrase until it became tempered Pétain steel. It says nothing but the truth—such a succession of fantastic, forgotten truths that it is utterly overwhelming. It doesn't bring tears to the eyes, but throws a glaring light on the past. It stirs up words which we now use only sparingly and which arouse a skeptical reaction today: service, honor, hope, faith, devotion, the whole vocabulary of official speeches which governments use to announce catastrophes or prepare the way for sacrifices. On any other lips than his, they would have sounded out of place. "What, Pétain, haven't you even the courage of your infamous convictions?" wrote Madeleine Jacob in her notebook. Coming from this exhausted, worn-out old king who was going back to the very sources of his being, who was not cheating or pretending, and whom the journalists stared at in utter fascination, these words finally made an impact.

"I asked for nothing and wanted nothing. I was begged to come; I came. I thus became the heir to a catastrophe for which I was not responsible, while those who were really responsible sheltered behind me to escape the wrath of the people. . . . Yes, the Armistice saved France and contributed to the Allied victory by ensuring that the Mediterranean remained free and the Empire intact. Power was entrusted to me lawfully and recognized by every country in the world from the Holy See to the U.S.S.R. I used that power as a shield to protect the French people, for whose sake I went so far as to sacrifice my personal prestige. I remained at the head of an occupied country. . . . While General de Gaulle, outside our frontiers, carried on the struggle, I prepared the way for the liberation, by preserving an unhappy but living France. . . ."

That idea too came from Isorni, who had persuaded the Marshal to amplify what he had suggested in his final message of 1944: de Gaulle was the sword, Pétain the shield.

"Your judgment will be followed by the judgment of God and the judgment of posterity. They will be sufficient for my conscience and my name."

He had originally intended to end his speech with the words,

"*Vive la France!*" On his manuscript these words are crossed out and replaced by the sentence, "I put my trust in France."

When he had finished his statement, which lasted seven minutes, the Marshal turned around and sat down, just as the Doge Marino Faliero, when he was unjustly accused of having betrayed his country, sat down before his judges in Venice, with the words Byron put into his mouth:

> Fortune is female . . .
> The fault was mine to hope
> Her former smiles again at this late hour. . . .
> I cannot plead to my inferiors, nor
> Can recognize your legal power to try me.
> Show me the law!

President Mongibeaux lost no time in destroying the effect which had been produced. With him the court returned to the world of postwar normality, in which retired marshals sent for in times of disaster return to private life and apply for official cars. The defense opened fire. Maître Isorni began to speak.

The temperature of the proceedings promptly rose. Bâtonnier Payen was reason itself, precise and orderly if rather boring, cautiously advancing through the undergrowth of legal procedure. Isorni had the rather bombastic eloquence of a preacher in his pulpit, raising his voice to make himself heard, but he also had courage and passion. At the risk of offending his chief and being dropped from the case, he had rushed to the Marshal's help, just as he had tried to save Robert Brasillach a few months earlier. He had done his utmost to breathe into the old man the strength which he possessed in abundance, and right from the start he had shown him a devotion verging on adoration. Almost every day he had cycled to the Fort of Montrouge to shake him out of his lethargy, to show him the facts, to awaken his sense of dignity, and to try to give that empty shell, governed by a wandering mind, the appearance of a sovereign.

Bâtonnier Payen wanted to plead diminished responsibility due to old age, and Isorni total responsibility for the acts in question, because those acts had saved the country. In his first speech he showed all the fire of his youth and faith. Tall and slim, he was handsome into the bargain. He had a way of stretching out his arms and gesturing with his long hands, with the sleeves of his robe thrown back like the folds of a Roman toga. "Being a trial lawyer means fighting constantly, running the risk of storm and shipwreck, accepting uncertainty and misfortune, and in misfortune, the only good fortune that counts, honorable solitude." Maître Isorni was already practicing what Jacques Isorni would later preach. In his opinion, the best form of defense was attack, and he proved it by protesting at the botching of the preliminary examination and the statements made by Monsieur Mongibeaux two days earlier.

Beside him, defense counsel Maître Lemaire raised his bald buccaneer's head, with its strong jaw attached to a thick neck rising above the starched neckband. Since the beginning of the hearing he had kept his shrewd gaze fixed on the man who personified the prosecution, and now he bluntly reproached the Attorney General for having expressed his opinion to the press three months before the opening of the trial. The Attorney General tossed his head and retorted angrily. What the *Journal officiel* delicately describes as murmurs arose among the public.

"I must say," exclaimed the Attorney General, "there are too many Germans in this courtroom."

There was a storm of protests and applause. Pinned down by the remark he had blurted out, the Attorney General was set upon by Lemaire and Isorni, and condemned himself out of his own mouth. The court learned that he had decided to demand the death sentence for Pétain before the end of the preliminary examination. But what regime cannot find a magistrate, when it wishes, to attack its chosen victims? One is born an attorney general just as one is born an executioner. A sense of vocation is required for both occupations, and in private life executioners are sometimes the gentlest of men, who love animals and weep when they see a tree being felled. After abandoning his Attorney General for a time to the attacks of the defense, the presiding judge finally came to his rescue and suspended the hearing.

When the guards came in, the uproar grew louder. A young woman lawyer loudly demanded freedom of speech, then pointed to the ceiling panels where the words *"Lex"* and *"Jus"* were painted in gilded capitals. The word *"JVS"* in which the letter *U* was written in the Roman style, as a *V*, looked like Christ's anagram, "JHS."

"Jus—the law—do you know what that means? We are the law, and order does not have precedence over the law!"

The chief of police hesitated at first, then decided to clear the gallery, although no shouts had come from it. The lawyers refused to allow themselves to be thrown out, and stood with their backs to the wall, making theatrical gestures. In the general confusion, a young Army captain who had lost one arm went up to Marshal Pétain and shook hands with him before the guards had time to push him away. A chorus of voices shouted: "Long live freedom!"

The incidents everyone had been afraid of had begun. In the corridors outside, someone said, "It's the Dreyfus affair all over again," and the remark was repeated over and over again. In the courtroom, the windows were opened and a little air came in. Outside, sight-seers were crowded on the balconies, with the lily-shaped railings, of the Sainte-Chapelle, whose gilded spire, above the pigeon-gray slate roof, could be seen between the stone crosspieces of the stained-glass windows. Atop the spire, a black angel leaned toward Notre Dame, above other angels blowing trumpets. Paris was calm, but the provinces remained in a state of unrest. People were still being killed in the name of the Resistance, without even being handed over to the law, although the law was wreaking swift justice and had recently taken only ten minutes to sentence the Stuttgart traitor, Paul Ferdonnet, to death. There was fear of rioting. In the offices of the President of the First Chamber, an ambitious young man with the face of a Spanish inquisitor, Monsieur Edgard Pisani, secretary general to the Prefect of Police, sat beside an inspector equipped with a radio transmitter, ready to call out reinforcements.

It took a fresh hearing lasting thirty-five minutes to still the emotion aroused by this incident. After which, in spite of the defense, which wanted to put off the examination of this witness to the next day, the judge suddenly decided to hear Monsieur Paul Reynaud.

A short, elegant figure in a striped suit with a large pocket handkerchief, narrow-eyed, his shiny, wavy hair barely turning gray, his voice solemn and clear, with a hint of grandiloquence, it was he who on May 18, 1940, had sent for Marshal Pétain, whom he had described in a speech full of deliberate pauses as the "victor of Verdun."

Monsieur Paul Reynaud, who had been Prime Minister at the time, had declared, "From now on he will be at my side, placing all his wisdom and all his strength at the service of his country. He will remain at my side until victory is won."

He now explained himself in curt little phrases, which he had spent four years polishing and preparing. Pétain in those days had been a myth. A "handsome marmoreal figure, surrounded by silence," he was considered to be thrifty with his soldiers' lives. Painlevé sent him to Morocco when Morocco was in danger, the Right applauded him, and the Left claimed him as one of their own. Léon Blum called him "the noblest and most human of our military leaders."

When Paul Reynaud summoned Pétain from Madrid and brought him into his government, the country went into a frenzy of enthusiasm. However, even if Pétain and Weygand could have changed the situation, it was too late now, and both men decided that since the battle had been lost, France should ask for an armistice. Monsieur Paul Reynaud found it hard to resign himself to this course of action, and wanted to continue the war in North Africa. He came up against the resistance of the experts, who in this case were the most famous soldiers in the French Army. To get the better of them, he thought at first of getting rid of them. But who would have understood him? You didn't solemnly include Pétain in your Cabinet, or place Weygand at the head of the Army, to dismiss them like a couple of servants a week later. He kept them, and that was the cause of all his troubles. Now the more illustrious of the two sat there, trying to disguise his deafness by pretending to stroke the back of his neck, or drumming his fingers on the arms of his chair. He could see nothing of Monsieur Paul Reynaud, six feet in front of him, but the back, the prominent ears and the wavy hair.

The hearing was adjourned to the following day. On the other side of the river the sunlight was falling on the façades of the Quai de la Mégisserie and the dark mass of the Théâtre du Châtelet. As he entered his room in the record office, the Marshal seemed in high spirits.

"I made a fine speech," he told his jailer, Joseph Simon.

This first day of the trial had left a feeling of malaise. The courtroom, too small for the occasion, did not measure up to the importance of the trial. Judges who had taken an oath of loyalty to Pétain were trying the case after making statements condemning the accused, and the Attorney General seemed to come straight out of those times when the country was torn by the wars of religion. Everyone said that the preliminary examination had been pushed through at breakneck speed, first by the Army lawyers, then by old Judge Bouchardon, a pale bent figure in a huge collar.

The cases of archives, which had arrived in whole trainfuls and been piled up in the corridors of the Palais Bourbon, had not all been opened. Rummaging through this mass of papers, with his bulbous eyes set under beetling brows and a narrow forehead, Judge Béteille, who was responsible for briefing the Pétain case, had extracted only enough documents to make a score of bundles. Important witnesses had not been heard, while others had been unable to check their statements. A great many documents had been burned or concealed, and the most precious of all had been found accidentally in a mysterious chest. This chest had been moved from one farm to another, for it was believed to bring bad luck, and had finally fallen into the hands of the police. It was the so-called "Pétain trunk," into which, for years past, the Marshal had stuffed papers he wanted to keep, and which his staff had saved from the Germans, before he left for Sigmaringen, entrusting it to some peasants who had no idea what it contained.

Twenty-four jurors, twelve members of Parliament and twelve members of the Resistance, together with their deputies, sat on the right and left of the presiding judge. Two days earlier, the defense had objected to two parliamentary jurors who were Communists and three others who had made statements suggesting that they had already arrived at their verdict. In the leading article in *Combat* on July 18, Camus had written:

> In spite of the serene declarations made to the press by certain magistrates of the High Court, the Pétain trial is not taking place under the best conditions. Attorney General Mornet cannot make a show of a clear conscience, or of complete self-assurance, or of haughty dignity without onlookers feeling a certain embarrassment on his behalf. He resembles one of those people who, as they walk along the street, try to look all the more dignified because they have stepped in excrement. This is rather the position of the Attorney General, who is going to find himself face to face with an accused to whom he has sworn an oath of loyalty.

As for President Mongibeaux, Bâtonnier Payen had seen him in his chambers after the first hearing.

"Obviously, Monsieur le Président, you never uttered the words Isorni put into your mouth."

"Why, yes," replied Monsieur Mongibeaux, "I did."

Maurice Clavel, in *L'Époque*, quoted Saint-Just: "Must we go and look for judges on the moon?" Only one man could decide on the means of sparing the nation the shame of punishing its fallen king: de Gaulle, who had become head of the provisional government and the new king—Charles XI in succession to Philippe VII—after an unhappy war which had ended well. All that was necessary was to find a formula.

"While General de Gaulle, outside our frontiers . . ." For the first time, the Marshal had openly expressed the idea of a tacit complicity between de Gaulle and himself. "Ah, if only he had wished!" the Marshal had often said to himself. Although the younger man had served him loyally, long enough to enter his circle, to take part in the deliberations of the sovereign's brain trust, and to prove himself a powerful and original thinker with a certain contempt for anyone who failed to keep up with him, de Gaulle had always been envious of his glory. Imperious and unbending, impatient to act and impose his opinions, capable of bold action to dominate men and events, too sure of himself to sail under any flag but his own, built for the high seas and rigged out for stormy weather, he had found it impossible to follow in the wake of the flagship and had quickly pulled away, with all sails set.

Yet submission was part of the ritual when you placed yourself under the protection of a great man: you gave and you received. De Gaulle had given very little, for no more than a season, and just enough to become aware of his value and forge his pride. He had received assurances of friendship from the most revered figure in France since Foch had died, together with his support against the scribes and Pharisees of the École de Guerre who turned up their noses at him. Without this illustrious backing, nobody would have agreed to offer a chair or even listen to that immensely tall captain, barely equipped with his Staff College certificate, who already played the professor and the strategist with the authority of a prophet. Worse still, he would have been completely crushed. In return, he was supposed to submit to the sovereign's authority and fill his granaries with his own harvests, just as a tenant farmer stores his grain in the barns of the lord of the manor, or makes wine in his plant under the name of his vineyard. After all, who had given de Gaulle his ideas? And, once they had been set to music with all the skill de Gaulle possessed, what name could lend them more distinction than that of Marshal Philippe Pétain, victor of Verdun and member of the Académie française?

De Gaulle's first act of insubordination had been to publish a new book, *France and Her Army,* under his own name, instead of retiring behind that of Pétain. When you are on a minister's staff, either you agree to write the speeches he makes or you hold aloof from the exercise of power. You don't show such cavalier independence. That is one of the conventions of official life. De Gaulle defied it. Why, he argued, should he attribute to a setting star about to vanish below the horizon a light which he considered came from him alone? When Pétain had received his Marshal's baton from Poincaré on the parade ground at Metz, on December 8, 1918, Foch had turned to Weygand and had spat out of his mustache, like a jet of tobacco juice, this ferocious comment which went the rounds of the staff officers: "To think we got him there with kicks in the backside." Between princes, as between wolves, there is no tenderness. Only sheep and cows sleep side by side. De Gaulle was willing to celebrate Pétain's well-deserved fame, crowned in old age with ancient honors, but he refused to serve it beyond acceptable limits.

Those who were close to the Marshal saw the faculties of the octogenarian declining. A legendary figure from a past epoch, he was now just a ghost greedy for praise and obsessed with protocol, whom Paul Valéry's speech welcoming him to the Académie française had placed on the pedestal of eternity.

His eyes still lively and sometimes roguish, his judgment quick at making assessments, his body and mind burdened by the apparatus of power and military honors, he lived in a sheltered atmosphere, lulled by flattery and servility. With his bushy eyebrows and his drooping jowls, the old man was the personification of established glory. He, too, would have a state funeral, like Foch. His bemedaled remains would be taken to the sanctuary at Douaumont, where they would rest on the mountain of his soldiers' bones. Whether or not Foch had been right to say Pétain would have broken the enemy attack, his name was linked with one of the most famous victories in history. If he had given way, his disgrace would have been on a par with his failure. "At that moment," Montherlant has declared, "France was admired by the whole world." After all, others before him had trembled, and Marshal Blaise de Montluc himself had not been ashamed of feeling fear when he was faced with a great decision. Every time Pétain

appeared in public, trumpets sounded, flags fluttered in the breeze,
weapons glinted in the sunlight. The old man's nostrils drank in the
smell of incense which hung around him.

He had liked de Gaulle for his bold opinions, but the young
officer's impatience irritated him. Pétain had known how to bide his
time. He found it hard to understand why anyone should take another
road or dare to hustle his august person, draped in the folds of his
sky-blue cape. "Patience, young man," he felt like saying. Since the
outrage which de Gaulle had inflicted on him by taking the credit for
work inspired by the sovereign and written for him, Pétain had taken
to exclaiming whenever he saw de Gaulle, "Ah! Here comes the
turkey cock." De Gaulle, in turn, spoke of the old man in tones of
commiseration. Why should he have patience? When you felt danger
approaching and saw a change taking place in military technology
which affected strategic principles, how could you refrain from
champing at the bit? And when you had a style of your own, why
shouldn't you satisfy that author's vanity which every writer secretly
nurtures at the beginning of his career?

Despising the grand old men of the French Army, without reflect-
ing that he would be one himself in time, and that he would know no
better than the rest when to retire from public life before it swallowed him up, de Gaulle could not forgive Pétain for sinking into the
feather bed of old age. The old man's vanity exasperated him. Yet it
was his pen, after that of Paul Valéry, which was to write his finest
eulogy:

> The day a choice had to be made between ruin and reason, promotion
> came to Pétain. Quick to grasp the essentials of every problem and to see
> what could be done to solve it, he was in complete intellectual command
> of the situation. What is more, he marked it with the stamp of his charac-
> ter. Between that clear-sighted figure and the supreme effort which was
> henceforth required from both the combat and the combatants, there was
> such complete harmony that it seemed like a law of nature. Moreover, men
> instinctively put their trust in a master known to despise the advantages of
> servitude. He had the strength of a critical spirit protected from common-

place favors. He had the grandeur of independence. He had the prestige of secrecy, preserved by deliberate coldness, vigilant irony, and the very pride in which his solitude was enveloped.

In retrospect, one might think that de Gaulle had painted his own portrait. What Pétain had been in the First World War he wanted to be too. Pétain was undoubtedly the master on whom he modeled himself. In his opinion, even Foch would not have succeeded if he had not had in his hands "the instrument designed by Pétain." But this new war had plunged the French Army into disaster before he, de Gaulle, had been able to show what he was capable of as a military leader; at the vital moment he had only an apology for an armoured division, and the two stars of an acting brigadier when he should have been handling whole armies. What future was there for him, seeing that the only politician who believed in him, Paul Reynaud, had decided to place the destiny of the country in the senile hands of Pétain, whom he had recalled from Spain, and of Weygand, who was outstripped by events?

III

❧

Tuesday, July 24, 1945

Thanks to a supplementary allowance of paper, the newspapers had
come out with full-sized pages, except for *L'Ordre* and *Le Monde*,
which had chosen to reduce the size of their pages in order to double
their number. They published photographs of the judges, the Attorney General and the accused. *L'Aurore* and *Le Figaro* devoted the
whole of their second pages to a transcript of the trial. *Franc-Tireur*
had a photograph of Monsieur Mongibeaux, looking twenty years
younger, with a bow tie and a splendid head of wavy hair.

The fine weather was continuing. In the First Chamber, long coarse
curtains the brownish-gray color of army sheets broke the rays of the
sun and let in a soft warm light. Paul Valéry had died the day before,
and the press announced that General de Gaulle was going to pay his
last respects before the coffin. Nobody pointed out that the great poet
to whom the new Republic was to give a state funeral, after a lying-in-
state on the esplanade of the Palais de Chaillot, could have been
called upon to appear at the trial as a defense witness.

When, in 1931, the author of *Mon Faust* had welcomed Marshal
Pétain into the Académie française, he had sharpened his quill on the
steely gaze of the victor of Verdun and had woven a noble garland of
words for him. The booklet reproducing the speeches made by Valéry

and Pétain on that occasion, now a great rarity, contained 136 pages of
mutual eulogies and, since Pétain was succeeding Foch, a précis of the
art of war, probably studded with a few phrases written by de Gaulle
when he had been in the Marshal's service. Pétain was the "rare man"
whom the harshest critics had been forced to spare, the independent
spirit who had preached the most rigorous doctrines, the heaven-sent
leader who had saved his country from catastrophe. "I cannot refrain
from pointing out here that it was the very general who has sometimes
been accused of looking on the dark side, of being a prophet of gloom,
who was unanimously called upon to restore our hopes and revive
our ardor."

In 1942 Paul Valéry had gone even further, in a work presented to
the head of state by the city of Paris as a token of esteem. In this
work, Valéry told the story of his first speech, and spoke of Pétain
the man, his goodness, his greatness and his destiny.

Who could have told me, on the twenty-second of January, 1931, at the
end of the sitting of the Académie française at which I had had the honor
of welcoming our new colleague Marshal Pétain, that that great career
which I had just been extolling was far from being over, that its most
tragic phase and its highest point had not yet been reached, that the
supreme military honors, the splendid fame of Verdun, the command of
all the French forces at the most critical and most decisive hour in our
history, were only a sort of preparation for more extraordinary destinies,
more poignant trials, and far higher authority, and that finally the total
defeat of France would oblige my illustrious new colleague, ten years later,
to assume a burden of crushing weight and fundamental importance, the
burden of responsibility for a nation whose strength was ebbing away, and
which had only an old soldier to maintain something of its unity and
preserve some future for it?

This was more convincing and more impressive testimony than that
of Monsieur Paul Reynaud, and it would have been enough to quote
it to intimidate Pétain's former ministers. For now that King
Philippe VII was accused of treason, they begrudged him even the
praise which they had formerly thrown around his shoulders like a

golden cloak. Paul Valéry spoke of a Prime Minister who had begged him, "in tears and on his knees," not to resign his portfolio as Minister of War.

Everyone knows the consequences: we are living them with him. What an extraordinary existence he has had! If one day a French Plutarch comes to write the lives of our famous men, this one will furnish him with a tremendous subject: a task which is the heaviest, the most uncertain, the most exposed, the most disturbing, and also the most grievous of all, undertaken in extreme old age, and accepted in the most difficult and sometimes the most painful circumstances—a task consisting of saving the order, honor and morale of the nation in the midst of confusion and general disarray. What a record of service!

This fresh eulogy didn't turn the old man's head. He commented with a smile: "I've given Valéry a chance to be clear for once."

Monsieur Paul Reynaud's mammoth hearing lasted over five hours. Monsieur Reynaud was sixty-six at the time, and his youthful appearance was already a subject of astonishment; he gave the impression that he would live to be a hundred, with the body of an athlete and the soul of a swordsman. In that assembly with its sinister complement of old men, he seemed the youngest of all the judges and witnesses. He had genuine youth, a supple body, a quicksilver mind and a feline face, to which a tan ostensibly due to the sun gave an appearance of health, together with the terrible artificial signs of some drug. Like so many other trial lawyers turned politicians, he had kept the monotonous eloquence and solemnly rounded sentences of his profession. To feel any quiver of emotion in him, you would have had to place your hand on his heart; there was no trace of feeling on that motionless Asiatic face or in that clear grave voice. Holding himself erect, and standing on tiptoe like all small men, in order to gain a fraction of an inch in height, Monsieur Paul Reynaud seemed self-assured and perfectly at ease, but his tongue, with which he kept moistening his lips, showed that the gravity of the occasion had blocked his salivary glands. At one moment he appeared to be out of breath and wiped away the sweat on his forehead. The presiding judge offered to let him sit down. Monsieur Reynaud grasped in mid-air the chair which was held out to him, but turned it round and remained standing, using the back of the chair as a bar.

One can only wonder today at that huge, detailed, skillful deposition, made in a shrill, hoarse voice. Once he had declared war on Pétain, Monsieur Paul Reynaud scarcely touched on the subject of the accused again. In his eyes, Pétain was a traitor first and foremost because he had put the speaker in prison. That crime had led to all the others, since it was behind the walls of the fortress of Le Portalet, at the foot of the Pyrenees, that the former Prime Minister's eyes had been opened to the Marshal's machinations. At first sight, Paul Reynaud's harangue seemed to be a speech in favor of a onetime Premier anxious to obtain a portfolio in future French governments.

No one would do Monsieur Paul Reynaud the injustice of taking him for a dishonest man. He once declared that he had left the post of Minister of Finance a poorer man than when he had taken it on, and it is true that it is still possible to find honest people in this world. So I shall do no more than say what reading his speech suggests twenty years later: that he defended and justified himself more than he accounted for and attacked the accused, almost forgotten behind him. Why didn't he turn around now and then? He would have seen an old man sitting impassively in his chair, his arms on the leather armrests with the gilded nails, and who, after taking out his watch and propping it up against his kepi, gave the impression of sinking into boredom. Finally an impatient juryman exclaimed, "I'd like to know whether we are trying Paul Reynaud here or Pétain!" Monsieur Paul Reynaud kept going back to prehistoric times, to the King of the Belgians, to General Corap, to the dangers represented by the Communist Party, to the Italian condominium in Tunisia. No one could make head or tail of what he was saying.

The real problem was not to be found in those confused days of fear during which the Third Republic disintegrated more from the inertia of its ministers than under the scourge of misfortune. Who

had brought Marshal Pétain back from Madrid? Monsieur Paul
Reynaud. Who had begged Marshal Pétain to join his government?
Monsieur Paul Reynaud. Could Monsieur Reynaud have been un-
aware that Marshal Pétain belonged to the Cagoule and had murderous designs on the institutions of the Republic? Could the police
forces of the Republic have forgotten to inform the Minister of the
Interior and his Prime Minister of that fact, or have shown themselves incapable of doing so? If not, what excuse had Monsieur
Reynaud for having admitted a traitor to his Cabinet? Or again, if he
had wanted to place alongside himself a legendary figure carved in
marble, who could forgive him now for having given way to naïve
hero worship? One can show indulgence to a rural dean, but not to
Monsieur Paul Reynaud. It was painful to hear him explain how he
nearly accepted the post of Ambassador in Washington offered to
him by Pétain, when he had become head of state but not yet turned
criminal.

The most striking fact that emerges from this deposition is that
when he found himself outvoted in the Council of Ministers, Monsieur Paul Reynaud resigned. Who was ruling the country? No one.
Generals and admirals declared that they were ready for anything,
except to repel the enemy who were advancing amid the thunder of
their armored divisions. God himself would have found the situation
confusing. Who was in command? No one, unless perhaps it was the
hard and beautiful Hélène de Portes, who was Monsieur Paul Reynaud's mistress and Egeria, as Madame de Crussol had been Daladier's—countesses and marquises played an important part behind the
scenes of the Third Republic.

To stop Hitler's tanks, the Republic had only two magic names:
Weygand and Pétain. Afterward Monsieur Paul Reynaud realized
that both were no longer anything but myths. Why didn't he find out
beforehand that, according to Joffre, Pétain was just a defeatist who
didn't believe in the importance of Verdun? A soldier can defend a
fortress even in the belief that it is unimportant, and the soldier's
merit grows in inverse proportion to the importance of the fortress.

According to Joffre, the real victor of Verdun was Nivelle. Why, then, had Monsieur Paul Reynaud waited to turn this knowledge to account, and what good will it do us later to learn that the real heroes of the battle of Egypt, of Bir Hakeim or of the landings of June 1944 were not Field Marshal Montgomery, nor General Koenig, nor Eisenhower, if those who know the truth, in the high places where history is made, remain silent? Monsieur Paul Reynaud quoted another remark by Monsieur Michel Clemenceau: "It was in spite of Pétain that we won the war." Whom can we believe, then, and who was being tricked?

The only people capable of thinking that the Armistice was unnecessary are those who did not live through those days, when half the French Army had been taken prisoner and the other half was falling back in disorder along roads cluttered with convoys and refugees. Panic had taken hold of a country to which no one dared to tell the truth and which had been prepared for war as if it were an everyday enterprise. Once the enemy had appeared, everything had collapsed into confusion. The disaster was put down to treason. The troops no longer obeyed orders, and those who still obeyed because they had leaders could no longer be used. "The choice is between victory and death. We must be victorious," said Gamelin in his order of the day of May 18, two days before he was sacked and replaced by seventy-two-year-old Weygand. The German tanks, which had been reassuringly described to us as sardine tins, were swamping the north, outflanking the Maginot Line, and crossing the Seine at Rouen, while Italy was rushing in for the kill. Mr. William Bullitt, the United States Ambassador in Paris, laid a rose on the memorial at Domrémy and made a speech which could have been written by Péguy. Without previous preparations, there could be no thought of making a stand along the Loire or the Garonne. As Bernanos had foreseen, we were in danger, not of defeat, but of annihilation.

I myself, a mere Air Force captain, knew like Monsieur Paul Reynaud that we had to withdraw to North Africa, in order to reconquer France years later with armored divisions dropped from the air and supported by thousands of bombers. It was only after he had lost all hope that Monsieur Paul Reynaud decided to call Marshal Pétain and the Virgin Mary to his aid by summoning his government, largely composed of atheists and Freemasons, to Notre Dame on May 19, 1940, and begging for divine protection before the relics of Saint Genevieve. Unless it was at the urgent request of Madame de Portes, who may have been a pious churchgoer in her idle moments.

In June, in those parts of France which had been spared, children made their first Communion just as in peacetime. On the outskirts of villages, flames rose from burning aircraft. *And another angel came out of the temple, crying with a loud voice to him that sat on the cloud, Thrust in thy sickle, and reap: for the time is come for thee to reap; for the harvest of the earth is ripe. . . .*

I was rereading the Apocalypse, so that nothing should surprise me. On June 16, when Monsieur Paul Reynaud resigned, what did he bequeath to Marshal Pétain? Failure. And the country called on Pétain to have Reynaud and Blum shot, as an example to others, and so that the men who were blamed for the national disaster should at least pay for that humiliation with their lives.

Pétain had accepted Monsieur Paul Reynaud's legacy, possibly out of ambition, perhaps in a spirit of self-sacrifice, or conceivably because he found it natural that a destiny which had begun only at the age of fifty-eight should be crowned with kingship at eighty-four. "I sought it not," says the Doge in Byron's *Marino Faliero;*

> . . . the flattering fetters met me
> Returning from my Roman embassy,
> And never having hitherto refused
> Toil, charge, or duty for the state, I did not,
> At these late years, decline what was the highest
> Of all in seeming, but of all most base
> In what we have to do and to endure.

I crossed the Mediterranean with my crew, at the same time as hundreds of other pilots, without being sure I had enough fuel to reach Algiers. On June 25 the Armistice was signed. Whether it was necessary or not, from the military point of view, is a question which can be discussed indefinitely. The Armistice didn't save the Army, which was out of action in any case, and only those units which were able to reach North Africa escaped the disaster. But it saved the country from extermination and total occupation. It allowed the refugees to return home, the prisoners to hope for liberation and the Resistance to organize.

At one point, like a ship, Monsieur Paul Reynaud seemed to be in difficulties, when, following Bâtonnier Payen, Maître Isorni opened fire on him with his somewhat wild broadsides.

"You remained and later you became a Munichite." (*Laughter.*)

"That's news to me! The defense is certainly being original. . . ."

"No! Kindly answer the question, Monsieur Reynaud. Don't try to give me the slip."

"Have no fear, I shan't try to give you the slip. I'm doing very nicely as I am."

This passage at arms between gifted lawyers brought out Monsieur Paul Reynaud's consummate art and his eloquent gestures, Maître Isorni's fine voice, and then Maître Lemaire's bald and bellicose outspokenness. The defense made the mistake of irritating the jury and harrying the Attorney General.

After this confused and futile tussle Monsieur Paul Reynaud disappeared like a fast-moving warship behind a smoke screen. He retired unharmed, without a single glance for Pétain. The Marshal beckoned to Bâtonnier Payen, who bent over him and then returned to his bench. When the judge suggested adjourning the hearing, Bâtonnier Payen stated that the Marshal was finding the heat oppressive and having difficulty in following the proceedings. At twenty past five the court rose. Everyone rushed toward the doors. A hubbub of voices arose in the gallery.

Twenty-five minutes later, sixty-one-year-old Monsieur Édouard Daladier, who gave his profession as "university graduate," came forward and took the oath. The accused ostentatiously turned his eyes away.

Stocky, long-eared, with heavy eyelids drooping over blue eyes, and dressed in a badly cut double-breasted suit, he bore an astonishing resemblance to his cartoons. His dignity of tone impressed the court immediately: "It is with no resentment but rather with a certain melancholy that I shall speak to you. . . ." The voice was warm, worn by centuries of debate, yet without having lost any of its strength, like those stone steps to which time lends grace while wearing them down. The Vaucluse Bull was done for and knew it. His horns lowered, his wind short, his chest tired and his hooves weary, he retained the high broad forehead and the strong jaws of his Mussolini mask. The unruly lock which he used to toss back out of his eyes now lay neatly with the rest of his thin gray hair. Placing his leather briefcase on the chair with the gilded back by which he was standing, he gradually moved forward until he found himself just below the judges. His hands outstretched, his mouth opening at times to cry out, his features taut, he gave his evidence in a spirited fashion.

What revelations the court heard! In 1934 Marshal Pétain was Minister of War in the Doumergue government. He was well aware of the country's weakness, yet he had agreed to reduce the Army estimates by 20 percent. That year, when Pétain could have overcome every obstacle in his way, by virtue of his enormous prestige, the French Government placed orders for the manufacture of only seventeen tanks. "Yes, that was a mistake!" exclaimed Monsieur Daladier, as if he were shielding with his body the bent old man behind him. "But we have all made mistakes. . . ." Monsieur Daladier spoke with the voice of experience. He had learned the hard way how to gauge human promises at their proper worth.

Had Pétain belonged to the Cagoule? The witness shrugged his shoulders. In 1939 Monsieur Daladier appointed Marshal Pétain Ambassador to Spain to avoid having a third frontier to defend in the event of war. Léon Blum alone had protested in *Le Populaire:* "The noblest and most human of our soldiers is out of place at General

Franco's court." Then Monsieur Daladier offered the Marshal a post in his government. The Marshal laid down a condition: that Pierre Laval should also join the government in order to make Italy more amenable. Monsieur Daladier refused, and although he nonetheless agreed to join the Cabinet, the Marshal changed his mind and set off again for Madrid. There, denigrating ministers and Generalissimo in turn, he said of Daladier, "He'll have to look after himself!" And then came the blitzkrieg.

The hearing was adjourned at 6:35. Everyone was puzzled by this refusal by the Marshal to join the Daladier government, to which Monsieur Paul Reynaud had referred the day before. According to General Laure, the Marshal didn't trust Monsieur Daladier. Yet what Prime Minister would not have been afraid of displeasing such an illustrious soldier by not following his policy for national defense? On the other hand, did Pétain have such a policy at the time? The article by him which the *Revue des Deux Mondes* published on March 1, 1935, under the title, "The Safety of France During the Quiet Years," reveals an unusual poverty of ideas: with a good deal of tub-thumping and a great many commonplaces, Pétain called for a two-year period of military service as a complete panacea. He simply smiled condescendingly at the revolutionary theories of his disciple de Gaulle, "Colonel Motor," who was then in command of a tank regiment and foretold the coming of mechanized warfare with the urgency of a prophet crying in the wilderness. In 1940 Pétain deplored the Army's failure to give courier pigeons a leading role in communications. "Old age is a shipwreck. . . ." Already the Marshal was sinking back on the soft cushions of his courtiers' flattery. How could he resist when he possessed everything, and when the whole of France expected oracular pronouncements from his lips?

On the balcony of the Opéra, that evening, under the warm starry sky, Grace Moore sang *Louise* and then the Marseillaise before a huge crowd which cheered her. The wind, which was blowing gently from the northeast, kept the stormy weather at a distance.

IV

❧

Wednesday, July 25, 1945

Monsieur Édouard Daladier's evidence lasted two and a half hours in all. That day, Monsieur Daladier no longer hammered the back of an ordinary chair with the palm of his hand, but the back of a cane-bottomed Louis Quinze armchair intended for Monsieur Albert Lebrun. He went on with his story.

The *Massilia* took the members of Parliament to Rabat. Monsieur Daladier tried to persuade General Noguès, who possessed the authority and the means of a colonial administrator, to go on fighting. General Noguès would have been quite willing to continue the war, but the fleet was at anchor in the harbors of Toulon and Mers-el-Kebir, and without the fleet . . . The British, preoccupied with defending their island, had no intention of lending their cruisers, and even if they had done so, that would only have provoked a conflict between the Royal Navy and the French Navy, which was loyal to Marshal Pétain.

Monsieur Daladier asked the court's permission to read out a few figures to show that the Republic had not handed over an unarmed France to Germany, and he put on his spectacles. The court thus learned that in 1940 the French Army possessed 3,600 tanks, nearly 1,000 armored vehicles, 6,000 light guns, over 7,000 heavy guns and 3,000 military aircraft. The Armistice listed in the Unoccupied Zone 4,238 aircraft, including 1,739 front-line planes, to which could be added 1,800 aircraft, including 800 front-line planes, which had been flown to North Africa.

The members of the jury exchanged glances. One of the judges heaved a sigh. There was a slight stir among the public. Why was it said that France had lost the battle of 1940 for want of war material? If it was true that the country had begun hostilities with so many aircraft, how had the Stukas been able to obtain aerial supremacy? Monsieur Daladier was telling the truth. France was not short of arms in 1940. It was simply that she lacked the time and the means to learn how to use them. Even Colonel de Gaulle, given command of a hurriedly formed armored division, had been powerless. All those guns, tanks and planes had counted for nothing, just as tractors and the most modern agricultural machines rust in the rain if the peasants only know how to use ox plows. The war machine had not been ready, and when he had taken over, Weygand had been struck by the demoralization of the Army leaders.

According to Maître Isorni's subsequent revelations, Monsieur Daladier had asked the defense not to attack him. In return, he had undertaken not to be too hard on the accused. Thus, when Monsieur Daladier had finished his deposition, the Bâtonnier stood up.

"Do you think that the Marshal betrayed his country?"

No lawyer would have risked putting that question to an enemy.

Monsieur Daladier turned around and took his time. Then, speaking slowly in his deep voice, alternately sad and good-natured, he said, "In all conscience I must reply that, in my opinion, Marshal Pétain betrayed the duties of his office."

"That isn't the same thing," the Bâtonnier said quickly, making as if to sit down again.

The next part of the reply stopped him.

"The word *treason* has many different meanings. There are men who have betrayed their country for money. There are others who have betrayed it by mere incompetence, and that, I believe, was the

case with Marshal Bazaine. Of Marshal Pétain, I must say quite
frankly, however much it pains me, that he betrayed his duty as a
Frenchman. . . ."

Some photographers suddenly approached the defense bench. A
woman in her sixties, who was taken for Madame Pétain on account
of her corpulence and dignified appearance, had just slipped in
behind the lawyers. It was Madame Payen.

A fresh incident occurred. Monsieur Mabrut, one of the parliamentary jurors, asked for the text of the telegram which Marshal
Pétain had sent the German authorities after the attempted British
landing at Dieppe. The presiding judge instructed the Bâtonnier to
ask the Marshal to stand up and answer this accusation. Maître Isorni
retorted that the answer had been given during the preliminary
investigation and was on the record.

"The preliminary investigation is now a dead letter. We are in the
presence of the accused. . . ."

There was a brief argument across the floor of the court, over the
Marshal's attitude and the text of the telegram. This was finally
discovered by the Attorney General's secretary, a young woman
archivist whom the presiding judge could not resist sending down to
history by calling her Ariadne.

The telegram, which could have been a blunder or a piece of
trickery, was then read out while the accused tapped his cheek with
his gloves. Maître Isorni asked the presiding judge for permission to
read out the statement the Marshal had made in this connection. The
judge retorted that as the accused was present he could give his
explanation himself.

One of the jurors representing the Resistance, Monsieur Perney,
lost patience and exclaimed, "That attitude can be kept up indefinitely. What we want is the truth, and it's the accused who must give
us the truth. . . ."

The defense again replied that both questions and answers could
be found in the record of the preliminary investigation. There were
murmurs of protest from the public.

"I am asking a precise question," said Monsieur Perney. "Is the Marshal prepared to answer when his honor is at stake, and to provide the explanations which are necessary if the truth is to come out?"

Bâtonnier Payen bent over the Marshal and repeated the question for his benefit. It was Maître Isorni who had conceived this idea of the Marshal's stubborn silence. Christ had said nothing before Pilate. In Isorni's eyes, the trial of Marshal Pétain was the trial of Christ.

"How can I give any explanations?" replied the Marshal in the midst of an oppressive silence. "I can't hear because I am very hard of hearing. I haven't heard anything. I don't even know what it's all about."

There were cries of indignation. In the sixteenth century, in Venice, Doge Marino Faliero also refused to defend himself:

I deny nothing—defend nothing—nothing
I ask of you, but silence for myself,
And sentence from the Court! . . .
What shall I say to ye,
Since my defence must be your condemnation?
You are at once offenders and accusers,
Judges and executioners!

"That's how things stand," concluded the Marshal.

"Since Marshal Pétain has heard my question, I shall read out the telegram to him. If you will be kind enough to pass it to me . . ."

"I must tell you that I won't answer."

"As far as I'm concerned, the incident is closed," said Monsieur Perney.

"I have already said I won't answer any questions put to me," repeated the Marshal.

"I don't even know what it's all about." How could this remark have failed to shock? In the stormy atmosphere of the courtroom it provoked an indignant outburst which the silence in which it was uttered made all the more striking. It alienated journalists who, like certain members of the jury, were looking for the truth. Bâtonnier Fernand Payen remained silent, and even the fiery Isorni did not press the point. They could have used a rhetorical device to reveal what the Marshal had said about that telegram during the preliminary investigation, but that would have been playing with fire. Maître Isorni preferred, a few moments later, to counter the description Monsieur Daladier gave of the Marshal's entourage by reading out part of the prose poem by Paul Valéry, who despite the passage of time had remained an admirer of his fellow academician:

> The extraordinary circumstances in which we are placed, our suspended destiny, our scattered power, our entire past lying around us, all this misfortune combines to turn an act of homage into an act of faith. As the capital, the intellectual center, the symbol and masterpiece of France, Paris offers herself and entrusts herself to him who has offered himself, in the midst of unprecedented disorder and unparalleled disaster, to maintain the unity which is the very existence of our country.

"That only goes to show that poets are not necessarily prophets," exclaimed President Mongibeaux with a touch of vulgarity.

In 1942 Valéry's eulogy had carried considerable weight. It overshadowed the end of Monsieur Édouard Daladier's testimony. Political justice, which Attorney General Mornet denied serving, was being meted out in hot blood, on matters which were barely closed, in courtrooms full of emotion. It was as if, separated from the court by only a curtain, the state were listening to the hearings, scrutinizing the judges' faces and spying on their consciences. And, indeed, every evening one of the jurors, Pierre Stibbe, met General de Gaulle's private secretary, Monsieur Gaston Palewski, as if by accident, in the corridors of the Senate, to describe the atmosphere of the trial.

At that moment, the linotypes of *Le Figaro* were setting up the leading article for the following day. In it François Mauriac wrote:

> We should be hypocrites if, before mingling our voices with all those raised in accusation, each of us did not ask himself: "What did I say, write or think at the time of Munich? How did I greet the news of the

Armistice?" After Munich, that huge crowd which cheered Daladier at
the airport (himself astonished not to have to wipe spittle off his face)
gave the hidden or declared accomplices of the Fuehrer an assurance that
they could go ahead and that they would be supported by the weakness
and abnegation of an entire people.

The poet whose body was lying in state on the esplanade of the
Palais de Chaillot also bore a share of the responsibility for having
lulled us with the illusion of a great unfinished destiny. It seemed
strange that General de Gaulle should take the salute at the parade of
troops in front of Paul Valéry's coffin, and should pay homage to the
memory of a writer who had sung the praises of King Philippe VII.
But de Gaulle was saluting the academician who had answered the
speech which, through the intermediary of Marshal Pétain, he himself had helped to write for posterity. Elevated above the Académie
française, General de Gaulle would always regret that he had never
read out a speech of thanks under the dome of the Institut, nor
inscribed his name on the marble of the Quai Conti, among those of
Chateaubriand, Victor Hugo and Sully Prudhomme. Still, Bossuet
was never a member of the Académie française, Clemenceau refused
to enter it, and Louis XIV could only honor it by his visits.

Adjourned after Monsieur Daladier had given evidence, the hear-
ing was resumed at 3:25 with the entry of Monsieur Albert Lebrun.
Meanwhile Marshal Pétain told Monsieur Joseph Simon in an aside,
"I didn't send that telegram. It came from Pierre Laval's office."

The former President of the Republic was obviously in the grip of
considerable emotion. In spite of his seventy-three years, he refused to
sit down in the armchair which was offered him and stood with his
hands resting on its wide back. With his bald head, his slack mouth
under the graying mustache, and his anxious, protuberant eyes,
Monsieur Albert Lebrun had never been anything but a kind, gentle
shadow, easily alarmed by any slip of the tongue and anxious to
maintain in all circumstances the dignity of his office. Meticulous,
elegant, narrow-shouldered, bent-backed, and ready to withdraw at

the slightest threat, he could have played the part of a starchy butler in any of the high-society films of the time. It had been for these very qualities and because he didn't dare to say no that he had been elected President of the Republic. His misfortune was that he had not been able to choose his time. He had allowed himself to be tossed about, shaken and jostled by events like a cork by a wave. The idea of relating those events to the court, and of giving a detailed account of that abnegation of power and command, which still shocked and surprised him, made him tremble. His teeth nearly started chattering. He had accepted everything, even being kept in ignorance of what was happening—"for you see, gentlemen, the position of the President of the Republic is rather special."

Consequently when, looking into the abyss of a new Cabinet crisis in the midst of a national disaster, he asked Marshal Pétain to form a government, and the Marshal, opening his briefcase, showed him a list of his ministers, "I must say," Monsieur Lebrun went on in his tired, solemn voice, "that however sad that moment was for me, I nonetheless felt a certain relief. I remembered during my eight years of office those difficult attempts to form a government which, as you will recall, used to last three or four days . . . whereas now I had my government at once. I considered that admirable. . . ."

Dear Monsieur Lebrun, terrorized by his title of Head of the Armed Services! The poor man, not knowing whether he should leave France or remain, did not dare to make a choice, and allowed himself to be harangued by Laval. ("Monsieur Laval," I said to him, "the louder you talk, the less clearly I hear you; please lower your voice.") In the hope of arranging matters, he surrendered his own office to the new Prime Minister. In short, he was pushed aside and deprived of the power to sign new laws; but as all this was done with a certain formality and seemed to be the wish of the Chambers, he did not protest.

Before taking his leave, he even paid a courtesy call on Marshal Pétain, in conformity with old-fashioned French politeness and his own temperament. In this way he obtained at Vizille, not the residence of the President of the Republic, which he said was "not very pleasant to live in," but a family villa. Why was this goodhearted notary, whose trembling voice seemed about to break into sobs, later thrown into a German camp? At the time, he had nothing but admiration and veneration for Pétain. In 1918 he had seen Raymond Poincaré hand him his Marshal's baton at the foot of the statue of Ney, whose career had also come to a tragic end.

"To rise so high!"

The accused smiled mockingly, raised his hand, then pointed down at the floor.

"And fall so low!" exclaimed Monsieur Albert Lebrun, choking with emotion as he concluded his depositon.

Monsieur Pierre-Bloch, Socialist Deputy for the Aisne and former Assistant Commissioner for the Interior on the Algiers Committee, asked how long the list of ministers in the Pétain government of June 1940 had been ready.

"Accused, stand up!" cried Monsieur Mongibeaux.

What had got into the presiding judge? A sudden desire to show his power had brought his musketeer's beard down onto his fur collar and set his aquiline nose quivering. Was the heat getting on his nerves? Yet, having acknowledged the solemnity of the occasion on the first day, by appearing in all the stifling splendor of his furs, he had removed the long squirrel trimmings from his red and black robes. In his shirt sleeves under his royal mantle, he was perfectly comfortable. With the movement he made, a thin lock of hair fell over his forehead.

Then, as the Marshal did not seem to have heard him, he said, "Guard, make the accused stand up."

The guard rose to his feet, very erect, his cheeks pink from a close shave, not daring to touch the Marshal. On the other side, Bâtonnier Payen stood up to protest. The Marshal did not budge.

"I know as well as anyone else that he is deaf. You are wrong to think that—"

"I am willing to put the question to him again," said the judge, with one hand on his blotter. "Repeat it to him. For how long—"

"Don't answer!" exclaimed Maître Isorni and Maître Lemaire, leaping to their feet.

"I can't answer since I didn't hear the question," the Marshal said slowly, tapping the arms of his chair.

"I shall repeat the question," the judge said in a loud voice. "How long beforehand had you prepared the list of Cabinet ministers you were going to submit to President Lebrun?"

This time everyone thought the Marshal was going to speak. His lips moved as if he were beginning his reply.

"What was the question?" he asked in a faint voice.

A murmur of disappointment ran through the courtroom. The Bâtonnier bent down again, grasped the Marshal's wrist, and rested his left arm on the back of the chair. In a photograph taken at that moment, the two old men's skulls, one crowned with white hair, like the head of a venerable abbot, the other furrowed with wrinkles and covered with winding blood vessels just under the skin, seem to be drawn together for a dramatic confession.

Thus once did stricken Carthage
See noble Marius distraught,
And each of these great ruins
Comfort to the other brought. . . .

"You were asked," said the Bâtonnier, "the date on which you drew up the list of ministers which you later submitted to President Lebrun. Do you remember that?"

The Marshal seemed to glance at Mongibeaux.

"I may have thought about a few names at first," he said, "but the list I submitted wasn't that one. . . . What I mean is that the list I had in my pocket wasn't the one I used in the end. . . . I have answered the question," he added after a pause.

There were murmurs in the courtroom.

"I don't think that is an answer to the question I asked," said Monsieur Pierre-Bloch.

"I can't obtain anything more," answered the judge in a resigned tone of voice.

Was the old King being cunning, or was he letting himself sink into the quagmire of the trial? Could the lucidity his lawyers forced out of him, by breaking through his monstrous indifference, still light up his mind for brief moments? There was a general feeling of discouragement. They were trying a dying man.

Three members of the jury tried to find out from Monsieur Lebrun whether the summoning of the National Assembly of July 1940 was legal or illegal, and whether he should not have asked Monsieur Paul Reynaud to form a new government. Among Monsieur Lebrun's embarrassed replies, this edifying remark stands out: "Oh, in those troubled times anything was possible. There were no Chambers; there was nothing."

Bâtonnier Payen, after a few unctuous gestures, put the same question as before: "Tell me, in all conscience, do you believe that this man is guilty of the abominable crime of treason toward his country?"

"You use the word *treason*," answered Monsieur Lebrun, constricted in his high stiff collar, his nose a little red. "That is a word which is very difficult to define. But I will say this: I cannot understand why . . . the Marshal did not stand up and say, 'No, I cannot. Either you agree or I go.' That's my point of view. . . . And then we should have had to face the consequences. France would have had a gauleiter and we would have known where we stood. . . ."

The court then learned that President Lebrun had sent New Year's greetings to the Marshal every year. It was pointed out that one didn't behave like that with a dishonest man.

"No one has used the word *dishonest*," said Monsieur Lebrun. Then, his eyes suddenly alarmed, his voice shaking, he denied having sent New Year's greetings to the very end. In fact he had shown his disapproval by his silence.

Had he been naïve? Or had he trusted the Marshal's intentions? Whatever the truth of the matter, after the Montoire meeting with Hitler, Monsieur Lebrun wrote a warm letter to Marshal Pétain, which Bâtonnier Payen read out with diabolical satisfaction. At

Vizille, came the reply, how could a former President of the Republic judge world affairs? If he had it to do over again, he would not have written that letter. And what about the handing over of the fleet? The fleet, he replied, had orders to disarm, while remaining ready to scuttle or to sail away to the United States. And what of the Armistice? Monsieur Lebrun had always spoken out against it. Twenty-two years before, he had heard Clemenceau, Foch and Joffre repeat, "War! War!" He remembered that Clemenceau wanted to fight on the Seine, on the Loire, on the Garonne, before the Pyrenees, at sea and in North Africa. But in June 1940 he heard the leaders of the French Army protest: "No, we must have an armistice!"

Yet Britain had kept back part of her forces for her own defense instead of risking them in a common struggle. In that case, France herself was no longer bound by the secret agreement of March 28, 1940. Maître Isorni had some trouble in extracting an admission to this effect from Monsieur Lebrun, who was said to have been devoted to the British royal family ever since the visit to Paris by the King and Queen in 1937. It was rumored that the President of the Republic, seized by an all-consuming passion for the Queen, was afraid of uttering a single word which might displease Her Gracious Majesty.

His voice died away in a last sob. The drama suddenly became as oppressive as the air in the courtroom. The presiding judge concluded in a few words.

"In the circumstances," he said, "I shall simply address Marshal Pétain once again and ask him whether he has any comments to make."

"No," replied the Marshal unhesitatingly. "No comment."

He put his watch back in his pocket, pushed the table away, picked up his kepi and stood up, while the Bâtonnier thanked Monsieur Albert Lebrun on behalf of his "poor old client."

The hearing was adjourned till the next day.

"History will say . . . We must rely on history to establish the truth. . . ." To escape from the thunderbolts which were splitting the heavens, the Third Republic sheltered under the lightning conductor of history. So did the Church. Paradoxically, *La Croix* had not printed the last words of Marshal Pétain's statement: "Your judgment will be followed by the judgment of God and the judgment of posterity." The only newspaper which, despite the Liberation, had continued to appear under the same title and the same editor, *La Croix* was careful not to show in a favorable light a man it had eulogized during the Occupation.

When the storm had broken and the rivers had burst their banks, the Third Republic had remained silent. Now that everything was returning to normal, it spoke up, but cautiously. At the time, how many of those who returned to the witnesses' bench with a sigh of relief, how many inscrutable judges, how many jurors had thought that the Armistice was a crime? "Among those men accusing Pétain," the leader writer in *Combat* had written on July 18, 1945, "among the judges and above all the witnesses, we can already see men whose previous record or connections with the accused do not particularly fit them for the role of expiators of wrongs."

Who had fought in France in 1940? A few units. Who wanted to go on fighting in June? A handful of men. The nation, floored in the first round, like a boxer ready to be knocked out, was staggering under its opponent's blows. Even if the Army had wanted to fight, the pitiful, hampering presence of the refugees on the roads, in both towns and villages, would have prevented it from doing so. A vast panic seized every soul. Everyone feared the worst for his family. There had been too many reports that as the Germans advanced, they burnt houses, raped women and killed children. Composed of countless individual misfortunes, the national misfortune covered the country with a darkness everyone had by now forgotten. All those who had given evidence so far spoke of the Armistice as of a medicine, discussing whether it had been beneficial or harmful. At the time, the prefects had still been able to requisition hotels and country houses for themselves, away from the huge migration which they appeared not to have seen. Pétain had placed himself between misfortune and the French, and in the glory of their liberation the French seemed to have forgotten that.

For my part, I remember, and the memory still hurts, I was an adjutant at the flying school in the Isère. I was given forty-eight hours to move my family from Chartres. At Lyons I jumped aboard a train. The station at Sens had been bombed. During the night I arrived in Paris, a deserted Paris. I discovered much later that the military governor of the capital was waiting for orders which never came. In the mass of traffic at the Porte de Versailles, a man who was going to Tours opened the door of his car for me. A vast procession of cars, trucks, cyclists and pedestrians was fleeing in total darkness. Soldiers kept threatening to fire at drivers who switched on their lights. Every now and then, the dented old moon emerged from the clouds and lit up the vehicles which had broken down and been pushed to the side of the road. At half past two in the morning I reached home and woke up my wife. Then, with our children, we in turn joined the disorderly column heading south.

Daylight revealed a lowering sky, torn by stormy squalls, which protected us against attacks from the air. I felt ashamed of finding myself in uniform at the wheel of a private car. At midnight in pouring rain, we reached Lyons, where I was lucky enough to find a room. That evening Monsieur Paul Reynaud spoke again on the radio to address an appeal to the United States of America. I didn't hear him. The next morning I rejoined my flying school with my family near me. What had all this achieved? Two days later I had to leave them there and we fell back. When the order to leave arrived, some of our men thought we were deserting them. The German divisions had already occupied Chartres and Dijon. Monsieur Paul Reynaud had resigned and Marshal Pétain had spared Monsieur Albert Lebrun a Cabinet crisis. We expected to see the tanks of the Panzer divisions arrive at any moment. We set fire to all the planes which couldn't take to the air. Some of our pilots were too impatient to warm up their engines before take-off, and crashed in flames.

It was no fault of ours if we flew to Algiers instead of to London.

Except for the fleet, which nothing had prevented from leaving, the Armistice changed hardly anything in the military situation. It saved the country from death. But did it also save it from despair and dishonor? In Brazil, Bernanos, who was better placed than myself to decide that question, did not try to evade a responsibility which he considered common to all Frenchmen, and of which he accepted his part, however shameful it might be. "Naturally," he wrote in June 1940,

I respect Marshal Pétain's glorious past. But it is not true—no, it is not true—that my country has chosen him. I admire that old man, who is proud of his past, and also, like all old men, given to sentimentalizing about himself, for agreeing to take power when no one else dared to assume that burden. But it was a real leader the country was hoping for, and the panic-stricken politicians, pending their return to the scene, have placed in power nothing but a liquidator. They have obviously persuaded that trusty old soldier that those same statesmen who have countless times declared their contempt for sentimentality in politics would be moved by the example of such nobility, and that Hitler would give up his claims to Alsace, Mussolini his claims to Corsica, and Franco his claims to Gibraltar and Morocco, to avoid hurting the feelings of an unfortunate octogenarian. When that old man has drunk the bitter cup to the dregs in their place, the politicians will all return together, under the protection of Fascist bayonets, and will send back into retirement that now too embarrassing witness of our dishonored victory.

V

❧

Thursday, July 26, 1945

The sky had been clouding over since midday. A pall of stifling heat covered the city. A storm was approaching. Everyone hoped for rain.

When the hearing was opened, at twenty past one, in an oppressive atmosphere, Maître Lemaire read out the answer the Marshal had given during the preliminary investigation in connection with the telegram about the Dieppe landing: "The instructions it contains are . . . contrary to my entire policy and incompatible with all my ideas." There was no comment, and eighty-one-year-old Monsieur Jules Jeanneney, preceded by a major of the Republican Guard, was admitted to the courtroom. Monsieur Jeanneney took the oath, settled himself comfortably in the witnesses' armchair, and stretched out his legs.

"Why, he's terribly young!" the Marshal whispered to his astonished guard.

The former President of the Senate was a shrewd-looking man with lively eyes behind his glasses and gaunt, mobile features. With a lace collar and sleeves, his pointed beard and splendid white hair would have given him the appearance of an El Greco figure. Dressed in a black jacket and striped trousers, with a bow tie, he was just a senator, mayor and former minister. It was he who had presided over the National Assembly which invested the Marshal with supreme power. He told the story, not without charm, in an unemotional, sometimes childish voice. The Marshal, one hand cupped around his ear, listened.

It was obvious that Monsieur Jeanneney could not have put up much of a fight. Isolated and bewildered, and subjected to the tirades of Pierre Laval, he explained his submission by the "conning"—that was the word he used—he had suffered. He, too, denounced the Armistice as an unforgivable error. At the time, even those deputies who were opposed to granting plenary power to Marshal Pétain recognized "the absolute necessity of continuing negotiations." Giving the Marshal supreme power in July 1940, he had assured him of his profound respect, and had put up less resistance than anyone else. Apart from General de Gaulle, who had dared to show the slightest opposition? Monsieur Jeanneney admitted that the powers granted to Marshal Pétain were perfectly legal, but read out a letter he had written to the head of state to protest the shooting of a hundred hostages at Châteaubriant. That Armistice which was now alleged to have brought nothing but shame on the country had been used as a means of exerting pressure. Bâtonnier Payen replied with René Payot's testimony: the Marshal had warned Hitler that if reprisals continued, he would go to the demarcation line and offer himself as a hostage. The lawyers bickered over the question of dates like dogs over a bone. A clap of thunder suddenly rang out in the distance, and everyone looked at the windows for the first slap of the expected downpour.

The Marshal, slumped in his armchair, was asleep. Bâtonnier Payen woke him up to ask him if he had anything to say. He waved his hand: "No, nothing." The examination of this witness had yielded nothing of any value. The Marshal stood up and Monsieur Jeanneney gave him a little bow which took Madeleine Jacob's breath away. The hearing was adjourned, then resumed. Rain was falling on the Sainte-Chapelle and dripping from the deserted galleries. The roofs were gleaming. Everyone gulped down the cool air coming in through the open windows.

Monsieur Louis Marin was only seventy-four, almost a young man in this assembly where so many bodies seemed ready to crumble into dust. The Deputy for Nancy, he had entered politics at the age of thirty-two and since then had spent his whole life as a deputy, a chairman of committees, a member of commissions, a budget spokesman, a social reformer and a minister. In 1940 he had been Vice Premier. This career had left him unknown, and his testimony resulted in no incidents, aroused no curiosity. His life had gone by without risk. With his polka-dot cravat, and his black suit smelling of mothballs, he looked like a bespectacled Latin master of the days before 1914.

His long deposition went unnoticed. No one was touched by what was said by that rather absurd figure with the dignified bearing and walrus mustache. And yet, twenty years later, his deposition assumes a strangely impressive character. The first of all those old men who had come to testify against another old man trapped in sleep like a ship in ice, Monsieur Louis Marin spoke with a clarity that the court had looked for in vain before. He placed the problem in its proper perspective and on its proper level, without blurring the issue and with an unexpected force. His words, probably because I didn't hear them from his own lips, now take on a new value.

"The Poles were massacred on all sides, but they went on fighting everywhere for a long time, and they did not conclude an armistice. Norway did not conclude an armistice. Belgium did not conclude an armistice. Holland did not conclude an armistice. Luxembourg did not conclude an armistice. And Yugoslavia, pulling out of the clutches of the pact the Regent had just signed, did not conclude an armistice either. We alone concluded one. . . ." Aside from the style, you might think you were reading Bernanos. But the court heard only Monsieur Louis Marin.

Monsieur Marin recalled the terms of the agreement of March 1940 with Great Britain, which Monsieur Paul Reynaud regarded as still binding on France in May. This was not, I think, a pact which had been given much publicity. Nor do I remember feeling ashamed, at the time, of belonging to a nation which broke its word. Monsieur Marin had asked Monsieur Paul Reynaud, "Tell us clearly, and tell everybody, if you still solemnly and sincerely consider that France is bound by that agreement." Monsieur Paul Reynaud had stood up and replied, "Yes, completely." Monsieur Marin rejected the excuses everyone had strained their ingenuity to dig up: "Come, gentlemen, are you really looking for extenuating circumstances? I hear people saying, 'England didn't send us enough planes. . . . England didn't give us sufficient support. . . . England this and England that. . . .' But I say that . . . breaking a pact like that is breaking the country's word of honor."

Pointing an accusing finger at the judges, while Marshal Pétain dozed behind him, and speaking in a quick voice which was occasionally drowned by the noise of the storm, Monsieur Marin analyzed the factors leading to the situation of July 1940. First of all, the leaders of the armed services would not hear of surrender or capitulation: surrender would involve a commitment on their part, whereas an armistice, decided on by the state and ordered by the government, would save their faces. Next, in order to by-pass the terms of the Franco-British pact, Monsieur Chautemps hit on the idea of asking the enemy, not for armistice terms, but for peace terms. It was argued that the French people, outraged by Hitler's demands, would then realize that the fight had to go on. In fact, according to Monsieur Marin, this was an attempt to disguise an approach that would inevitably lead to an armistice. Finally, Pétain, like Weygand, declared that he would not leave the mainland of France. According to Monsieur Marin, this was proof that both men wanted the Armistice, because an armistice would have been out of the question if the government had gone to Algiers. It was important to remember that Weygand was obsessed with the idea of public order; he announced at a meeting of the Council of Ministers that the Communist leader Thorez was at the Élysée. Like him, Pétain preferred an armistice to disorder.

"Which are the countries who said, 'We are at the end of our tether'?" cried Monsieur Marin. "Only our own country." And he recalled that a law passed in 1793 laid down the death penalty for anyone who spoke of negotiating with an enemy who had not previously recognized the nation's independence and security, her unity and indivisibility. Monsieur Marin inveighed against the collapse of the Army and the nation. He maintained that the Army was still capable of fighting and that while it had little hope of victory, the French people greeted the Armistice with despair. Contrary to what Monsieur Paul Reynaud had declared, Monsieur Louis Marin claimed that most of the ministers, like most of the Army, spoke out against the Armistice.

This man who had spent nearly the whole war in a Vichy hotel under the Marshal's patronage, before traveling to London in April 1944, only to see the collapse of his political hopes, concluded his deposition with an attack on the accused. It was said that this was his revenge for not having been given a ministerial portfolio or even the post of Governor of Lorraine. He was one of the few who had not stood up when the Marshal had appeared on the first day of the trial.

Bâtonnier Payen asked for the opinion of Monsieur Paul Reynaud, who got to his feet from the witnesses' bench. Had there been a majority in the Council of Ministers for or against the Armistice? In Monsieur Paul Reynaud's opinion, the question was insoluble and the argument was still going on. The President of the Republic had not called for a vote. According to Monsieur Louis Marin, Monsieur Paul Reynaud had misinterpreted his ministers' opinions and had made a mistake.

"It is obvious," Attorney General Mornet suddenly barked, rising from his seat, "that the situation was, to say the very least, confused. . . . What I am concerned with is establishing the responsibility of those who asked for the Armistice and subsequently accepted its provisions. That is the crux of the trial."

Reading the transcript of the proceedings twenty years later, I have the impression that at this point the Attorney General was trying to help Monsieur Paul Reynaud. A member of the jury, whose name is not recorded, took it upon himself to ask a leading question. From what he had heard, it appeared that there had been fifteen ministers against the Armistice and only twelve in favor of it. What had Monsieur Reynaud to say about that?

"It's possible," came the reply. "That question, the question of the majority, was of no interest to me. What did interest me was governing, and in order to govern we had to have a new government."

Monsieur Paul Reynaud, who had just contradicted what he had said two days before, then fell back on shy, worthy Albert Lebrun. Monsieur Lebrun had told him, "I should like to keep you, but you must bow to the majority opinion." Yet that majority opinion had not been expressed. Nobody knew exactly what it was. It now seems that even Monsieur Paul Reynaud himself didn't want to know what it was. That man who was always ready to attack, and whose blows, when he struck out, came thick and fast, was suddenly confused and muddle-headed. There is a mystery surrounding Paul Reynaud.

Monsieur Louis Marin tried to solve it while at the same time getting in a dig at the Attorney General. The question, he said, ought to be put to all Monsieur Paul Reynaud's former ministers.

Maître Isorni, sitting watchfully on his bench, stood up.

"I should like to put Monsieur Louis Marin's mind at rest," he said. "All the ministers in Monsieur Paul Reynaud's Cabinet have been questioned, and they have all declared that they were opposed to the Armistice."

There was a roar of laughter and the deposition tailed off miserably. Monsieur Louis Marin puffed out his chest and withdrew. He had not proved adequate to the occasion. He had leveled accusations in the hope of parrying any accusation which might be leveled at himself. What Monsieur Louis Marin lacked was not force of argument, but style and weight. What did Monsieur Louis Marin stand for? Nothing. He had set no example, save that of prudence, and also that of a silence which he suddenly broke once all danger had disappeared. He was the sort of man who always fights with someone else's blood. And yet, at this stage in my examination of the transcript, it struck me that a piece of sleight-of-hand had just been carried out under the eyes of jury and spectators, without drawing a word of protest from the judges who had caught the conjuror in the act.

Perhaps the Paul Reynaud mystery bore the name of Hélène de Portes. The Prime Minister had changed his mind under the influence of his Egeria. If she had stood firm, he might have been the Clemenceau of 1940. One day in Bordeaux Madame de Portes had waited for the Marshal to come out of his hotel, and had thrown herself weeping at his feet.

"Please stop Paul from spoiling everything," she had begged him.

"What could I do?" the Marshal asked later. "I took a handkerchief out of my pocket and handed it to her. And to comfort her I said, 'I will, Madame.'"

His mustache and cravat debonair and triumphant, Monsieur Louis Marin returned to the witnesses' bench where everyone forgot about him.

The next witness had been an attaché at the French Embassy in Madrid when Marshal Pétain had been Ambassador. His forty-eight years lent him the appearance of a prematurely aged adolescent. A diminutive diplomat bearing the name of an antelope and just as timid as that animal. Of his timorous features and receding hair no trace has remained in the photographs of the trial, and his barely formulated statements have vanished from the minds of those who heard them. All that is left of him is a cartoon in the newspaper *Libres*.

Flattering the presiding judge in order to get into his good graces, he tried not to incriminate himself and thus spoil his prospects of promotion, just as he tried not to criticize the accused while taking care not to defend him. How could the Marshal have shown the list of his future Cabinet ministers to a colleague such as that? Through the naïveté which soldiers display when their career happens to take them outside the world of the fighting man.

The hearing was adjourned at 5:35. In the crush the Marshal spoke to the witness.

"Didn't you enjoy your stay in Spain, Monsieur?"

"Monsieur le Maréchal, I told the court what I remembered, the good and the bad."

"The bad, the bad," growled the accused, as Bâtonnier Payen drew him away.

The storm had died down. The sky remained cloudy, but the air was fresher. The newspapers carried photographs of the accused, Monsieur Lebrun and Monsieur Daladier. They gave a list of the foodstuffs which could be obtained from the shops in exchange for coupons, and announced that to heat Paris the following winter two thousand trains would have to bring a million tons of wood from the Ardennes and the Morvan.

VI

❖

Friday, July 27, 1945

It was very hot when Monsieur Léon Blum gave his evidence. People were fanning themselves in the courtroom. The sky was leaden with the threat of another storm. Irritated by the photographers who were waiting with one knee on the floor to take shots of him, the Marshal once again made a gesture of annoyance. For some reason a good many journalists smiled when Léon Blum raised his right hand to take the oath, and he himself smiled under his splendid white Gallic mustache. Possibly President Mongibeaux had made some witticism when asking the witness to step forward, or when questioning him as to his identity. Turning toward Bâtonnier Payen, the Marshal asked a question which no one else heard.

To say that Monsieur Léon Blum was perfectly at ease would be an understatement. The Socialist politician had lost none of his old self-confidence. He was completely at home in a public assembly, and behaved with elegant assurance. He wore a handkerchief in the breast pocket of his jacket, which despite the heat was buttoned over his waistcoat. A slim, dark-suited figure, he gave the impression, as soon as he started speaking, of such extreme weakness and vulnerability that it seemed a puff of wind might blow him over. A stormy career, hard work, political warfare, the burden of authority, and then imprisonment and deportation appeared to have taken their toll of his physical stamina and his seventy-three years. Yet he had refused to sit down in the armchair and was not even leaning on it. At his very first words, everyone strained their ears to catch his thin voice with the inflections of a dying cello.

Near the witnesses' entrance, someone cupped his hand around his ear. A member of the public called out, "A little louder, please."

"I'll speak louder as I go along," came the reply.

Monsieur Léon Blum had played no part in the events of June 1940. He had not been a member of Paul Reynaud's Cabinet, but he had had friends who were, and Georges Mandel, the Minister of the Interior, had asked him to come to Bordeaux. There he was appalled by what he found:

"What struck me about the very first conversations I had was the degree to which the leaders of the Army already considered that all resistance had become impossible. We plied them with questions. We said, 'What do you mean? Is there nothing to be done? Aren't you defending the Seine? Aren't you going to defend the Loire? What then?' And we always got the same reply: 'General Weygand says there's nothing to be done.' "

Monsieur Léon Blum gave Saturday, June 15, as the date of the Chautemps proposal: that France should ask the enemy for their terms in order to justify rejecting them, and then go to North Africa. On Sunday, June 16, Georges Mandel announced that at ten o'clock that evening the members of Paul Reynaud's Cabinet were due to vote. No vote was taken. When the ministers arrived at the Prefecture, a new government was already being formed.

To anyone reading the transcript of the trial, the Paul Reynaud mystery thickens. Why was that vote, which was supposed to enlighten the Prime Minister as to the state of mind of his Cabinet, never taken? Why did Monsieur Paul Reynaud, who was opposed to the Armistice, give up hope of imposing his point of view? No questions on this point were put to either Monsieur Léon Blum or Monsieur Paul Reynaud. Did no one know the extent of the influence exerted on the Prime Minister by the steely Comtesse de Portes, who dictated the choice of generals and ambassadors? Her ambitious nature led her to discuss matters of state and indulge in palace intrigues.

If the authorities had dared to bring Monsieur Camille Chautemps from his prison to give evidence, he could have testified that at Tours Madame de Portes had already been very active, interfering in government business, and that he actually had to refuse to sign a decree which she had initiated. To rescue the Prime Minister from her influence, Monsieur Chautemps invited her to lunch at Blois. Full of somber forebodings, she spoke to him feelingly about the military situation and the need to conclude an armistice at once. True, Monsieur Chautemps's testimony might have appeared suspect. The ardor which had consumed Madame de Portes so far should have given Monsieur Paul Reynaud added strength of mind. And yet that fiery woman, who for a time had advocated holding out in Brittany, suddenly seemed to lose heart. On June 8, at Le Verdon, she had put her children on a boat for the United States, where she intended to join them. For Monsieur Paul Reynaud, who was intelligence incarnate, the drama was being played out, not only on the national stage, but also in his heart. Madame de Portes was his courage. Isn't it reasonable to suppose that without her he weakened in his turn, despite de Gaulle? When political matters are decided in the rooms of a woman who is loved and admired, the results can be unexpected, and the private life of the great men of this world, when it affects affairs of state, ought to weigh in the scales of justice.

Léon Blum had sworn to tell the truth, and he told it bravely and serenely. Even Maître Isorni later described him as bearing himself nobly.

In July 1940, at Vichy, the irremediable became law. "There, in the space of two days," said Léon Blum, "I saw men change and go rotten before my very eyes, as if they had been plunged into an acid bath. What was affecting them was fear: fear of Doriot's gangs in the street, fear of Weygand's soldiers at Clermont-Ferrand, fear of the Germans who had reached Moulins. . . . And the rumor going the rounds was: 'Those who don't vote won't sleep in their beds to-night.' "

The former chairman of the Council of State maintained a modest silence as to the nobility of his own attitude, and did not utter a word of complaint about all that he had suffered. Standing in a thoughtful posture, his chin resting in his right hand, his elbow in his left, he attacked the Riom judges to whom Monsieur Daladier had shown a certain indulgence. The defense lawyers suddenly sat up in their seats.

"How could they have given a decision in conflict with the oath of personal loyalty they had sworn to the Marshal? . . . I want to say here what I think: speaking for myself, I don't regard an oath of loyalty as a ridiculous formality. I once read that after the *coup d'état* of December 2, 1851, the young Duc de Broglie refused to take the oath as a councilor, and the aged Chancellor Pasquier told him, 'It is just as absurd to refuse a political oath as it is to demand it.' For my part I don't consider it would have been absurd to refuse it. . . . For a quarter of a century I myself have belonged to a profession whose members have not shown much courage. . . ."

The Attorney General bristled at this attack and scribbled a few notes. Everyone wondered whether he was going to reply. He chose instead to bide his time. President Mongibeaux, suddenly very pale, gripped his beard in his hand. Then, forestalling the questions he was going to be asked, Léon Blum gave his definition of the treason the accused had committed: "To betray means to hand over." The Armistice gave the French people the protection of certain guarantees. "That Armistice was handed over like all the rest, point by point, item by item." He went on to state clearly what he regarded as the crux of the matter.

"In June 1940 I saw a country . . . which was dazed and bewildered by its defeat and the vast, brutal, incomprehensible nature of that defeat. . . . The people were dumfounded, utterly crestfallen, prostrate with stupor and despair. And they were told, 'No, you are wrong. The Armistice we are proposing, which dishonors you and delivers you into the enemy's hands, is not a shameful act, but a natural act in conformity with the country's interests.' And the people of that country, not knowing the terms of the Armistice, believed what they were told because the man who told them these things spoke in the name of his victorious past, in the name of glory and victory, in the name of the Army, in the name of honor. Well, in my eyes, that is the heart of the matter, and I consider that that vast, abominable breach of a nation's trust deserves the name of treason."

There Léon Blum concluded his deposition, and silence fell on that terrible word.

A member of the jury hesitantly asked a question about the atmosphere at Vichy. Then the Attorney General raised the matter of the oath. He asked Léon Blum who would have taken the place of the judges if they had refused to take it.

The reply was framed at first in cautious language, then suddenly became cutting.

"I have always condemned the men at Vichy who gave in to that argument. . . . It would have been better for the administration of justice to be interrupted in France than for justice to be meted out, as it was in certain cases, for the enemy's benefit!"

"Which of the two men, Laval and the Marshal, influenced the other?" asked Bâtonnier Payen.

There followed a few important exchanges between the witness and the defense. Léon Blum knew Pierre Laval but not the Marshal, in whom he distinguished an impenetrable mystery. He did not know what lay behind Pétain's actions: ambition, the desire for personal power or some emotional experience. Léon Blum had not been chary of praise of the Marshal before 1940.

"I lived under the same illusion as the rest of France. . . . It is precisely the fame enjoyed by Marshal Pétain, that national fame composed of so many elements—his martial bearing, his stature, his limpid gaze, whatever you like—it is that fame, used to deceive France as to the purpose and implications of the Armistice, and endowing it with the misleading appearance and false prestige of honor, when in fact the country was being led into disgrace—it is that which in my opinion forms the crux of this trial."

"You are right," said Maître Payen, "that is indeed the crux of the affair. We are confronted with two hypotheses . . . you will, I trust, admit that in the face of the one you have just put forward there is another, to wit, that this man, the Marshal of France who is here before us, never meant to betray his country, but wished to act for the best. Whether he was mistaken or not is another matter, but that he wished to act for the best is something that I hope to be able to prove to you a little later. . . ."

"You stated that Marshal Pétain had created an illusion," said Maître Isorni in his turn. "Don't you think that when an illusion can last from 1914 to 1939, in other words for nearly twenty-five years, that illusion may nonetheless conceal a certain reality?"

Léon Blum turned toward the Marshal, and the two men gazed intently at each other.

"I think one can be mistaken for a very long time as to the real nature of a man. I also think that men sometimes change, that the balance of motives and passions can alter. I think, too, that men can change when, after living a life of everyday responsibility, they find themselves involved in new activities and preoccupations."

The Marshal made a gesture of denial with his hand.

Monsieur Paul Reynaud was called forward to explain why Paris had not been defended. He came and stood next to Monsieur Léon Blum, in his well-cut light-gray suit, and leaned on the back of the armchair. He replied that he had not wished to immobilize forces in Paris which he preferred to send to North Africa.

"I am going to ask Marshal Pétain a question," said the presiding judge. "Has he any comments to make? Has he any questions to put to the witness?"

The Marshal shook his head.

"A frosty silence," said the judge, pushing away his cap.

Slim and elegant, with a noble forehead and a long intelligent face above a high stiff collar, obsessed with himself and what he was saying, the next witness had the courage to bow to the Marshal, who held out his hand to him. Monsieur François Charles-Roux, Secretary

General for Foreign Affairs from May to October 1940, knew a great many state secrets and had witnessed a great many government dramas. His deposition, given in a monotonous voice and interrupted by an adjournment, lasted nearly two hours. Plied with questions, he sidestepped them neatly. An ambassador knows the art of walking on thin ice without breaking it, of avoiding taking up dangerous positions or putting others into such positions. Diplomacy is a subtle mixture of firmness and evasion, of half-lies and banal or high-sounding truths. Never to do or say anything which might compromise somebody, never to risk basing action or argument on hypotheses, and never to rely on the facts without remembering that they have no sooner been established than they may collapse—such are the rudiments of the profession. Once a man has mastered these rules, he can serve princes or republics.

"Men sometimes change," said Monsieur Léon Blum. But had the Marshal changed? At Vichy he was nicknamed "The Triple S": serenity, sovereignty, simplicity. Could anyone imagine that he had dark designs which he had kept hidden all his life, at the very age when mind and body become set in a concrete mold? The fact was that when he appeared on the political scene, virtues were attributed to him which he did not possess. At a certain moment in their lives, men have been known to force destiny, but fortune is a whore, and like all whores goes from one bed to another. It was no fault of his if he was urged to mount a throne which nobody wanted. On the point of leaving this world, with every day that passed taking him one step nearer the shadows, he was suddenly offered a crown of light. How could a man who had begun living and commanding only after his retirement have refused the undreamed-of role that was proposed to him? "Oh, to accept and perform such an act of abasement," exclaimed de Gaulle on the London radio, "they had no need of you, Monsieur le Maréchal, they had no need of the victor of Verdun. Anybody would have done." True. But de Gaulle was then in the prime of life. What octogenarian can resist a display of interest in himself, and why are Academy meetings so well attended if not because old men are afraid of solitude and boredom? All of a sudden the Marshal found himself a magus, kneeling before the star of a grandiose redemption.

Greeting Marshal de Villeroy after he had been defeated by Marlborough at Ramillies, Louis XIV said to him, "Monsieur le Maréchal, at our age no one is happy." But Madame Pétain, receiving Monsieur and Madame Massis at Vichy one day, made this terrible statement about her husband: "If only you knew how happy he has been these last two years!" He was reigning over a country which had been bled white, danger was threatening on all sides, the enemy kept carrying off the young men of France, and war and disaster were spreading, yet he was radiant with happiness. He was still alive. People asked for his opinion, he issued messages in his quavering voice, and when he moved around the country, the homage of a whole nation warmed his old bones. How could he have failed to cling with all his might to the Frankish battle-ax which he gripped in his hand like a scepter?

The Armistice and the disaster of 1940 were not so terrible as all that for a memory purring in the sunshine of former triumphs. Old age helped him to forget the present and dwell among the victories of which he remained the hero. Already he possessed the ability to ignore unpleasant events and to bury them in the mists of sleep. His serenity was based on the monstrous indifference of old men toward misfortunes which strike down others and spare themselves, and that wisdom of his which was so greatly admired was simply extreme prudence, which had helped him to attain the highest positions and now enabled him to deceive the enemy. Yes, he was made of marble, and it was as marble that he countered the onslaughts of misfortune with an icy refusal to adapt himself to anything and a stubborn determination to gaze into the future with empty eyes.

In any event, no misfortune could ever have drawn him away from that despicable throne which had become his reason for survival. Why should he stay in Switzerland and give up the first place in the land, just to please de Gaulle? Why should he sacrifice the revenge which old age had given him over so many fools? As a young man, he had been forgotten, and, despite all his talent, relegated to subordinate positions. As an old man, he reigned supreme, and his old age was in the image of his prime. He remained just as he had been when fame had come to him: conscious of his worth, unshakable in his determination, a little lecherous and given to indulging in fanciful hopes, not in the least senile and never second-rate, full of common sense and endowed with a ready wit. If someone he regarded as unreliable asked him to autograph a book, he would do so with a stub of pencil he took out of his pocket, saying apologetically, "It's easier to rub out." At the end of the day, his will power would suddenly collapse for a few hours; but the next morning he would once more be keeping a close eye on the affairs of state. No, he had not changed.

Some people, like that simpleton Louis Marin, thought he was an idiot. Perhaps that was because Pétain the farmer's son had entered Saint-Cyr with one of the lowest grades and, like Charles de Foucauld, had been the butt of the "bright boys" of his year. De Gaulle, who saw him at close quarters, would not have chosen a fool as his master.

How could he have shone right from the start in an army where an initial grading follows a man like a star or a ball and chain? Who would ever have seen a future leader in that modest officer, full of good-natured or fierce wit, who ate like a horse and had only two passions in life: women and the infantry? Like a peaceable bull, he pawed and sniffed at the problems he met, cropped the grass while scanning the countryside with moist eyes, and then slowly chewed his cud. It had taken a war to give him command of the herd. Fixed in his habits and his mealtimes, faithful to his moods, opposing the hierarchy by sheer bulk, he showed himself stubborn, inaccessible and hard to shake, but once he was on the move, head high and quivering with irresistible anger, he would seek out the enemy, measure him up, then charge straight at him and fell him to the ground.

He had realized that the great secret was to endure. To do that, he had to avoid anything that might wear him down, from emotion to white wine. Now an unshakable Buddha, skeptical and smiling, he rested his gaze and his hands on his empty table, drew men and events toward him, then flicked them away into the void. A king, he reigned with sovereign dignity. He had, moreover, made a gift of his rather tired person to the country: a mere trifle. What more did France want of him? Victory lay in the past and the past was enough for him, still lulling him with its golden dreams. Monsieur Léon Blum himself had sung the great man's praises and would have voted for him if the occasion had arisen. Marshal Pétain had committed no breach of trust. It was rather the ministers of a moribund Republic who had sinned through excessive trust. Where, then, did treason lie?

VII

✤

Saturday, July 28, 1945

Nothing could be drearier than reading the seventeen pages of the
Journal officiel for that date. What, for example, despite his exem-
plary conduct and the care with which he had watched over his
spiritual inheritance, did the court learn from Georges Clemenceau's
son, another little old man of seventy-two, bald, dignified and
mustachioed like his father? Simply that the Marshal could hear what
was being said, since, as on the previous day, he waved his hand in
denial when the witness accused him of handing over Georges
Mandel and Paul Reynaud to the Germans. Again as on the previous
day, and however boring the witness might be, he listened. While
Monsieur Michel Clemenceau was reading out a letter, he displayed
an attentiveness tinged with irony. At the end of the deposition, a
member of the jury from the Resistance, bearded Monsieur Perney,
asked what the Marshal thought of it.

"Accused . . ." said the presiding judge. Then, disheartened, he
said to Bâtonnier Payen: "Kindly pass on the question to your client."

The Bâtonnier bent down and whispered into the Marshal's ear.
To everyone's astonishment the Marshal spoke.

"I have no intention of answering," he said, putting his hands on
his knees. "I cannot answer a question I don't understand."

"It seems to me that the question is not as difficult as all that," retorted the presiding judge.

"These repeated incidents are pointless," said Bâtonnier Payen, "seeing that the Marshal has decided not to answer."

A few minutes later, Monsieur Perney returned to the attack.

"He can hear. I have taken note of the fact that no more questions are to be put to him . . . but he can hear."

"That is correct," said Maître Isorni. "He can hear more or less clearly what the witnesses say, but he cannot really hear what Monsieur le Président says."

"My voice probably isn't loud enough," said the judge. "I'm sorry about that."

It was true that under the gilded canopy of the lofty ceiling voices tended to get lost.

General Doyen had led the French delegation to the Armistice commission at Wiesbaden. One day the Marshal had said to him of Laval, "That man is a shit." With or without Laval, the French delegation had given way on every point and handed everything over. The defense lawyers and Monsieur Paul Reynaud argued for twenty minutes about what Marshal Pétain could or could not be blamed for during the five months he had been Minister of War in 1934.

Everyone started yawning. General Doyen was trying to obtain forgiveness for the zeal he had shown under the Vichy regime. He had come to give evidence in uniform wearing the insignia of a Grand Officer of the Legion of Honor. The court took pity on him and the presiding judge called the next witness.

He came in rather stiffly, dressed in a dark striped suit with the buttonhole of a Commander of the Legion of Honor, and stood in front of the Marshal's table. When he turned toward the court, the light falling from the lofty windows lit up a frozen face and the steely gaze of a prosecuting counsel, behind narrow-rimmed spectacles. In his hand he held a folded sheet of paper. This was Pierre Frédéric Caous, former President of the Supreme Court of Justice of

Riom, who somewhat defiantly presented himself under that title. An even more important figure than was generally believed, he had previously belonged, together with Admiral Auphan, the Rector of the University, the Attorney General of the Audit Office, Ambassador Léon Noël and General Weygand, to the council empowered to govern the country in the event of Marshal Pétain's incapacity. "A Vichy pastille soaked in vinegar," was how Madeleine Jacob described him.

He had asked to give evidence in order to reply to Monsieur Léon Blum's attack on the judiciary. The Riom judges, he pointed out, had taken the oath in its old form and had not sworn loyalty to the person of the head of state. Speaking in a metallic voice, Monsieur Caous launched into a lengthy explanation of the text of the oath and of the powers and dignity of his profession. The court finally learned what he was holding gripped between his fingers like the host. It was a copy of the text of the law of August 1940, which he proposed to leave for the court's consideration.

He was about to withdraw, after receiving the presiding judge's thanks, when the Attorney General took the opportunity to praise the Riom judges, and then sat down again. Immediately Maître Isorni, with an innocent air, invited Monsieur Caous to give a public denial to the rumor going around Paris that the Attorney General had applied to serve in the Riom court.

"That's a foul lie!" yelled Monsieur Mornet, leaping angrily to his feet.

A murmur rose from the public.

"May I answer that question?" said Monsieur Caous, turning stiffly toward the judges.

The murmur died down, and was followed by a silence as deep as an abyss.

Monsieur Caous declared that he had never heard that Monsieur Mornet had asked to serve in the Riom court. He, Monsieur Caous, had invited him to do so, and Monsieur Mornet had accepted. To the accompaniment of sarcastic laughter from the public and an ironic smile from the accused, Attorney General Mornet replied that he was always to be found where treason had to be denounced, but that when he had discovered what was expected of the Riom judges, he had regretted writing the letter in which he had not refused that office.

"I am sure of one thing, Attorney General," said Monsieur Caous, "and that is that in that matter you could not have done any more or any better than we did."

"The incident is closed," cried the presiding judge, putting on his cap.

It was half past four. Journalists and lawyers rushed into the anteroom of the judges' chambers, convinced that they were going to see a quarrel between Monsieur Mornet and Maître Isorni. His eyes glittering under his shaggy brows, his beak in the air, the Attorney General tapped the trial lawyer on the shoulder and shook hands with him.

"My dear Isorni," he barked with a hoarse chuckle.

A brief smile touched Bâtonnier Payen's lips.

Resumed forty minutes later, the hearing became bogged down in trivialities. Another attaché at the French Embassy in Madrid, who never stopped taking off his spectacles to wipe them with a big white handkerchief, reported that at a ceremony at the Escurial the German section of the Spanish National Socialist Party had dipped their flags when Marshal Pétain passed by, and he had replied with a military salute. On another occasion, he told the court, the Marshal had shaken hands with the German Ambassador, in a monastery near Burgos.

"I must say," added the diplomat, "that the Marshal explained, 'I shake hands with an opponent before a fight.'"

As confidences go, this one sounded very solemn. In fact, on the day in question, seeing the shocked expressions of the officers accompanying him, old Pétain said to them, "I've given the Germans a hell of a beating. I'm entitled to shake hands with that young man." The attaché had translated this comment into diplomatic language.

No one could understand why another witness, the director of the *Opera mundi* agency, had chosen to appear before the court. He was a man of Czechoslovakian and Alsatian parentage, who had served with the Austrian Army in 1918. Two days later, the defense scored a minor victory when Maître Lemaire accused him of having spied for the Nazis.

The Marshal's eyes appeared to light up when a secretary on the General Staff came in, dressed in a skirt and tunic in coarse army cloth, with a Cross of Lorraine pinned over her heart. Today one can only wonder how the woman could have had the nerve to level such a flimsy but determined accusation at a Marshal of France. A former singer, she had performed seventeen years before, in parish halls in the suburbs, in an operetta by Louis-Gabriel Robinet, André Lavagne and Jacques Isorni. Perhaps she hoped that this time she might make a hit. Possibly she had been pushed into coming forward on this occasion. As it happened, she showed no lack of eloquence, guile and wit. But Maître Lemaire had no trouble in showing the unseemly and frivolous nature of her allegations.

VIII

❧

Sunday, July 29, 1945

Boredom was creeping in. The press, thoroughly disillusioned, was losing interest in this parody of a trial, in which the accused was only the shadow of a great name and a great destiny, and was giving less space to reports of the hearings. Anonymous letters were pouring in from all sides, addressed to the judges and the Marshal. Veterans of Verdun called for an acquittal, members of the Resistance for the firing squad. The defense lawyers themselves were threatened with death by fanatics on both sides. Revolvers had been issued to the members of the jury, whose lives seemed to be in danger, and the police were protecting those who considered themselves most seriously threatened. They were picked up every morning and taken home every night by car.

That day the accused had a cold and stayed in bed. His doctors certified that he was suffering from a mild attack of laryngitis. He could have echoed the plaintive words of King Lear: "They flattered me like a dog, and told me I had white hairs in my beard ere the black ones were there. To say 'ay' and 'no' to everything I said! 'Ay' and 'no' too was no good divinity. When the rain came to wet me once, and the wind to make me chatter; when the thunder would not peace at my bidding; there I found 'em, there I smelt 'em out. Go to,

they are not men o' their words! They told me I was everything. 'Tis a
lie—I am not ague-proof."

Canon Pottevin, a prison chaplain, came to say Mass in the
Marshal's room. Referring to the statement he had made on the first
day of the trial, the Marshal asked the canon if he was pleased with
what he had said.

"Oh, Monsieur le Maréchal . . ."

"But will God be pleased with it?"

This was a question worthy of a child in a village catechism class,
and it must have warmed the chaplain's heart. The Marshal had
stuffed piety into his saddlebag like a flask of brandy, but as his
faculties declined was his old-fashioned Christianity turning into
bigotry? In any event, he insisted on keeping his religious practices
secret, and no one knew that he was taking Communion.

After a whole week of hearings, the prosecution witnesses had
done nothing but defend the Third Republic, without laying any
serious charge at the Marshal's door, while the accused had said
nothing. "This is the Maginot Line of silence," declared the leader
writer of *Combat*, who recalled the attitude taken up by General
Gamelin at the Riom trial and expressed astonishment that it had
proved impossible to find a prosecuting counsel in France whose
conduct during the Occupation had made him fit to call the former
head of state to account. Like the Army, the entire judiciary had
sworn loyalty to the state, ready to recant at any time and swear a new
oath of loyalty to the new king.

The storms had brought about an improvement in the weather.
That Sunday, there were some sunny periods during the afternoon,
and sight-seers came to the Palais to gaze at the apparatus of law and
justice protected by the lofty turreted walls. They admired the angels
at the top of the black façades, the scales and swords and branches of
oak and laurel carved in stone, and the shield with the three fleurs-de-
lis surmounted by the crown of the kings of France, above the
gateway into the courtyard where the clerks used to dance every
springtime round a maypole. On the Quai de la Mégisserie, near the

Théâtre du Châtelet where *L'Aiglon* was billed, birds, guinea pigs and tame white mice were still being sold. On the other side of the Pont au Change, the flower market was overflowing with roses and geraniums.

"Flowers, lovely flowers, ladies!" shouted the stallkeepers.

Lovers gazed into each other's eyes. Here the war was over. But it was still going on in Japan, where thousands of Flying Fortresses were bombing Tokyo.

IX

❖

Monday, July 30, 1945

Monsieur Édouard Herriot was the last witness for the prosecution. Despite his tiredness and the gout which obliged him to keep one foot in a slipper, he did not accept the presiding judge's invitation to sit down in the armchair. Women's heads could be seen leaning forward in the gallery to get a better view of him. Square-chinned, his face furrowed and emaciated, his thick hair barely graying at the temples despite his seventy-three years, he had lost none of his massive good looks. Throughout the entire war, for fear of being poisoned, he had never allowed himself to be parted from Césarine, his cook.

The former President of the Chamber of Deputies, dressed in a black jacket and striped trousers, with a gold chain across his waistcoat, spoke in a deep loud voice. He had the disadvantage of following the principal actors. Breathing hard, he was alternately vague, bombastic, short-winded, shrill and tearful. It was hard to recognize in him the determined adversary of the Armistice which he claimed to have been. In point of fact, his sole preoccupation had been to spare his constituents the horrors of war; he had even waked up the Marshal in the middle of the night to persuade him to declare

Lyons an open city. It was impossible not to distinguish in him a certain naïveté mingled with a great deal of cunning. In a speech a few days before, he had made a good-natured attempt to obtain indulgence for the members of Parliament who had laid the immortal principles of which they were the guardians at the feet of Marshal Pétain.

He was no match for the defense lawyers, who reminded him of the terms of another speech which he had made to his colleagues immediately after the Armistice: "In its distress, our nation has gathered round Marshal Pétain, united in the veneration which his name inspires in one and all. Let us take care not to disturb the concord which has at last been established under his authority." Behind him, very pale, his fingers following the edges of his table and the arms of his chair, the Marshal listened with a contemptuous smile on his lips, then dozed off.

The witness was about to withdraw when the presiding judge asked once again whether the accused had any comments to make. "This is the period when he doesn't hear," he added, "but I am obliged to put the question to him."

Before the hearing was adjourned, one of the jurors asked for more witnesses to be called to testify to the tragedies caused by the Armistice and the deportations.

When the hearing was resumed, twenty minutes later, Bâtonnier Payen objected to the proposal to hear witnesses for the prosecution after the defense witnesses. The judges withdrew to consider the matter. A few minutes later they returned and overruled the defense's objection. The extra witnesses would be summoned by virtue of the presiding judge's discretionary powers, and at his will. Then the Attorney General read out a brief letter from Mademoiselle Mandel, who was barely fifteen years old. She apologized for not appearing before the court, for she was incapable of asking anything of it and could only weep.

"What was all that about?" the accused asked his lawyers.

Then he took some papers out of his pocket and read them. They were messages of support which had arrived that very morning from America.

The man approaching the judges was walking with the aid of canes and swinging his legs forward like a robot. Under his close-cropped hair, his smooth, hollow-cheeked face seemed to be covered with dark scars left by burns. An old suit hung loosely about his body. This was Major Loustanau-Lacau, the former head of the Legion of Combatants. After taking the oath, he lowered himself laboriously into the armchair. He gave his profession as "political deportee," and he had in fact just come from Mauthausen.

With his fierce, toneless voice, broken by dramatic pauses, and his seemingly blind eyes gazing straight ahead, barely moving his hard, lofty brow when a member of the jury questioned him, he held the court's attention as if he were an apparition. This former Saint-Cyrian, who had obtained his Staff College certificate at the same time as General de Gaulle, and who like the General possessed a remarkable command of the French language, had served his country and two marshals with passionate devotion. Abandoned by Marshal Pétain as soon as he risked compromising him, he had been arrested in North Africa, had escaped and joined the Maquis, and had finally been recaptured, imprisoned, interrogated fifty-four times and sentenced to death.

"I owe nothing to Marshal Pétain," he said, slowly stressing every syllable, "but that doesn't prevent me from being nauseated by the sight of those who, in this courtroom, are trying to unload the responsibility for all their mistakes onto a near centenarian."

One of the canes gripped in his nervous hands fell to the floor. He picked it up with a tired gesture.

He cleared Marshal Pétain of the accusation that he had belonged to the Cagoule. In 1937 there had been a plan to overthrow the institutions of the Republic by a *coup d'état*. Communists and putschists were laying in stocks of arms. Army officers had formed secret societies to supervise political action in the barracks.

"What did Marshal Pétain know of all this?" he asked in a harsh, sneering voice. "Nothing. Why should we have informed him of our secret activities? This wasn't out of distrust on our part, but rather for fear that he might mix up his files, or that his forgetfulness, which was sometimes catastrophic, might lead him to make some enormous blunder."

He went on to paint a revolting portrait of Pierre Laval, imitating the latter's accent. He gave the impression of stirring up the mud of the Third Republic with the rubber tips of his canes, and, every now and then, of thrusting into it one of the personalities he had had occasion to meet.

"The Marshal," said one of the jurors, "ought to be asked once more if he did anything to save his former staff officer."

"Bâtonnier," said the presiding judge, "do you think you can pass the question on to your client?"

"Yes, Monsieur le Président, but I think I can give you his reply: the Marshal will not answer that question any more than the others that have been put to him."

"That's very probable, but I would be grateful if you would put the question to him all the same."

The Bâtonnier went up to the Marshal, whispered in his ear, listened for a moment, and then said, "He doesn't know anything about that business."

Major Loustanau-Lacau seemed to turn pale.

"With regard to Marshal Pétain," he said after a brief passage at arms with the Attorney General, "I would like to say that although he let me down in the most despicable way, I must ask the court to reflect that France's escutcheon is sufficiently stained with the blood of Marie Antoinette and Marshal Ney."

He pulled himself to his feet, pushed the armchair away and, without saluting the court, turned his back on the judges and walked away. In the silence his canes could be heard tapping on the floor. He left the courtroom and the Palais de Justice, and disappeared into the crowd like a ghost. His destiny followed him. He died a deputy in

1954, the very day Mendès-France promoted him to the rank of brigadier on the Reserve List.

The emotion he had aroused was still gripping the court when Madame Henriette Psichari-Renan touched every heart again.

"I had a son who was a sublieutenant. He was twenty-five. After an inner conflict which he related to me before he died, he decided to obey the government which in his eyes represented the government of France. For ten days, like every other sailor in the French Navy, he had felt sure that he was going to join the Free French forces, but on the tenth day an order arrived from their Commander in Chief telling them to put that idea out of their minds. My son obeyed."

One day he had been tempted to come back to Paris to see his mother, his brothers and his sister. The idea of meeting enemy officers and being forced to salute them discouraged him. I remember that feeling. In 1941 I traveled to the Unoccupied Zone to collect some planes for Morocco. My heart started beating wildly every time I met a German serving with the Control Commission. This was no longer the honorable Armistice of our imagination, but an unbearable physical reality. It was only then that I understood.

Henriette Psichari's son had died, or at least so she had been told, in an engagement with some American ships off Oran, on November 8, 1942, for having obeyed Admiral Darlan's orders. His name was Michel Revault d'Allonnes.

"Gentlemen, that is why our children died. They died, I am grieved and ashamed to say, in the service of Germany."

Pastor Marc Boegner, the head of the Reformed Church of France, gave evidence for the accused in a solemn, unemotional voice.

"The Marshal," he said, "was clearly kept in ignorance of what was happening, and on repeated occasions, gentlemen, I observed that at Vichy, in the highest quarters, nothing was known of the dreadful, horrible things taking place not only in the Occupied Zone, but also in the Unoccupied Zone."

The hearing was adjourned at 5:45.

"This is a fascinating business," the Marshal said to his lawyers. "I've learned a lot of things I didn't know."

Pierre Laval, whom Franco had expelled from Spain, where he had taken refuge, had returned after a few minutes as the result of a technical hitch. The weather had turned fine again.

"In your opinion," the Marshal asked his jailer, Monsieur Simon, "am I going to be shot?"

He gazed thoughtfully at a picture, hanging in the entrance hall, which has since disappeared.

"Do you know that place?" he asked. "It's a picture of the Île d'Yeu."

He had been there once on a brief visit.

X

✣

Tuesday, July 31, 1945

I have to draw breath before I can embark on an account of this day. No one can read the twenty-three pages of the eighth section of the *Journal officiel* without feeling depressed and disturbed. When you come to the end of the transcript of the day's proceedings, you no longer know where things stand, and it seems impossible to take in the whole vast panorama at one glance. The trial of Pétain was the drama of a prostrate and divided France. Order would be restored only with the end of a scourge destined to spread over several continents, and with a confrontation between those forces which would decide whether the world was to be free or dominated by a single party.

At the opening of the hearing, two witnesses, an electrician and a lawyer, recalled the consequences of the Vichy regime: the country's police forces busy hunting and torturing patriots, and France's honor grotesquely represented by the Legion of Volunteers and the militia. Then General Weygand came in.

A gaunt figure, but strengthened by an inner force, that little man, whose very birth was something of a mystery, walked stiffly forward, leaning on a stick. He clicked his heels and bowed to the Marshal, who had been following him with his gaze and returned his salute.

Weygand had come from the Val-de-Grâce where he was in the prison hospital. He seemed to share Paul Reynaud's physical characteristics: slanting eyes, a hollow face, prominent cheekbones, a sharp, bitter mind, and teeth and claws ready to savage their prey. When the presiding judge invited him to sit in the armchair, he appeared to bristle. Alone, but nobler than ever in his isolation, he stood apart from all that had brought about his ruin, yet face to face with it. The public held its breath. As alert as a cavalry brigade setting off at a trot to take up position for a charge, he began his story.

Now a witness, but himself likely to face a treason charge before long, he warned the court that his deposition would be a lengthy one, because he did not wish to leave anything unexplained. On the witnesses' bench, Paul Reynaud tugged nervously at his collar. To begin with, General Weygand dismissed the allegation which had been made about him to the effect that he had plotted to gain power. It seems obvious now that he was telling the truth. Like Pétain, he had not asked for high office. He was Commander in Chief in the Middle East when he was begged to return to France. He would have preferred to remain in Beirut, where it is now known that, giving way to an old man's caprice, he had fallen in love with a married woman, who incidentally was extremely ugly. When the order came to return to France, and his aide-de-camp discreetly begged him to leave for the airport, where the British had placed a plane at his disposal, Weygand urged his Egeria to go with him. She refused. Finally, three hours late, he set off by himself.

General Weygand's deposition in itself lasted three hours. The first hour went slowly, as he outlined the situation and sketched in the characters. Then, all of a sudden, the course of events quickened. On June 13, 1940, at the Château de Cangé near Tours, where the government had installed itself, while the Comtesse de Portes intrigued and General Weygand sent off love letters to Beirut, uncertainty reigned supreme.

Weygand spoke of the telegram which announced that the Germans had entered Aubervilliers and Thorez had moved into the

Élysée, but in fact he was anticipating events. In his report to the Prime Minister that day, Weygand stated that it was important that the fleet should leave port before the Armistice. At the close of the hearing, Monsieur Paul Reynaud would say he could no longer remember, and would place the responsibility for this episode on his successor's shoulders with this astonishing remark: "How can you talk about putting the fleet out of the enemy's reach if you don't ask for an armistice?"

On June 15 Monsieur Paul Reynaud announced that he was going to follow the example of Queen Wilhelmina of Holland, who had taken refuge in England. He ordered General Weygand to capitulate. But was the General, who had signed the Armistice of 1918, to dirty his hands? Was the great commander, who had been hurriedly flown home from the Middle East, to admit that he was incapable, because the French Army, trained and led by other men, had been defeated? He exploded with indignation.

"Ah, no, I can't agree to that! I am still General Weygand!"

At one meeting of the Council of Ministers after another, Paul Reynaud insisted.

"I refuse," said Weygand, "and come what may, I shall always refuse to bring that disgrace upon our colors."

He told the court: "I repeated that there was no power on earth which could make me surrender an army which had fought as the French Army had just been fighting. . . . Gentlemen, if we are to understand this question of honor, we must shed as much light on it as possible. . . . I can understand my own actions and Marshal Pétain's completely, and now that I have thrown what light I can on what I did, I ask for light to be thrown on what others did."

"You must be feeling tired," said the presiding judge. "Do you want to go on?"

The hearing was adjourned. The Marshal asked General Weygand to go with him, but the lawyers pointed out to him that this was against the law. Weygand stayed rooted to the spot, his heels together, his features inscrutable. On the other side of the courtroom, like a bantamweight waiting in his corner for the bell, Paul Reynaud, who had never stopped stirring in his seat, sat thinking out his answer behind his expressionless mask.

A heavy shower of rain wet the steps of the Palais and sent journalists and public back to the First Chamber. The hearing was resumed. Once again Weygand ostentatiously saluted Marshal Pétain.

Paul Reynaud had thought first of all of sacking Weygand, then of relieving him of his command. Finally, on June 16, he resigned, asking the President of the Republic to send for Marshal Pétain, who wanted an armistice. Weygand had made his choice between an armistice and capitulation.

"Gentlemen, capitulation is a shameful act. People talk to you of honor and ask you for capitulation. . . . A country which capitulates never recovers. Our code of military justice lays down the death penalty for any Army leader who capitulates on the field of battle."

Capitulation would have handed the entire country and its army over to the enemy. French North Africa had neither men nor material. Could it have stood up to a fresh German offensive, to unscathed Italian forces, or to an attack based in Spanish Morocco?

Could the French and British fleets have defended the Mediterranean? Only one man could answer these questions: General Noguès. From Portugal, where he had taken refuge, refusing to shirk his responsibilities, and in spite of the fact that he was accused of treason by both sides, a sick and disillusioned General Noguès declared his readiness to give evidence in writing. The prosecution took good care not to put any questions to him, and the defense dreaded his testimony.

On June 17, 1940, he had tested the government's reactions by sending a certain Bataille, the captain of a corvette, to Bordeaux to encourage the spirit of resistance which seemed to be on the decline. A few days later, General Koeltz had been dispatched to make him see reason and prevent him from making contact with the *Massilia* envoys. Under pressure from Weygand he had given way. When

General Catroux, the Governor General of Indo-China, sent him a cable congratulating him for continuing the struggle, General Noguès replied that he was not continuing the struggle, and at that moment Weygand seemed to give up all hope of victory. Struck by the swiftness of the Nazi onslaught, he lost heart and admitted defeat in advance.

As a man who felt nostalgia for a legitimist past, he was incapable of breaking with conventions and institutions. Perhaps it was the royal blood which was rumored to flow in his veins which gave him so much respect for established authority and so little taste for rebellion. He served only lawful governments. When a member of the jury asked him which of the two governments, that of the French Republic and that of the French State, he regarded as the lawful government of France, he replied: "Why, both of them, of course, Monsieur . . . I consider that any government which has succeeded a previous one is a lawful government."

He was a traditional soldier of the old guard, a man as unbending as the law, who expected himself to see clearly and others to obey promptly. He gauged the enemy's strength too dogmatically and refused to admit that the future might tip the balance in his favor. At one point in the trial, he would say sarcastically to a juror, "Forgive me, imagination is not my strong point. I prefer facts." De Gaulle was entitled to speak, in a broadcast from London, of his "morose skepticism." Because, at a tragic moment in history, he had accepted a tragic legacy which ended in tragic fashion, Weygand was blinded by pessimism. He swept aside every argument in favor of resistance. In any case, who, at the time, believed that it was possible to halt Hitler's advance? There was a danger, too, of Spain entering the conflict, and Franco, torn between Marshal Pétain and a house painter turned brilliant strategist, had begun casting envious eyes on the province of Oran and altering the gauges of his railways for the benefit of the German divisions. If Noguès had insisted on holding out, the Axis could have occupied the south shore of the Mediterranean.

True, French North Africa possessed neither industry, nor reserves, nor raw materials, and had never been prepared for war. This fact had occurred to the government on May 19, 1940.

"And do you imagine that such things can be done in a fortnight's time?" cried Weygand. "War isn't an intellectual pastime; war is a matter of strength."

De Gaulle would say the same thing on June 18, 1940. But de Gaulle was under fifty. Weygand, at seventy-three, acted with all the prudence, sadness and resignation of an old man.

What would de Gaulle have done if Monsieur Paul Reynaud, who admired him and had promoted him to the rank of brigadier, had also, in a moment of courage, made him Commander in Chief? The question could not arise. But if it had, would de Gaulle have turned all Weygand's arguments around to his own advantage? "We would have lost Africa if we had agreed to capitulate," declared General Weygand. Would de Gaulle have decided to hold out in Brittany for a while? In order to fight, he would have needed an army of lions, and he no longer had anything but rabbits. The Armistice filled us with despair, but it left us alive. For that stroke of luck—since history has shown that in agreeing to the Armistice Hitler made the biggest mistake of his life—whom have we to thank? One would be tempted to reply: Monsieur Paul Reynaud, but that would be placing too heavy a burden on the frail shoulders of that man who always saw so clearly and acted so wrongly. How could Monsieur Paul Reynaud have swum against the current of men and events when Madame de Portes thought only of negotiating with the enemy? Later on, forgetting that he had sent de Gaulle to offer the post of Commander in Chief to General Huntziger, he would cynically tell the court that there was no military leader who was an obvious choice.

Who would have given his approval to the slightest revolutionary measure? The former Minister of War, General Maurin, went on record as saying: "If you want to fight a war, you have to begin by respecting seniority!" Would sixty-eight-year-old Monsieur Lebrun, seventy-seven-year-old Monsieur Jeanneney, or sixty-nine-year-old

Monsieur Herriot—all respectful of law, seniority, custom and tradition—ever have agreed to the replacement of a lieutenant general by an acting brigadier? At Vichy, Pierre Laval used to quote this remark by Paul Reynaud, not without a certain irony: "Who are the three men responsible for France's misfortune? Daladier for making Pétain Ambassador in Madrid, me for making him a minister, and Laval for making him head of state." At least eighty-five-year-old Marshal Pétain would be obeyed. He would be hailed as the victor of Verdun. A soldier who had conquered once would conquer again, and the nation's morale would be miraculously stiffened by the thought that an illustrious warrior was taking the country's destinies in hand. Everything was decided by a constellation of old moons circling in the dark around a dying star.

The Armistice temporarily removed any threat to Africa, and saved an army of 100,000 men in France and of 200,000 outside France. With total disaster averted, there remained some hope. As for the fleet, if it was captive, disarmed or sunk, that wasn't Weygand's fault. Admiral Darlan had said to Herriot, "Is it true that the old man and General Weygand want an armistice? If that's the case, Monsieur le Président, then I go off tomorrow with the fleet." Far from going off with the fleet, he had left his ships at Toulon. He had even become a Vice Marshal pending the award of the golden belt of a Grand Admiral of the Reich. It was he who was the villain of the piece.

A year later I greeted Weygand when he visited the air base at Sétif where I was in command of a reconnaissance squadron. We didn't feel dishonored. We were secretly plotting revenge, and Weygand needed revenge himself. However convinced a man may be of the grandeur of self-sacrifice, he doesn't like to finish a lifetime of honorable service on a note of humiliation. At the time, draped in a cape which hung down over his polished leggings, General Weygand looked out from under the peak of his gold-braided kepi with the sharp, pitiless gaze of a hunted animal.

As for the Armistice itself—dare I admit it?—it didn't cause us overmuch anguish. Until then the word had held holiday connotations for us, since we used to commemorate the Armistice of 1918 with fanfares and parades. However inglorious this new Armistice might be, it didn't fill us with shame, for we could not hear the vengeful insults de Gaulle was hurling at Pétain over the air. We didn't know that the Marshal had thrown down his cards as if he hadn't a single trump left, that he had emptied our pockets and drained the cup of shame to the dregs. Pétain himself heard all this, but didn't care. "He's a fool to talk so much," he used to say of de Gaulle. "He'll give himself a bad name."

"I must apologize for presuming on your attention for so long," said General Weygand. "I hope I may have convinced you that the decisions which were taken were taken only for military reasons and only in the highest, noblest interests of the country."

He seemed to be leaning rather heavily on his stick. In spite of the heat, there was not a single bead of sweat on his forehead.

For ten minutes he gave brisk answers to the presiding judge's questions, and defended the Marshal. In 1942 the Marshal had a secret cipher which enabled him to annul the orders he appeared to be giving Admiral Darlan to continue hostilities against the Allies.

Monsieur Gabriel Delattre, the foreman of the parliamentary jurors, questioned him about the Marshal's state of mind in November 1942.

"The Marshal never told me of any intention he might have had of leaving."

"Were you with him when Hitler invaded the whole of France?"

"Yes, I was with him."

"And the two of you never talked about that together?"

"I said that Marshal Pétain never indicated to me any intention of leaving."

Weygand didn't want to say that he had urged the Marshal to fly to Algiers.

"Did you receive a letter from General de Gaulle?" Monsieur Pierre-Bloch asked Weygand.

"Yes."

"What did you do with it?"

"I kept it. It ended with these words, 'I send you my respects if your answer is yes.' Well, nobody writes to me like that!"

De Gaulle had infuriated Weygand. The letter had been returned to the sender with this note: "If ex-Colonel de Gaulle wishes to communicate with General Weygand, he must do so through the proper channels."

That was how to deal with a young brigadier and Under Secretary for State for National Defense who presumed to speak like the head of a government and interfered in matters which were no concern of his. . . .

"All right! So they cross the Somme," de Gaulle had said to Weygand on June 8, 1940. "And after that?"

"After that? They cross the Seine and the Marne."

"Yes. And after that?"

"After that? Why, it's all over!"

"What do you mean, all over? What about the world? What about the Empire?"

Weygand later denied that this conversation took place, but it rings true. Other leaders might tolerate insubordination, but not Weygand. Refusing to take any notice of an acting rank which the Armistice had made null and void, he had called upon Colonel de Gaulle to return to the ranks of the defeated, and de Gaulle had replied in that cavalier, authoritarian style which ignored the rules of seniority. Had Weygand actually thought of having him arrested on June 16? When he was asked this question, in the preliminary investigation before his own trial, he retorted, "I had other things to do than bother about that great booby."

Weygand was now almost enjoying himself. He had forgotten his tiredness. These people were no match for him. Not even that juror from the Resistance who wore a squadron leader's uniform and tried to trap the General by asking him what he thought of the Marshal's treason in connection with the legions recruited to serve against the Allies. "Because the whole trial hinges on that," added the juror.

General Weygand swung smoothly around toward his right. His

steely features, speckled with large brown patches, were suddenly
exposed to the light and looked as if they were marked by the blows
of fate.

"No, Monsieur, the whole trial does not hinge on that. The whole
trial hinges on the choice between an armistice and capitulation."

"Oh, no!" cried the juror, drawing shocked protests from the
public.

"You are interrupting a witness," snapped the General, and he
paused for a moment to make it clear that he was only replying out of
sheer magnanimity.

"I tell you that I know what this trial is about. It is about the
choice between an armistice and capitulation. That is the crux of the
trial and you can't avoid it, because if you do, then the trial becomes a
farce."

"The crux of the trial is treason," said the juror, looking very
pale.

"No, Monsieur. In any case," he went on, thumping the floor with
his stick, "nobody will ever get me to utter that word in connection
with Marshal Pétain, because my conscience forbids it. . . . You
will never get me to say that the Marshal is a traitor. And you mustn't
lay traps for me either."

The Marshal stirred in his armchair and motioned that he wished
to speak. "There is a question that . . ." he began. The Bâtonnier
rushed over to him. The defense lawyers stood up uneasily. There was
suddenly a profound silence. The guard glanced sideways in surprise
at the old man as he rose to his feet.

"Monsieur le Président," said the Marshal, "I have never before
felt such regret that I am hard of hearing. I sometimes hear my name
mentioned, and I catch a phrase here and there, but I cannot tie up
the various snatches of conversation. Consequently I cannot take part
in the proceedings. All the same, from what I could hear of General
Weygand's testimony, because I was the person closest to him, it
seemed to me that he was in complete agreement with my policy. So I
could have supported him if I had been able to speak up. I am very

sorry that I didn't do so. General Weygand is a man one can trust. He deals with military questions in a clear, apposite way. On the basis of what I was able to hear, because I wasn't able to see [*sic*] everything, I give him my entire support."

General Weygand gave a nod which could have been interpreted as a gesture of thanks or as a sign of annoyance. The Marshal had stumbled over certain words, and he repeated himself, his mind caught in a trap. His faltering delivery lent added distinction to the curt elegance of Weygand's style.

After a pause, the presiding judge spoke up. "I shall sum up what he has just said about those rather irritating questions. He said . . ."

Weygand's lip curled slightly. The presiding judge had not even taken the trouble to say "the accused." It was typical of these vulgar times that this irreverent pronoun should be used to refer to a Marshal of France.

"Are you in a position to clarify this point?"

"Me?" asked Weygand irritably.

"No, the Marshal, since the Marshal answered."

The Bâtonnier went over to the old man, who shook his head.

"I didn't hear," he said.

A member of the jury wanted to know whether Weygand had been responsible for the formal application made in November 1940 for General de Gaulle to be stripped of his French nationality.

Weygand replied that all the witnesses before him had recognized that Marshal Pétain's government was the lawful government of France and that it had been required to defend the country's interests.

"All those," he went on in a cutting voice, "who at that time persuaded parts of the French Empire to flout the authority of the lawful government of France were regarded as traitors by the French Government."

Everyone was waiting impatiently for Weygand and Paul Reynaud to cross swords. Maître Isorni provided the occasion for the expected duel.

"It follows from your deposition, does it not," he said, "that the first mentions of the Armistice in the War Committee were made neither by you nor by Marshal Pétain, but by the President of the Republic and the Prime Minister?"

"That is correct."

Paul Reynaud sprang up from the witnesses' bench and went over to the desk dividing the floor of the court.

In the lengthy statement which he proceeded to make, it is impossible to discover a single phrase which answers the question. Like all politicians, Monsieur Paul Reynaud possessed the art of enveloping reality in formulas which hide it from view. Eloquence sometimes serves to put out smoke screens behind which warring monsters move. When hatred enters into the situation, with each adversary waiting for the moment to fire off a murderous broadside at the other, it is difficult to discover the truth. Each man defends his own version of the facts.

For over a quarter of an hour, Monsieur Paul Reynaud answered General Weygand. He repeated the reasons which had prevented him from sacking him. Nobody was any the wiser. On June 16 Paul Reynaud had said to Weygand, "You state that a cease-fire is contrary to the Army's honor. But if a cease-fire is written into the Armistice terms, will you still consider it in that light?" Weygand had replied, "We shall see when the time comes." The President of the Republic himself had protested. "No," he said, "we must see right now."

The Marshal spoke up. "There's a question I would like to ask the General," he said. "When I went and joined him in the next room, did I agree with him about the cease-fire? I'm not sure I agreed with him about the cease-fire," he repeated.

"You argued about it, Monsieur le Maréchal," said Weygand gently.

"I can't remember at all."

Among cease-fire, armistice and capitulation, how does one weigh the question of honor or dishonor? Finding himself in difficulties for a moment, General Weygand retorted with the problem of the fleet

which had not put to sea although it had asked the Prime Minister to
order it to do so. The discussion which followed between the
witnesses, the defense lawyers, the Attorney General and the presiding judge led nowhere. Everyone felt bored. The hearing was adjourned at a quarter past six, in the midst of general confusion.

Surrounded by his own lawyers, an exhausted Weygand sat taking
smelling salts. The rain had stopped, but the sky remained dull and
cloudy. This trial of embittered old men was dragging. The princes
of the realm were settling futile quarrels between themselves and
tearing each other to shreds under the eyes of Philippe VII, whom
one might have wished to hear uttering King Lear's appeal for pity:
"Bear with me: pray you now, forget and forgive: I am old and
foolish."

Nobody had pity on him because the country had expected salvation from him, and indeed from his age. Laval himself had wanted
him to be elected to the Presidency of the Republic in 1932, in place
of Monsieur Lebrun, who wept whenever a cloud passed over the sun.
Laval believed that this would have prevented the war. The Marshal
had repelled these advances, though it was not known whether it was
to avoid being a nonentity or to go on leading a quiet life. At the age
of eighty-five, and thanks to a defeat, he had obtained supreme
power. Because he had begun life as an old man, because he had
remained a lieutenant for ten years and because he had won his
laurels in the midst of disaster, and at an age when conquerors have
usually turned to dust, he thought he was proof against time and
misfortune. Since he was assured that he was the savior of France,
since he was urged to accept the crown held above his head, and since
refugees stopped his car to beg him to bring the war to an end, how
could he refuse? Now women loved him, crowds cheered him. People
tried to touch him as if he were a saint, and the whiffs of incense
which rose toward him from the masses intoxicated him. No honor
was too great for him.

And now . . . Bâtonnier Payen touched his elbow. He instinc-
tively looked around for Francine Bonitzer, the beautiful reporter

from *L'Aurore,* who usually sat on his right, quite close to him. Maître de Moro-Giafferi, who had seen her one day on the beach at Deauville, used to say, "She is Venus rising from the waves." She had disappeared, and he had to go back to the record office of the First Chamber. It was almost like going back to prison.

XI

❋

Wednesday, August 1, 1945

The trial was getting bogged down, and the press was beginning to lose patience with it.

When the hearing started at twenty past one the presiding judge admitted that the arguments about the Armistice were becoming tiresome.

"I think it is time the Pétain trial began," said the Attorney General, to sarcastic applause from the public.

After some acid exchanges, the court decided not to recall General Weygand. A few minutes later, as soon as Monsieur du Chayla, a former attaché at the French Embassy in Madrid, had begun giving evidence, it decided the opposite.

General Weygand promised he would be only a few minutes. He stayed half an hour, quivering with anger, exchanging blows with Monsieur Paul Reynaud. Face to face, or sometimes contemptuously turning their backs on each other, they stood like two fighting cocks on their steel spurs, with the inscrutable, dry-eyed Marshal slumped in his armchair between them, and fought a pitiless duel.

General Weygand considered himself insulted by the remarks Monsieur Paul Reynaud had made to the press the day before. Interrupted by his adversary's sneering exclamations, the former Prime

Minister, casually leaning on the rail around the courtroom floor, expounded his theories about certain comments made by General Gamelin and an embassy official who had served as an officer cadet in the Air Force at Bordeaux.

"Have you finished?" cried General Weygand, leaping from his armchair. "That's what I mean by capitulation!"

Then, changing his mind, he resumed his seat, and with a shrug of his shoulders let the storm blow over.

Invited to reply, he stood up and pointed his finger at his enemy. A glutton for power, Paul Reynaud, he declared, had not shown any eagerness for responsibility. The name of Madame de Portes was not mentioned, and no one learned why Monsieur Paul Reynaud had given way so easily to those who advocated an armistice, or how, injured in a strange car accident in which Madame de Portes had been killed beside him, he had abstained from voting on July 10, 1940. Then Weygand asked for permission to remain silent. The two men withdrew, bristling with hatred.

"I need scarcely say that this is just the beginning!" exclaimed Paul Reynaud.

"Come now, gentlemen," said the presiding judge in a loud voice, like a headmaster scolding a pair of schoolboys.

"How can the public have failed to greet with jeers and catcalls the sneers, sniggers and eye-rolling of the General responsible for the biggest military disaster of all time?" wrote Georges Bernanos in *Combat*. Why attack Weygand and not Paul Reynaud? Weygand had been powerless to save the situation. He had come, he had seen, and he had been conquered. His sole mistake had been to believe—he, who knew the state of the French Army—that he had only to appear on the scene, riding crop in hand, to change oxen into bulls and North African troops into armored divisions. At his age, a man is easily intoxicated by the idea that he can read his fate in a woman's shining eyes.

Monsieur du Chayla came back to read out a translation of a letter Admiral Leahy, the former American Ambassador in Vichy, had just

sent Marshal Pétain. The Marshal cupped his left hand around his
ear. The letter was laudatory, well intentioned, honest and ingenuous.
Listening to it as he sat in the second row of journalists on the right,
his chin in his hand and his mane of hair thrown back, Joseph Kessel
smiled.

With his bald, birdlike head, his pince-nez and his bow tie,
General Héring spoke for an hour. To begin with, the Marshal
listened to the witness singing his praises: his influence, his calmness,
his caution, his forethought, his style, his vigilance, his preparations
to meet the threat of war, his strategic theories, the mutual esteem felt
by Pétain and de Gaulle, the reasonable, humane policy pursued after
defeat, and the factors governing the use of arms. General Héring
had been in command of the École de Guerre at the time when the
Marshal had imposed Captain de Gaulle on that institution as a
lecturer. The defense lawyers took care not to press him on that point.
What he said bored his listeners. The Marshal's forehead weighed
more and more heavily on the palm of his hand, and finally he fell
asleep. The adjournment of the hearing woke him up.

"That's enough!" he growled as he shook hands with General
Héring.

L'Humanité expressed indignation that the General should not
have left the Palais de Justice between a couple of gendarmes.

The next witness was extremely violent in his opinions. According
to him, all the patriots who had been betrayed, imprisoned and
handed over to the Germans had Pétain to thank for what had
happened to them. Pointing at the Marshal, his lips flecked with
foam, he shouted, "If he had the slightest feeling of honor or love
for his country left, then before going to his execution he would fall
on his knees and beg forgiveness. . . ." Some accounts of the trial
report that a member of the jury cried, "Bravo!" The accused shook
his head in amazement.

Next, General Georges, a moon-faced figure with round spectacles
and a shining pate, gave the court another lecture on strategy which
put everyone to sleep.

"What would you have done if you had been Commander in

Chief?" the presiding judge asked him, to find out whether he would have chosen capitulation or an armistice.

"I can understand General Weygand asking for an armistice," said General Georges. "Capitulation in the field brings disgrace upon an army."

The witness had tried to persuade the accused to go to North Africa in 1942. "The whole of France is going to be invaded," the Marshal replied. "My duty is to stay with the French people."

In 1944 General Georges had met Winston Churchill, who had told him, "In June 1940 England had no arms left. . . . The armistice in fact did us a service. Hitler blundered when he granted it. He could have crossed over to French North Africa and seized it in order to invade Egypt. Then we would have had a difficult job on our hands."

The Attorney General tried to get the witness to betray the secrets the accused had confided in him when, as French Ambassador to Spain, he had come to spend three days incognito in Paris.

"That's the plot!" cried Maître Isorni.

The Marshal woke up with a start.

"What part did General Georges play in it?" he asked Bâtonnier Payen. The Bâtonnier took the trouble to explain it to him. The General withdrew almost immediately, after saluting the accused.

General Vauthier's deposition finished off the day's proceedings, and almost finished off the court.

"I don't think there would be any objection by the defense," said the presiding judge, "if I asked you to cut your testimony short."

The Marshal made an irritated gesture.

"Yes, we've had enough tactics," he said.

The hearing was adjourned at 5:45.

How could the press have published a full transcript of each day's proceedings in newspapers which at that time were generally limited to a single sheet? A dramatic incident was reported during the evening: the German plane which had taken Pierre Laval to Spain had brought him back to Innsbruck, where the former Prime Minister had been arrested by the Americans. Now he had returned to Paris, his soft hat pulled down over his eyes, with his wife and fourteen trunks. "I am going back to France to defend myself and to accuse," he had declared in Barcelona. Crowds by the roadside had shouted for his death. He had been shut up at Fresnes, where his cell had been isolated from the rest of the prison. The Marshal's lawyers decided to do all they could to prevent his being called as a witness.

A year before, Antoine de Saint-Exupéry had disappeared on a reconnaissance flight between Corsica and Grenoble. If he had lived, he would have given evidence for the accused. In January 1944, from Algiers, where General de Gaulle had banned his books, he wrote to a woman friend:

The climate here is terribly unhealthy for me. I have never had such a feeling of wear-and-tear to no purpose. Besides, my crime is always the same one. I proved in the United States that a man could be a good Frenchman, anti-German and anti-Nazi, and yet not support the government of France by the Gaullist party.

On July 30 he had been even more bitter: "Their arguments bore me stiff and I can't think of anything to be said for them." General de Gaulle had never deigned to receive him.

XII

✿

Thursday, August 2, 1945

A little man with protuberant eyes and a face aglow with self-righteousness, Monsieur Léon Noël, former French Ambassador in Warsaw, called as a defense witness, took the oath with an air of authority. He had just been elected a member of the Academy of Moral and Political Sciences. It was said that before signing the decree admitting to the Institut the man who had negotiated the Armistice, General de Gaulle had waited to find out what he was going to say before the High Court. It is now known that Monsieur Léon Noël had telephoned the day before to Bâtonnier Payen to warn him that he intended to criticize the Marshal's policies severely. Maître Isorni had rushed around to see him. Monsieur Léon Noël had promised not to indulge in any critical comments.

Who could blame a former chairman of the Council of State for having served with dignity in the various positions of principal private secretary, prefect and ambassador? The desire to don the green coat of the Institut at so early an age—Monsieur Léon Noël was fifty-seven—to crown so many titles with yet another, and to attain the highest offices of state, led to every sort of recantation. In the courtroom of the First Chamber, with its blue walls decorated with fleurs-de-lis and the curtains pulled back to reveal a gray sky pierced by the spire of the Sainte-Chapelle, when Monsieur Léon Noël made his way toward the witnesses' armchair, pretending not to see the accused, it should have been possible for anyone who strained his ears to hear a cock crow. How many cocks, both in the French countryside and in the Paris suburbs, where people still kept poultry because of the food restrictions, must have crowed at that time to celebrate betrayals!

In Monsieur Léon Noël, cleverness and prudence were allied with determined ambition. A consummate tactician, he never missed an opportunity to be in the forefront of affairs, without asking to be, every time that matters of state reached a critical point. As plenipotentiary minister in the Armistice negotiations, he had been clever enough to let the military chiefs sign the agreements. As the government delegate in occupied France, he resigned as soon as he sensed that Pierre Laval was on the wrong tack.

Speaking in a low voice, he took care to avoid passing any judgment on the Armistice itself. In his opinion, giving way on the terms of the signed agreement had done nothing to lessen the country's suffering, and General Huntziger deserved to be criticized for not standing up to the German commissions. He declared that he had turned down all the posts which had been offered him. Baffled and dismayed by his *volte-face,* the defense did not dare to remind him that he had belonged to the council appointed to govern the country in the event of the Marshal's being incapacitated, or to quote the letter he had written to the Minister of Foreign Affairs asking for any post he could offer him.

"In fact, right from the start of the Armistice, you had been working for the Resistance?" asked a member of the jury.

Without giving a straight reply, Monsieur Léon Noël was skillful enough to derive all the advantage he could from this pluperfect indicative. Today Monsieur Léon Noël, who was President of the Constitutional Council of the Fifth Republic after nearly governing Franche-Comté under the Vichy regime, is still a government counselor. I should not like to be in his place on Judgment Day.

With General Sérigny, Pétain's former chief of staff at Verdun, the court suddenly parted company with the men who were afraid to compromise themselves. The General, who talked as if he were drinking a bowl of country soup, ignored all considerations of prudence. He had served under the Marshal and admired him. He still admired him, and didn't care who knew it.

In 1941 Hitler was determined to enter Spain, attack Gibraltar and occupy Spanish Morocco. Pétain opposed this plan. In exchange he offered to hand over all the food stocks, oil, guns and munitions in French North Africa to the German Expeditionary Corps in Tripolitania.

"An egg in exchange for an ox," the General said in his sententious voice. "And even the egg was broken."

"An omelet, in fact!" said a voice.

Everyone laughed, including the General.

Nothing was handed over that had not been sabotaged or put out of action. At that period there had been complete and absolute complicity.

"I therefore consider and roundly declare that, in those circumstances, the Marshal served his country well. I will go further than that. It is said that General de Gaulle recognizes that North Africa was the springboard of victory. By protecting that springboard . . . Marshal Pétain became in fact one of the secret architects of victory."

On November 12, 1942, General Sérigny left Paris for Vichy, with the intention of persuading the Marshal to accompany him to Algiers. Pétain refused. "Every time I oppose Hitler," he told the General, "he threatens to put a gauleiter in my place. Do you know what a gauleiter is like? Ask the Belgians. . . . No, it is my duty to stay here to deaden the blows."

"Instead of the crown of glory which I offered him and which it would have been so easy for him to take," said General Sérigny, "he chose a crown of thorns."

No member of the jury dared to ask him any questions. He turned round, saluted his old chief and held out his hand.

"I haven't any right to shake hands with you," said the Marshal. The witness took his hand by force, and then calmly withdrew with an ironic smile on his face.

Monsieur Charles Trochu, who had been President of the Municipal Council of Paris during the Occupation, was a striking figure. Tall, sturdy and well dressed, with his massive head framed in a dark mane of hair, sharp, thin lips, a clear gaze and a noble forehead, he gave his evidence with a brave eloquence, tinged with a harsh southern accent. Together with Charles Vallin, one of the Paris deputies, he had proposed to accompany the Marshal to the demarcation line to offer himself as a hostage with him at the time of the Châteaubriant executions, and he had kept the bust of the Republic in his office in the Hôtel de Ville. The same plaster bust, surrounded by laurels, was enthroned on his right, on a level with the judges, over the great oak stalls, lit up by the August sunlight and looking as if it were possessed of a truth which would last for centuries.

In 1943 Monsieur Trochu had almost persuaded Marshal Pétain to transfer the lawful French Government to Algiers in the person of some nonentity who would last long enough for General de Gaulle to prove that he represented the majority of the French people.

"How can anyone see the debonair grandfather celebrated by Claudel as an old crowned cannibal?" asked Monsieur Trochu in a sepulchral voice.

There was a roar of laughter. The Marshal laughed too. The witness was rebuked for pleading the cause of the accused.

"When Monsieur le Président asked me to speak without hatred," he retorted, "instead of promising like Monsieur Paul Reynaud to testify without hatred, I could have promised rather to plead without love."

He was asked if he would ever again wear the francisc which the Marshal had presented to him, and which he had returned in December 1942. With an Olympian look in his eyes, and his fists clenched on his chest, he replied, "Do you think that if I considered I ought to wear it, I wouldn't have put it in my buttonhole when I came here?"

The juror pressed the point. The public protested. I myself, in my innocence, would have worn the francisc at the time, if it had been given to me. And then, like Monsieur Trochu, I would have discarded it.

The hearing was adjourned at 3:40. The corridors hummed with conversation. The adjournment lasted an hour and a half. What could the court be discussing? The answer was on everyone's lips: Pierre Laval, who had been headline news for the past few days. What bomb had he brought back with him in his luggage? He was quite capable of setting it off at the trial and taking Marshal Pétain and a few other people with him to his doom. Sure enough, the presiding judge announced that the court had been discussing the question of Monsieur Pierre Laval's testimony. Everyone held his breath. His head glistening with sweat, his features twitching convulsively, Bâtonnier Payen asked the court not to hear Monsieur Pierre Laval without a fresh preliminary investigation.

The judges withdrew for a few minutes. On their return they rejected the plea made by the defense. Pierre Laval would come and give evidence. The reporters made a rush for the telephones. It was still quite light.

"Does this mean I am free?" asked the accused.

Bâtonnier Payen gently disillusioned him.

The legal correspondent of *Combat,* Georges Altschuler, walked to the Cité Métro station by way of the flower market. He was in a hurry and saw nothing of his surroundings.

He was impatient to write his copy after the leading article by Albert Camus which the paper had published that morning. Everyone was still astonished by the masterly skill with which the author of *The Stranger* tackled the gravest issues of the day. Camus asked questions, read proofs, looked through the latest cables and the other newspapers, sometimes letting out a short laugh which sounded like a cackle, and then, once he had found his subject, locked his door and unscrewed his fountain pen. In a few minutes, his forehead furrowed with concentration, he would cover at one go a page of the coarse *Combat* notepaper with his small, thick handwriting.

"It was a stroke of cruel irony," he had written the day before,

to choose a prosecutor and witnesses for the prosecution who have no right whatever to accuse. The fact remains that this irony is unbearable, as is this insistence on looking for plots for which there is no evidence, and on focusing a treason trial on an Armistice which may be said to have been a mistake, but which cannot be proved to have been a crime. On this point, only one witness was entitled to speak, and it is a great misfortune for the country that decency now obliges him to keep silent. . . . The whole of the truth remains to be established. . . . It is a matter of establishing whether Pétain served Germany, whether his policy helped the interests of the Hitler war, whether he was responsible for the deportations, tortures and executions . . . and finally, whether, willingly or not, he was the enemy's servant and the agent of his infamous deeds.

With Laval present, the country was perhaps going to find out. The trial which had achieved nothing was possibly going to reveal a truth. In one of the offices where he had arrived under escort by way of a maze of underground passages, Laval was weeping. The Bishop of Versailles had had to intervene to prevent the parish priest of Villiers-le-Bel from saying a Mass for Marshal Pétain.

XIII

❧

Friday, August 3, 1945

The courtroom was crowded, like a theater on an important first night. Pressed together even tighter than on the first day of the trial, everyone was suffocating. For fear of an attempted assassination, rows of armed guards were pushing the public back, and the reporters were brought in by way of dark corridors. At half past one the judges finally came in to the accompaniment of a rustling of ermine hoods. With his brief under his arm and his beard bristling, the Attorney General made his way to his seat, occasionally getting entangled in the folds of his red robes. The accused was sitting in his armchair, looking very pale, his hands trembling violently. "Thou tremblest, Faliero," a judge says to the Doge of Venice. " 'Tis with age, then." The reply which Byron put into his mouth was the same reply that Bailly, the Mayor of Paris, gave to his executioners. The presiding judge lost no time in calling Pierre Laval.

Evil genius, sorcerer, swine—all the words which had been hurled at the witness had added to the spectators' curiosity. They almost expected him to come rushing into the bull ring with steaming nostrils and foam-flecked lips, looking around to decide whom to charge. Then, on the edge of an abyss of abrupt silence, he appeared, pale and haggard, and walked forward with faltering steps into the glare of the flashbulbs. Dressed in a crumpled, gray striped suit, his skinny neck protruding from a wide collar pinned together under a grubby white tie, his cheeks tinged with bile, his gray hair plastered down, his mustache yellowed by tobacco, clutching a black leather briefcase and a soft hat, he was no longer anything but a wounded animal who had been dragged out of his cell at dawn to be taken to the central police station, mercilessly harried by the photographers.

"I shall not ask you to take the oath," said the presiding judge. "I am hearing you only in order to obtain certain information, and I have no intention of asking you any questions which might be regarded as the premature interrogation of an accused person. . . . You are sufficiently familiar with public assemblies to understand what I mean when I tell you: No diversions, no digressions. . . . When did your political relations with Marshal Pétain begin?"

Despite his boastful threats, he was already a humble penitent with a rope around his neck. After all, a man whom Franco had sent back, with his Junker 52 and his German crew, to the base he had left with fifty million francs taken from the secret funds, had little enough to boast about. The Marshal had turned away scowling, and was twisting his gloves in his hands, looking at him out of the corner of his eye and pretending not to be listening.

"We were expecting a combination of vice and crime," wrote Maurice Clavel. "What we had before us was a village idiot from Auvergne, speaking to the local magistrate for the first time." Little by little his tired, otherworldly voice grew stronger. He began to regain his self-assurance and to look for the support he needed in words, those magical instruments he had always used to persuade, captivate and conquer. His rustic accent with the rolling r's added to his charm: you could scarcely distrust a peasant who, hand on heart, protested his loyalty to his country. Shifty-eyed and loose-lipped, he tried to gauge the atmosphere in the courtroom as he spoke at length of France's relations with Italy.

"Forgive me for interrupting you," said the presiding judge, "but it seems to me that you are not answering the question that was put to you."

"Forgive me. . . . It seems to me . . ." Laval gave a slight smile as he heard the telltale phrases, and his anxiety diminished. In 1934 he had been Minister of Foreign Affairs, and in 1935 Prime Minister. He talked about the Duke of Windsor, the defense of the franc, his hatred of war.

"I have a profound respect for human life. . . ."

A shudder ran through the courtroom. He went on. His deposition had already lasted twenty-five minutes.

"I must interrupt you again," said the judge, "to remind you that this is the trial of Marshal Pétain."

How could he know what he was supposed to tell the court? He knew nothing about the proceedings so far, had not heard the radio or read any papers.

"If the things I have been saying don't interest the public, I apologize. . . . But they do concern the French people."

The public protested, and behind him, he heard boos and catcalls heralding a storm. At the press table Madeleine Jacob was writing: "Pierre Laval! Philippe Pétain! Both in captivity before our eyes! There they are, together: shame in a uniform and shame in a gray suit. . . ." She raised her pencil. Lucile Augeron, the correspondent for *Ce Soir,* was comparing the witness to a Barbary pirate and a slave dealer.

"I didn't say you weren't French," he continued, turning slightly to the left. "I said that these things concerned the rest of the French people."

And he went on as before, scattering his sentences with interjections like little nasal coughs. The prestige and authority of the Marshal's name, he said, had raised the country's standing abroad. Laval had seen him occasionally before the war. He sometimes went to the Hôtel des Invalides to chat with him. He couldn't remember what he had said to Loustanau-Lacau, and in 1940 he had not been in the center of things. At Bordeaux the Marshal had offered him the Ministry of Justice. He had asked for the Ministry of Foreign Affairs. Then Weygand had intervened, the Marshal had gone back on his word, and Laval had refused to join the new government.

Once again it became obvious that the presiding judge had not mastered the details of the case and was letting himself be out-maneuvered. "I am going to put some questions to you," he had said to begin with, "which I shall try to make as precise as possible and which I must ask you to answer briefly, yet in sufficient detail to shed light on the case."

What was easygoing Monsieur Mongibeaux, who loved his country house in Dordogne, his sheep dog and his cats, doing in this affair? After beginning the trial in a sarcastic mood, he had grown much milder, and every evening he bitterly regretted accepting what seventeen judges before him had turned down—the exalted office of President of the Court of Appeal which obliged him to preside over the High Court. It was said that de Gaulle had swept away his final objections with the words, "Do it for the Republic and for your children." He no longer found any pleasure in life. The gibes hurled at him in the press hurt him. After the bad start it had made, how was this trial going to finish, and what credit would he derive from it? Already he had the impression that some of his colleagues were avoiding him. Behind his pretense of submissiveness, Laval kept slipping through his fingers.

"Let's return to the Pétain trial, since that's what this is supposed to be."

"It's also my trial to some extent . . . hmm . . . Monsieur le Président."

He said "M'sieu" for "Monsieur." Several times he had even said "M'sieu le Maréchal" instead of "M'sieu le Président," but no one had laughed.

"It may be your trial one day—indeed, it certainly will be—but for the moment it's the trial of Marshal Pétain."

What distinguished Laval from Pétain was that the people of France would never have believed Laval, whereas they had followed Pétain on his white charger like an army gradually breaking up. Laval was seen as a dangerous Gray Eminence who, as a result of the King's weakness, had become first a prince and then his evil genius.

At this point Monsieur Mongibeaux mixed up his dates and referred to Pétain as the President of the Supreme War Council, which he had ceased to be many years before. He was rapped over the knuckles by the witness and the defense, impaled himself on a trivial question, was disowned by the Attorney General, and only just managed to fall on his feet again.

As for Laval, his mouth parched and his throat constricted with anxiety, he was visibly choking. Speaking in a whisper, he asked the journalists near him if he could have something to drink. One or two foreign correspondents turned to the presiding judge and called for some water.

"Why, of course," said Monsieur Mongibeaux in a fatherly tone of voice, and he called out to one of the ushers, "Jules, did you hear that?"

A court official went out and, with unconscious irony, returned with a bottle of Vichy water. He struggled for a long time with the cap, but finally Laval was handed a large glass, which he grasped in his left hand. He drank only a few mouthfuls and then put it down on one of the press tables, practically under the Marshal's nose.

"I almost feel like sitting down," he said to the people around him.

"Then sit down," said Madeleine Jacob. "You're an old hand here."

"Can I? Good!"

He sat down, his fleshy ears hanging loosely against his cheeks. "I've got Buddha's ears," he used to say. "They bring me luck."

"You may remain seated," said the presiding judge.

He promptly stood up again, placing his gray hat and his briefcase on the armchair.

"No," he said. "It's more correct to stand up."

He denied having organized a *coup d'état* against the Republic in July 1940. The Marshal had given him a letter in which he declared that Laval spoke in the Assembly on his behalf, but none of the constitutional acts signed by the Marshal had any validity because they were not preceded by the formula, "After consultation with the

Council of Ministers." In his opinion, they were all null and void, even the act which appointed him the Marshal's successor.

"That wasn't the Marshal's fault," he said indulgently, turning toward the accused. "You mustn't blame him. He didn't know anything about it," he added, his yellow face twisted in a grin. "The Marshal used to sign everything that was put in front of him. Sometimes I pointed that out to him. He never paid any attention."

"You mean to say that the Marshal reigned without governing?"

"No, M'sieu le Président. He let the government act under his supervision. Hmm. That isn't the same thing. . . . I didn't agree with the Marshal on a lot of questions. Is that what you wanted to know?"

He mopped his brow, picked up the glass on his left, took a sip of water and gave a little cough.

"I feel a certain embarrassment and something like regret at being confronted with the Marshal like this, because he is the Marshal and because he was my chief. But it is my duty to tell the truth. Hmm . . . One thing is certain, in any case, and that is that the entire National Assembly accepted the law . . . on the tenth of July. At no time, and in no form, direct or indirect, was there the slightest objection to the Armistice. . . . Yet it was perfectly possible to raise objections, since the Assembly was in secret session. Nobody said anything. That is a fact."

He had not been a very close adviser, he told the court. The Marshal did not consult him often and appointed or dismissed his ministers as he wished.

"Yet you were his evil genius."

"I am here to try to correct that false legend," he said with a smile which bared his black teeth.

He was concerned with the question of relations with the Occupation authorities, but discussion of the laws lay outside his province. The presiding judge tried to get him to talk about Alsace-Lorraine.

"I haven't finished talking about home affairs, Monsieur le Président," he said, bristling.

"I see. You haven't finished."

He would have been quite capable of conducting the trial himself. He kept fingering his white tie surreptitiously. "What is Laval?" Weygand used to say. "A white tie." He gesticulated with his beautiful delicate hands, slipping them into the pockets of his jacket, then resting them on the back of the armchair. Everyone gazed at him in fascination. This man who had been destroyed was coming back to life; this man who had been felled to the ground was getting to his feet. Some of the journalists and jurors watching him rested their chins in their hands, utterly astonished.

He had asked for more liberal treatment of the Freemasons in the laws concerning them—laws he had played no part in drafting. As for the Marshal . . .

"They went to see the Marshal and he said, 'All right.' "

"He said, 'All right'?"

"I presume so; I wasn't there. Hmm . . . You are free to give a monologue, Monsieur le Président. I could give a monologue myself, but I'm not obliged to answer a question like that. . . . My knowledge of the Marshal allows me to tell you that he possessed no political experience at all."

"But he could think clearly and make up his own mind?"

"There's no doubt about that."

Laval had protested to the German authorities, and Germany had made no reply. That silence was an indication of France's plight.

The hearing was adjourned after two hours. Everyone exchanged glances with his neighbor. The defense lawyers heaved a sigh of relief. Laval appeared to have changed his tactics: far from attacking, he was dodging out of the way, taking care not to come to grips, his heavy eyelids scarcely blinking. The Marshal stood up, looking thoughtfully at the Attorney General, and Laval fell into step with his guards, holding his soft hat and his worn briefcase. Soiled, crumpled and ravaged, he still exerted considerable charm with his good-natured language and his Auvergne accent, polished like a pebble by years of parliamentary life.

When the hearing was resumed, Monsieur de la Pommeraye, the Secretary General of the Senate, was admitted to the courtroom. He had witnessed the signing of the constitutional acts which Laval had presented to the Marshal. He was a frail old man in a dark suit, with a pair of spectacles perched on his nose, a piping voice, and parchment-like cheeks dotted with white hairs which had escaped the razor.

"What acts are you talking about?" asked Laval.

"I'm talking about the three constitutional acts signed in the morning. You got the Marshal to sign those acts in my presence, and then you turned to me and said, 'And that's how you overthrow the Republic.' "

There was a gasp from the public.

"Oh! Oh!" said Laval. With his hands in the pockets of his jacket, he glared at his accuser.

In ordinary circumstances the Secretary General of the Senate would have simply shriveled up, but now he stood firm, looking his adversary straight in the eyes, with a faint smile on his lips.

Laval no longer remembered anything. Laval could not even recall presenting the acts in question to the Marshal for signature. Monsieur de la Pommeraye had no need of his services as a postman.

"Overthrow the Republic? I'm not a Fascist. I'm not a Nazi. . . ."

The public gasped again.

"Monsieur de la Pommeraye has reported a remark which he states you made," said the presiding judge. "Do you deny that you made that remark?"

"I love freedom, the Republic. . . ."

A roar of laughter came from the public and cut him short.

"You can laugh if you like," he snarled.

Even the jury found it difficult to keep straight faces. Laval must have imagined he was back in the Chamber when a squall had blown up and suddenly, from the government bench, he had to face the jeers and catcalls of the Opposition. As if intoxicated by the danger, he narrowed his slanting eyes, dropped his lower lip, and waited for a lull into which to hurl a word which would restore silence.

"The Republic—"

"I did not ask you whether you loved the Republic," said the judge in a loud voice. "I asked you whether you said what you are alleged to have said."

"I've no idea. After an interval of four years it's quite impossible for me to remember. Monsieur de la Pommeraye's personal relations with me were not particularly friendly."

"Oh!" said Monsieur de la Pommeraye.

"It was—how shall I put it?—a joke in rather poor taste. That will do," he said, to dismiss Monsieur de la Pommeraye.

He faltered for a moment, losing the thread of his ideas. He floundered about, repeating twice that his personal relations with the Secretary General of the Senate had been unfriendly. He couldn't remember anything. He let his mind rest for a moment and then start up again. He had never envisaged any regime for his country other than the Republic, but he considered that the 1875 law made it too easy to overthrow a government and that it wasn't possible to pursue a policy at home and abroad for any length of time. He made a face.

"One day the Marshal asked me if I had any objection to his receiving the Comte de Paris. Constitutionally, of course, that was impossible. As pretender to the French throne, the Comte de Paris is not allowed to enter France. But this was during the Occupation. The Marshal told me, 'He insists.' I said, 'Send somebody to see him. Considering his family connections, he may have some useful information to give us.' A colonel went to see him. Hmm . . . The Comte de Paris told the colonel, 'I have nothing to say to you. I want to see the Marshal.' "

The Comte de Paris had duly arrived and the Marshal had asked Laval to receive him. The royalists were ready for action and the pretender was watching for the moment when he might seize the throne of Vichy.

"In the course of our conversation, the Comte de Paris told me he had been waiting a long time. 'I have been waiting for twelve years,' he said. I replied, 'You will have to go on waiting, Your Royal

Highness. France is a Republic and France does not want any other regime.' "

Laval had recovered all his old self-assurance. In his opinion, it was not on account of Montoire that the Marshal had had him arrested on December 13, 1940, but because his successor, Monsieur Flandin, had seemed more likely to collaborate with the royalists. Laval had not asked to go to Montoire. He had been going to call on von Ribbentrop, the Foreign Minister of the Reich, when he was taken to the Fuehrer, who expressed the desire to see the Marshal. Laval had rushed back to Vichy.

"I told the Marshal what had happened. I said that the Chancellor was expecting us the next day at the same place . . . and the two of us set off again for Montoire."

"Did the Marshal go there of his own free will?" asked the presiding judge.

"Yes, of his own free will. I didn't take him along by force."

"Without being taken along by force, he could have shown a certain reluctance, he could have raised objections. . . ."

"I fully understand your position, which is very different from mine. You want to get me to say things you would like to know. But all I can say are the things I know. And what I know is that when I informed the Marshal of Hitler's desire for a meeting the following day, he fell in with that desire without raising any difficulties."

"Without any reluctance and without raising any difficulties . . . that's what I wanted to get you to say."

"If he felt any reluctance, he didn't express it to me. I don't know anything about it. He didn't express any reluctance, and he came to Montoire. . . ."

Hitler wanted to know the feelings of defeated France toward victorious Germany, and to work out a general scheme of collaboration with France, if she was willing. He dismissed the idea of a vengeful peace; England would pay the piper.

According to Laval, nothing was decided at the meeting. The two heads of state simply explored the idea of an entente, which came to nothing. The Occupation costs were reduced from 400 million francs a day to 180 million, and it was agreed that two million prisoners would be returned to France in batches of 150,000.

"Do you think that in 1940 any intelligent man could imagine anything but a German victory?" added Laval.

The public exploded. He stopped, puffing out his bilious cheeks in contempt.

"I can hear you. I'm sorry if I've said something that offends you. I'm talking about the facts at the time."

And what did I think about collaboration, from the evidence of the notes I made at that time? Nothing. Toward the end of the summer of 1940, I returned to France by boat to collect the rest of my group. I seized the opportunity to take my family back to Algeria with me. One of our generals who came to bid us farewell asked us to train for the day when our forces should be thrown into the balance. After the Crémieux decree was annulled, the Jews of Algeria became natives once more. The Arabs, and the French settlers, of whom I was one, were secretly pleased. Paul Reynaud, Georges Mandel and Jules Moch were arrested and charged. I wrote in my notebook: "The Marshal is cleansing France with the torrent of his justice." The Freemasons fell into disgrace. I was pleased at this news too. To obtain promotion in the French Army before the war, a man had to have the backing of the lodges.

At the time of Montoire, I saw a photograph in the papers of a smiling, uniformed Pétain shaking hands with Adolf Hitler, who, with an Iron Cross pinned over his heart, was looking him straight in the eyes. Between the two men, the gleaming figure of von Ribbentrop and the peaked cap of Field Marshal Keitel seemed to set the seal on the new alliance. I did not flinch, nor did anyone who saw the photograph with me. The two heads of state probably had to pose several times in front of the photographers, for the benefit of posterity. It was, I admit, rather embarrassing. When, in 1854, Marshal Saint-Arnaud and Lord Raglan, allied for the first time against the Russians after a thousand years of warfare, exchanged salutes, there must have been some French soldiers who felt that they were betraying the memory of Crécy and Agincourt. After the war, the English, wiser than ourselves, gave a peerage to the Bailiff of Jersey, who had extended a courteous welcome to the Germans invading his island. Why shouldn't Marshal Pétain have been the new Talleyrand of a new Congress of Vienna, or indeed our Metternich?

I was no worse and no more stupid than the average French officer. In 1940 some of my fellow officers had their doubts about Pétain and gave him a very lukewarm loyalty. I admit, without pride but without shame, that, with the same naïveté which had made an officer of me, I thought we were living once more in times when the Army obeyed the great rules of its order: honor, integrity, self-sacrifice. Yes, I actually believed, and still believe now, in that kind of nonsense. In my opinion, as also in the opinion of Léon Blum and Paul Reynaud, one man personified all those virtues: Pétain. I gave lectures at the base to propagate my faith. I even collected them together in a pamphlet which was published anonymously because the regional Chief of Air Staff, a more cautious man than I, had the sense to warn me not to put my name to it. Far from having the stylistic quality of Captain de Gaulle and Paul Valéry, my eulogy was worthless. Indeed, it revealed a rare stupidity, and I do not feel proud of it.

Those were the days when Saint-Exupéry, meeting his friend Guillaumet, bade him not to despair. "The Armistice is the only possible solution just now," he said. "If we had gone on fighting, France would have been knocked out for a century." I thought the same. We knew that the Germans had demanded Bizerte in vain. Laval had been arrested, while Pétain had refused to dismiss Peyrouton and was said to have declared, "Good, if you go on annoying me, I'll leave you with a France in revolt and go off to Africa. . . ." In *The Profession of Arms,* where I explained all this at some length, I compared myself to a donkey circling around a chain pump to draw water from a well. I wonder now if I hadn't simply bent my back under the harness and allowed my eyes to be blinkered by blind obedience. There were millions of donkeys like me. Perhaps there are more now—who knows?—who are tempted along with different carrots.

It was only later that Dr. Paul Schmidt, the Fuehrer's official interpreter, revealed how stubbornly the Marshal had rejected all Hitler's proposals at Montoire. On the other hand, he shook hands with the Chancellor. At the same time—it is not known whether the timing was deliberate or not—Pétain sent a special envoy, for whom incidentally he felt a certain dislike, to assure Churchill that France would do nothing incompatible with honor against her former ally. The mention of honor was almost inevitable. If he had been a pretty woman, Pétain would have found an honorable way of going to bed with the Chancellor, and, while pretending to surrender to him, giving him nothing he had hoped for. The trouble is that later, when the husband comes home, if he not unreasonably considers he has been deceived and demands compensation, the wife has to pay.

"What we, the judges of the Pétain trial, want to know," said Monsieur Pierre-Bloch, "is whether the former Prime Minister accepts all the charges Marshal Pétain's lawyers are laying at his door."

"If I made a mistake," Laval replied, "and if events have not worked out as I foresaw and logic suggested, well, let me tell you one thing. That is that when the country's life and destiny are at stake, France must have a full hand of cards. She must not be missing a single card, and even if the German card was a poor one, it had to be in France's hand. De Gaulle put his money on the other side. Hmm. He was right, and never, Monsieur le Président, never has anyone heard me utter a single insulting or disobliging word about any Frenchman who thought differently from myself."

"The question I am asking you is this," the presiding judge broke in irritably. "Was the Marshal in full agreement with you, as in fact he said he was in his messages?"

"He was in full agreement with me when he came to Montoire," said Laval, turning toward the Marshal as if to seek his approval. "There can be no doubt about that."

Then, in a self-assured, sarcastic, amused tone of voice, he related how he had been arrested and then released. He had gone back to see the Marshal, who had said, "Me? I didn't know anything about it. I didn't know you had been arrested. I don't know anything." Laval, coarse and quick-tempered by nature, had reacted sharply. It was the first time he had shown a lack of respect for the Marshal. Refusing the Ministry of the Interior which he was offered, he went off with Abetz, the German Ambassador, slamming the door behind him.*

Eighteen months later he came back. He explained all the circumstances in detail. What he said makes poor reading; Laval was no writer. His eloquence, consisting of banalities, repetitions, outbursts and evasions, has vanished from the paper yellowed by time, and the man is no longer there to give life to his remarks. But the reader can sense him clinging to the insane hope of convincing his audience, as he had always succeeded in doing, and of obtaining once again a vote of confidence.

"You rejoined the government on the twenty-second of April, 1942, and exactly two months later—as you must remember, for it was an important event in your life and the life of your country—you made that notorious remark—"

"Yes," he broke in mockingly: " 'I hope . . .' "

"Did you make that remark?"

"Yes, M'sieu le Président."

"In agreement with the Marshal?"

"Let me tell you all about it. . . ."

He was not in the least alarmed by the lengthy interruption. A star to the very end, he was enjoying defending himself and exerting his charm. Why should he deny the facts? He was speaking in front of his judges, but also in front of the press, and the press was the whole country. He had recognized Géo London, a former contributor to

* In fact, Marshal Pétain offered him only the Ministry of Labor.

Gringoire, who had taken advantage of the adjournment to approach him. "Pierrot!" he had exclaimed, throwing himself into Laval's arms. So Laval still had a few friends! It was up to him to help them by eating humble pie, for he had backed the wrong side: Germany had been defeated. He, Laval, had allowed fate to trick him, not to mention men. . . .

At that period Laval needed a certain authority in order to speak to the Germans. He had to give guarantees of his sincerity if they were to believe in him. And he hit on the idea of making a statement on the radio. He read it beforehand to the Secretary General for Foreign Affairs, Monsieur Rochat, who told him, "If I were you, I wouldn't include that phrase." Together they went to consult the Marshal about it, and he told Laval, "You aren't a soldier, you haven't any right to say, 'I believe.' You don't know anything about it. . . . If I were you I would leave out the phrase, 'I believe in a German victory.' " He had accordingly omitted the words "I believe in" and substituted "I hope for."

Deeply compromised in the eyes of his fellow countrymen, he could now stand up to the Germans. Would he conclude a military alliance with Germany? No. Would he send hundreds of thousands of workers to Germany? He would think about it. Would he form a French SS? On certain conditions.

"And when the attack on Normandy took place . . ."

There was a sudden explosion of laughter in the courtroom, which took him by surprise. He stopped, thrusting out his lower lip and narrowing his eyes, and made a grimace. Tiredness was the only possible explanation for such a blunder.

". . . When the Normandy landings took place—I beg your pardon, but I've been speaking for a long time. Naturally I didn't mean an attack on Normandy, I meant the landings in Normandy— the Germans wanted to send in the French SS and the Legion and make them fight on the Western front. I refused. . . ."

A good many leaders had used phrases like "I hope"—such as Churchill referring to the Russians and Marshal Molitor referring to the Germans. In *Les Décombres* Lucien Rebatet had written the same

words: "I hope for a German victory because the war Germany is
waging is my war, our war." In his opinion, by fighting the Muzhiks
and the Jews, Germany was saving the white man.

Laval laid his hand on his heart, paused, and let a tear moisten his
slanting eyes.

"I used those words, M'sieu le Président. I was born at Châteldon,
a little village in Auvergne. I love the soil of France. My feet are
rooted in the soil of France. As I told you earlier, I love my country.
How can you imagine that I could ever want anything but victory and
happiness for my country?"

Legend had it that his little Château de Châteldon was built on the
bones of English soldiers slaughtered in the Hundred Years' War.
"A real case of predestination," Laval used to say.

"Usher," said the presiding judge, "kindly take the witness away."

Laval was quite pleased with himself for leaving the judges on this
emotional note. He picked up his hat and his briefcase, glanced along
the rows of journalists, and bared his teeth at the jury in what could
have been a smile, a greeting or a threat. He turned around, ready to
bow to the old man, but Bâtonnier Payen was already standing
between them, bending over the Marshal. Laval slipped away in
complete silence and disappeared.

"If the Marshal is willing to answer, I should like to ask him how
he reacted when—"

"He is just telling me now," said the Bâtonnier.

"Then let him speak up. It's quite an important question."

Everyone had been shocked and surprised to hear that he had not
protested violently when Laval had gone to see him and told him, "I
believe in a German victory." The explanation was that that phrase
had been followed by an amplification which had justified it completely in his eyes: ". . . for without that victory, the whole of
Europe will fall under Communist control." On the back of the
translation of a statement made by Sumner Welles, the acting Secretary of State, on June 23, 1941, the Marshal had penciled the
following words, without a single correction:

We, the Americans and the French, are confronted with two doctrines, neither of which we wish to see put into practice: Nazism and Bolshevism. For Europe Bolshevism represents the greater danger. We Europeans have no reasons to regret the blows which are being inflicted on it today. Nazi supremacy too is undesirable, for the peoples under Nazi rule would be subjected to almost unbearable constraint. In view of that constraint and the vast extent of the undertaking, it is reasonable to prophesy that cracks would soon appear in the Nazi edifice which would bring it crashing to the ground.

The Marshal stood up, suddenly looking very pale.

"I reacted very strongly," he said in a voice quivering with anger, "when I heard in Monsieur Laval's speech the phrase, 'I hope for a German victory.' He said just now that he came to see me with Monsieur Rochat, who represented the Ministry of Foreign Affairs, to consult me about that phrase. The fact is that Monsieur Rochat would never have agreed to keep that phrase, and I was in complete agreement with him. Besides, when I heard it on the radio—thinking it was all over and that he had arranged matters—when I heard that phrase repeated on the radio, I was furious. I hadn't understood. I thought the phrase had been struck out and I was appalled that it had been allowed to stand."

On several occasions, faced with the indignation which had swept the country, the Marshal had condemned Laval's unfortunate pronouncement. He assured the court that Laval regretted making it.

Unfortunately Monsieur Rochat was in Switzerland, and the authorities refused to allow him to enter France.

The hearing was adjourned at 5:40.

Was Laval a traitor? Twenty years later, now that we are no longer blinded by political passion, how can we maintain that he was? The word *treason* always sent Laval into a fury of indignation, and there are people today who consider that he worked in his way for the good of his country, and that his only misfortune was to have backed the wrong side. After all, he went to Berchtesgaden to talk to Hitler as one statesman to another. Why should we refuse to pay tribute to that realism and opportunism which take no account of morality? "You are the stronger of our two countries," he had said to Hitler. "If you want to crush us, we will suffer and one day we shall rebel. Conquered now, we may conquer you in the future, as has happened before. On the other hand, if you offer us a just peace, a great deal may be possible." This sort of cynical talk is justified in a man who believes the enemy is going to be victorious and wants to protect life at the expense of honor and friendship. In politics, honor consists of making the right decisions. For mankind, it consists of dying rather than committing treason. For my part, I shall always be on the side of mankind.

Alternately booed and cheered, standing up to his opponents and answering their reproaches with a coarse gusto, never traveling anywhere except in a bulletproof car, and never happy except when chatting with the peasants of his village, playing for high stakes and compromising himself to the hilt—was Laval really the mean, greedy, cunning, audacious politician Monsieur Albert Lebrun had described, or had he simply backed the wrong horse, as Weygand maintained? It is impossible to deny his boldness in trying to help the French people in spite of themselves, or his courage in braving unpopularity. That power-hungry politician who lived a Bohemian life in a smoky den which the Marshal loathed, and who hated the conventions, stubbornly believed that Germany could not lose the war. Perhaps Occupied France was lucky to have Laval to sully himself in her place, but there are some fornications to which a man never descends, even to save an inheritance. Attacked by all his enemies as soon as he was defeated, a scapegoat bleeding from the blows he had endured, he still stood firm, spitting out scorn and contempt.

The entire press fell on him. In *France-Soir,* under the caption "Call Pierre Laval," a cartoon showed judges, gendarmes and journalists holding their noses as he came into the courtroom.

XIV

❀

Saturday, August 4, 1945

That day, at 9:34 in the morning, Ferdonnet was shot in the ditches of the Fort of Montrouge. He died bravely. The police arrested fifteen railway workers who had looted a load of shoes in the station at Villeneuve-Saint-Georges. Gabriel Cosset, lord of the manor of Quistenic, and former leader of the Finistère militia, was sentenced to death at Quimper. And finally it was announced that fifty leading war criminals were to be tried at Nuremberg in October, and that the Pétain trial was costing 200,000 francs a day in emoluments and allowances for the judges, jurors and police.

The feverish atmosphere of the previous day had abated. When Laval reappeared he created less of an impression. He greeted the court humbly, like a medieval villager appearing before a company of noblemen. Nobody was afraid of him any more. His briefcase was empty and they knew that nothing would come out of it which could blow anyone up. He was floundering around the heavy embroidered kepi, clinging to it as to a gilded buoy which was his only chance of survival. His daughter, Madame de Chambrun, had been allowed to embrace him. She had whispered to him that he had a friend among the defense lawyers. Perhaps it was that which gave him more confidence than he had shown the day before. This time he had taken the measure of his audience. There was still some hope, despite the vicious hostility of the press—for even his friend Géo London did not dare to defend him; indeed, under the name of Georges Lesur, he had attacked him in the Communist paper *Ce Soir*.

It is no use trying to convince oneself that he was a monster. A photograph of the Council of Ministers taken at Vichy five years before shows him in a drawing room hung with tapestries of rural life, sitting opposite the Marshal, who is taking notes. With his hair brushed low over his swarthy forehead and one shining lock hanging over his right temple, with his full cheeks, half-open eyes and drooping mustache, the man Céline called "the Arab of the Third Republic, with his ebony lock of hair" is talking, and the ministers are listening spellbound. In five years, misfortune had wreaked havoc with his appearance. If he had been victorious, would he have shown no pity to the vanquished? This time he stood in front of the arm-chair, close to the judges, as if in order to be more persuasive.

He defended himself boldly. In his town hall at Aubervilliers he, too, had kept the bust of the Republic, and after the lunch celebrating their reunion, the Marshal had said, "All the disagreements and all the misunderstandings which may have arisen between Monsieur Pierre Laval and myself have been settled. From now on we go forward hand in hand." Laval was confronted with the statement the Marshal had made the day before about his phrase, "I hope for a German victory."

"Let me tell you one thing," he retorted, "and that is that Monsieur Rochat, who had thought the Marshal would act as an umpire, was quite annoyed, as he came downstairs with me, that the Marshal hadn't forbidden me to use that phrase. . . . The Marshal showed no indignation whatever. He made me drop the words 'I believe' and keep the word 'hope.' "

Although the Marshal had declared in the preliminary investigation that on that particular day he had called Laval a "shit," there was apparently no record of any repudiation of Laval's statement at the next meeting of the Council of Ministers. If there had been any such repudiation, the Germans would have known about it. On the contrary, a letter from Admiral Darlan congratulated Laval on his "brave and moving speech."

In Laval's opinion, collaboration could be justified in a few words. Without the help of the Germans the country was in danger of wasting away. The prisoners of war who had been repatriated might be interned again, and without coal or oil the economy was dying. What right had Laval to force a recalcitrant France to display heroic endurance for four and a half years? In exchange for easing the country's sufferings, the occupying power demanded labor. Whereas the Belgians sent 80 percent of their workers to Germany, the French provided only 16 percent of theirs. To avoid being sent to do hard labor in Germany, thousands of men joined the Maquis. This in turn enabled Laval to tell the Germans one day that the mass deportation of workers was stirring up feelings of revolt which fed the forces of terrorism. He was asked what Pétain's attitude had been.

"The Marshal's attitude, M'sieu le Président, was what you would expect of a man of honor. He was as indignant as I was. He protested. . . ."

"Protested and yielded!"

"But yielded what, M'sieu le Président?" asked Laval with an aggressive sneer.

Monsieur Mongibeaux made no reply. During the Occupation all he had done was hide his head under his hood.

On October 11, 1940, before meeting Hitler at Montoire, the Marshal had broadcast a fresh appeal for international collaboration:

France is prepared to collaborate in every sphere of activity with all her neighbors. She knows in any case that, whatever changes may take place in the political map of Europe and the world, the problem of Franco-German relations, so criminally mishandled in the past, will continue to decide her future. After her victory over us, Germany is faced with the choice between a conditional peace of oppression and a new peace of collaboration . . . and she may prefer a living peace for the victor, a beneficial peace for all. The choice lies first with the victor, but it also depends on the vanquished.

If every road is closed to us, we shall wait and suffer. But if, on the contrary, hope is given to the world, we shall overcome our humiliation, our sorrows, our misfortunes. In the presence of a victor who has overcome his victory, we shall overcome our defeat.

These were exactly Laval's sentiments.

How could the Marshal have shown any surprise when, eleven days later, Hitler informed him that he wished to see him in his train at Montoire-sur-Loire? Hitler himself, in a letter cited in the preliminary investigation, would tell him again, on November 27, 1942, that he had merely complied with the Marshal's wishes. The translation of the record kept by the Foreign Ministry delegate shows that Marshal Pétain stated that the time had not come for France to declare war on England, but that he was prepared to consider the idea of collaboration with Germany along the lines suggested by the Fuehrer.

Writing to Pétain from Paris on October 27, 1940, General de la Laurencie, who led the French delegation in the Occupied Zone, declared: "I venture to tell you, Monsieur le Maréchal, with pained and respectful emotion, that this constitutes the first blow to your prestige, which had so far remained immaculate and intact."

It was at that point that Pétain had broadcast an explanation to the French people: "I am honorably taking the road of collaboration, and history alone will be my judge. So far I have spoken to you as a father; today I speak to you as a leader. Follow me!" How many times have we since heard the words "Follow me!" from the lips of another Frenchman! I for one followed obediently. I was neither intelligent enough to learn from world events nor rebellious enough to shake off my yoke. I accordingly went on circling around my chain pump like a donkey.

That day *Le Figaro* published an article by the writers Jérome and Jean Tharaud telling how they had been invited to lunch by the Marshal at the Hôtel du Parc a few days after the Montoire meeting.

The Tharaud brothers had asked the Marshal about his impressions of the Chancellor.

"Hitler is horrible!" the Marshal had replied, raising his hands in front of his face. "I never once saw his eyes, and I didn't hear his voice."

And when the Tharaud brothers had asked him what Hitler had said, he had answered, "Oh, it was really very simple. He told me, 'Somebody has got to pay. If it isn't the English, it will have to be you!' "

In a handwritten letter dated November 9, 1940, which was not cited in the preliminary investigation and was only published in 1950, Pétain had explained to Weygand the spirit in which he was acting:

I, too, have received numerous inquiries from Winston Churchill and Lord Halifax regarding the subject of my conversations with Hitler. I was able to tell them, for it was the truth, that the collaboration we had discussed was purely theoretical. We had not considered any means of putting it into effect. I had confined myself at that interview to asking for an improvement in the lot of our prisoners, in food supplies, and in communications between the two zones, and for the abolition of the demarcation line. The question of collaboration will probably be raised again one day. I shall make sure that it applies only to economic matters or to the defense of our African Empire, rejecting any idea of an attack on England. I am fully determined not to join in that task with either the Italians or the Germans. . . . The situation of our country makes it essential to maintain a prudent balance between collaboration with Germany (which is inevitable in the economic sphere) and the solicitations made by England and America. That is an obligation which I shall not forget.

For his part, Weygand had never made any secret of his hostility toward Laval, and through the British Consul at Tangier he had told Churchill: "General Weygand will not hand over the Empire to the Germans. He will not be the gravedigger of French Africa."

A year after Montoire Pétain had written to Hitler:

No doubt Franco-German collaboration has not yielded all the results which you foresaw and I hoped for. It has not yet been able to shed its comforting light on those dark regions in which the soul of a wounded people is rebelling against its misfortune. Our people are suffering cruel hardships and our prisoners have not come home. Finally, foreign propaganda is doing its utmost to drive a wedge between the occupying power and the occupied people. . . . Even more than a year ago, your victory over Bolshevism offers our collaboration an opportunity to assert itself in peaceful works for the formation of a great new Europe.

"Was the Marshal aware of the aims of this policy of collaboration?"

"M'sieu le Président, I never took any measures of any sort, of any kind. . . ."

"Without consulting the Marshal?"

". . . not only without consulting the Marshal, but without discussing it at a meeting of the Council of Ministers presided over by the Marshal. That goes without saying."

Monsieur Mongibeaux, his bow tie showing above the collar of his robes, kept allowing the discussion to go astray, when he wasn't leading it astray himself. A case in point was the telegram to Hitler, after the failure of the Dieppe landing, suggesting that France should be allowed to take part in her own defense.

Neither Laval nor Pétain admitted signing that telegram. Both declared they were in no way responsible for the congratulations addressed in their names to the German troops, and there was no written evidence that they had in fact played any part in that episode. That day, discussion of the Dieppe telegram lasted a quarter of an hour without yielding the slightest result. Laval asked for a glass of water and took a few sips.

On November 8, 1942, it seemed that the situation was going to be cleared up at last. When the Allies landed in Algeria, Admiral Darlan happened to be in Algiers visiting his son, who had been struck down by poliomyelitis. He could not possibly order the French troops to fight the Allies, since General Juin and General Noguès both told him repeatedly that they would never agree to fight side by side with the Germans. As for the messages from the Marshal and Laval, they were simply blinds which took nobody in. Nobody, that is, except fools like myself. Nobody except an innocent like Admiral Esteva, hopelessly lost among all the other admirals in that drama. The stock joke at that time was that Admiral Darlan had never known the sea, Admiral Abrial had never known defeat and Admiral Esteva had never known love. As for Admiral Platon, General Weygand told him one day in a phrase like a slap in the face, "You are a disgrace to France."

Admiral Esteva, the French Resident General in Tunisia, was a pious upright man, very like the Bey in his fragile appearance and type of hair, who had a collection of clocks which he kept in his palace in the Tunis suburb of La Marsa. He carried out Pétain's orders to the letter, as we did for a time, and as the course of events speeded up was relieved of his command. To his great surprise, he found a letter of congratulations from von Ribbentrop, the Foreign Minister of the Reich, waiting for him at Vichy. Choking with indignation, the poor man could not believe his eyes. Yet that was where the head of state had led him, and had nearly led us too. With his fan-shaped beard and soulful eyes, he had carried out the orders of his king, and had stopped his ears to shut out the summons to rebellion, working unwittingly to obtain victory for the Axis powers.

"Like our ancestors," the Marshal wrote to him, "you have shown that patriotism consists above all of loyalty. . . . In years to come, when men look for models of moral worth among all the weaknesses of mind and heart which characterize our times, the example you have set will be noted and taught. I embrace you." One can only pity the poor Admiral, who wore over his heart an image of the ruined Cathedral of Reims, and came within two votes of being sentenced to death after the Liberation. How many were there at the time who claimed to speak for their country, and among those, how many honest men, how many fools and how many rogues?

Laval took good care not to send any orders to the services. He left that to the Marshal, who issued a succession of appeals followed by anathema. My ears have retained the memory of that broken voice still shaken by a stubborn ferocity: "Frenchmen, a few generals have refused to obey my orders. Generals, officers, noncommissioned officers and men of the African Army, do not obey those unworthy leaders. Once again I order you to resist the Anglo-Saxon invasion. . . ."

"We were not free agents," said Laval, "and the Marshal was not a free agent either. The German Minister came and knocked at his door and told him, 'Broadcast a message.' The Marshal spoke to me about that message. We resisted, but finally he was obliged to give in."

In his armchair, the Marshal raised his hand as if he were going to ask permission to speak.

"I'm trying to help you, Monsieur le Maréchal," whispered Laval, to reassure him.

At least Laval didn't talk about honor. That man without shame showed some sense of shame on that point.

The Marshal had been asked to issue an order to resist the Americans and he had obeyed, "to spare the French people fresh misfortunes." A long, futile argument ensued between the presiding judge and the defense lawyers. There existed a secret Admiralty code, and when he heard of it on November 10, the Marshal used it to give Admiral Darlan a free hand. Laval admitted that he knew about this, and the Marshal, in his armchair, nodded his head with a conspiratorial air. Darlan was disowned only to deceive the Germans. "In fact," said Laval, "the Marshal approved of his conduct." But a few days later, when Admiral Platon was about to leave for Tunis to comfort poor Admiral Esteva and asked for instructions, he was told: "You must manage as best you can."

On November 10 Dr. Ménétrel, the Marshal's personal physician, noted in his diary that when he was informed of the order the Marshal had given to resist the Americans, Pierre Laval telephoned Berchtesgaden: "The Marshal has saved France!" At which Weygand exclaimed, "I hope to God they don't ruin her!" and went on to condemn the Prime Minister's policy. Why was Dr. Ménétrel's evidence heard only in the preliminary investigation? Why should the Attorney General, who solemnly presented the court with the tittle-tattle of staff secretaries, have failed to subpoena Dr. Ménétrel unless he had seen that his evidence would help the defense? As for the defense lawyers, they had not dared to contradict Dr. Ménétrel's lawyer when he had advised him against giving evidence.

On November 27, 1942, at four in the morning, refusing to listen to General de Gaulle, Admiral Auboyneau or even Darlan, who all urged it to sail to Africa, the French fleet scuttled itself at Toulon, on the orders of the head of state. It was not until half past four that Laval heard the news in his village of Châteldon, from the lips of the German Minister at Vichy, Herr Krugg von Nidda, who was accompanied by Monsieur Rochat.

"If the German Government had trusted me," said Laval with a grimace, "it wouldn't have taken that precaution. On the contrary . . . it would have informed me soon enough for me to give orders . . . to save our ships from being scuttled and to enable the Germans to use them. But the German Government knew very well what my attitude would have been. . . ."

"Among the papers you have mentioned," said Monsieur Mongibeaux, "I see one that originated with you. It says: 'An American general presumes to give us orders. . . .' "

"Read it out," said Laval.

"I am reading it out. Thank you for being so kind as to give me instructions."

The public laughed. The scoundrel had recovered all his old arrogance. He thought he was back at the tribune of the Chamber of Deputies, and was speaking once more with his curt, sneering tone of voice and the familiar gestures of a cattle dealer feeling the fat of a cow or lifting a horse's lip, judging beasts and men at a single glance. In the preliminary investigation before his own trial, he told President Béteille how he had learned from the Auvergne peasants how to pick out a cow which would give good butter: "You put your finger in her ear. Hmm, hmm. If there's wax there, well . . ." And he sneered at the Russians on the kolkhozes he had visited, who didn't know that particular trick.

"Monsieur le Président," he suddenly protested, "there are cameras in front of me. That seems a trifle excessive in a courtroom. You're going a bit far," he added, speaking to the cameramen.

They were filming his protruding lower lip, his half-closed eyelids, the lock of hair falling over one temple. He turned away. Free of the cameras at last, he returned to the state of the country during the Occupation. One day, harried on all sides, full of bitterness, and tired of being criticized by all and sundry, he hit on the idea of a referendum on the simple question, "Do you want me to go or to stay?"

During a brief visit I paid to Lyons in 1941, I met only humble officials who were obeying orders and waiting for things to improve. The heroes very naturally remained in hiding. It was unfortunate for Laval that he was unable to provide the court with the evidence of a referendum approving his policy. For at that time the vast majority of the French people showed little taste for rebellion.

"Would you like me to tell you, M'sieu le Président, what their reply would have been? . . . The French people would have answered, 'Stay and suffer in our place, and defend us.' I was there in fact to defend them . . . hmm . . . and the Marshal too. . . . And now we stand here before you. I realized at the time that a sacrifice was called for, and I sacrificed myself. Today you ask me for a further sacrifice. I love my country, I stand before you, I shall answer all your questions."

One day the Germans had urged him to deprive all Jews of their French nationality.

"I realized all too well what they wanted: as soon as they had been deprived of their nationality, the Jews would be arrested and deported. I told the Germans, 'I refuse.' They said, 'There's no room for argument; this is an order.' . . . The whole business took such a serious turn that I thought it over. I said to myself, 'After all, this is no concern of mine,' and I told the Marshal. I said to him, 'This is

what the Germans want. But we mustn't do it.' I need scarcely tell
you that the Marshal agreed with me."

Who knows? Perhaps even the Jews would have answered yes to
Laval as well as to Pétain.

At ten past three the Marshal, who was feeling tired, asked for an
adjournment. The judge granted his request.

When the hearing was resumed, the court went on muckraking for
an hour and twenty minutes, recalling the murders of Georges
Mandel and Jean Zay, the arrests of Paul Reynaud, Daladier, Léon
Blum and General Gamelin. Laval's voice grew misty with sadness
and thick with disgust. He had stood up for his former colleagues
and protested to the Germans. When Darnand, who had taken an
oath of loyalty to Hitler, was appointed Secretary General for the
Maintenance of Order, he had been afflicted with scruples and had
actually started examining his conscience. Shouldn't he resign? he had
asked himself.

"I said to myself, 'If I go, what will happen?' I asked myself who
would be given control. . . ."

Darnand had assured Laval that his oath of loyalty to Hitler was
meaningless. As for Laval himself, he maintained that, although he
had been begged to do so, he had never sworn an oath of loyalty to
the Marshal. In the nineteenth century some government officials had
sworn nine different oaths under the Empire and the Restoration. In
his opinion, any oath, whether you swore it or not, was futile.

The Attorney General stood up and read out a letter from the
Marshal to Laval: "We shall have to envisage severe measures to deal
with breaches of the peace. I have often told you that I have no
objection to the setting up of courts-martial to try killers. It is better
to have a few spectacular executions than rioting and bloodshed."
And with regard to the appointment of Darnand, he wrote: "With
reference to the police, General Bridoux might do worse than call on
Monsieur Darnand, whose courage and energy are well known to
me. . . ."

Like the Marshal, Laval knew nothing about all this. "I hadn't seen the list. . . ." "I didn't know about that. . . ." "I haven't the faintest idea. . . ." "I only said what I had been told. . . ." The whole record of his evidence is studded with similar protestations of ignorance and innocence. He only just refrained from claiming that he had stood up for the Communists and the Resistance. In any case, he had condemned the jurisdiction of exceptional courts. Faced with fresh German demands, he had resorted to trickery and procrastination, keeping the Marshal fully informed. And when the squeeze had come and Monsieur de Brinon had asked for a delegation of powers, Laval had refused and so had the Marshal.

"I refused all his demands," the Marshal agreed, breaking his silence.

The strange old man obstinately refused to answer any questions, but kept intervening whenever he thought fit, despite his lawyers, shaking off his apathy as soon as he thought he could help his own case. For another quarter of an hour Laval went on answering the jury's questions with calm self-assurance. From now on, who could dissociate the Marshal from what he had done? Like a patient, cunning spider, he had trussed up the Marshal in his statements and insinuations in bonds which could never be untied. No one, after all, had forced the Marshal to take him back, or to put up with him, even to the point of preferring him to Weygand.

"No more questions?" asked the presiding judge.

Laval blandly looked the defense lawyers up and down. Bâtonnier Payen bowed his head.

"Kindly take the witness away."

Then, with a slight shrug of the shoulders which may have implied regret, Laval picked up his hat and his briefcase and walked slowly away, after a vague smile which revealed his black teeth. In front of the embroidered kepi, and the old man who turned his eyes away, he gave a little bow.

"*Au revoir,* M'sieu le Maréchal," he said in a syrupy voice. Then, very slowly, to give the court plenty of time to remember him, he went off, with humble steps which nonetheless made the floor creak, and disappeared through the witnesses' door. All of a sudden the stage seemed empty.

On August 2, during Monsieur Trochu's deposition, a member of the jury had asked to hear a draft message written by the Marshal which it had proved impossible to find at the time. Today the Attorney General read it out, wetting his lips as he savored every word:

Reports from abroad have drawn my attention to a disease spreading throughout our overseas possessions, and working on the masses like a subtle poison which disturbs their sense of reality and turns them away from their duty to the motherland. That disease is called Gaullism, from the name of ex-General de Gaulle of the French Army. . . .

This document, written in pencil by the Marshal on five pages numbered in his hand, had been corrected at a few points. It had been found in an envelope on which Dr. Ménétrel had written: "Document belonging to Dr. Ménétrel (MS message on Gaullism, April 1942—not broadcast)."

At the period in question the number of desertions was growing and the Marshal was about to recall Laval to power. One is reminded of the words which Israel Bertuccio throws in the teeth of Doge Faliero in Byron's play:

> Know then, that there are met and sworn in secret
> A band of brethren, valiant hearts and true;
> Men who have proved all fortunes, and have long
> Grieved over that of Venice, and have right
> To do so; having served her in all climes,
> And having rescued her from foreign foes,
> Would do the same for those within her walls.
> They are not numerous, nor yet too few
> For their great purpose; they have arms, and means,
> And hearts, and hopes, and faith, and patient courage.

It was probably to reply to reproaches of this sort that the Marshal wrote the message of April 1942. Did he have the idea of writing it or did someone suggest it to him, and if so, was it he who discarded it or was he persuaded to delay broadcasting it? In any case, it contains a condemnation of Gaullism; de Gaulle had taken the wrong turning, and Pétain accused him of entering a dead-end street out of stubborn pride.

The Attorney General went on reading out the message in his loud, arrogant voice:

He has gathered around him some young Frenchmen whom he has tricked into believing that the way to save France is by taking up arms again. . . . What shame lies in store for those unfortunate renegades, condemned to end their days on foreign soil! What unhappiness awaits their families whose names will remain forever marked with the shameful stain of desertion! . . . To enhance de Gaulle's propaganda, some people have presumed to suggest that I am cooperating with him in carrying out a common plan of action; and they have even gone so far as to assert that we are related. There is no truth in any of these suggestions and . . .

The draft stopped there, at the end of the eighth line on the fifth page, as if the old man's thoughts had suddenly dried up.

"What is that document supposed to be?" asked Bâtonnier Payen. "A message broadcast by the Marshal?"

"It's a draft in the Marshal's handwriting," replied Monsieur Mornet.

"Was anything ever done with it?"

"I have no idea."

"Was it ever broadcast?" thundered Maître Isorni.

"That's really going too far," exclaimed the Marshal.

The lawyers did battle with the Attorney General over the nature of the alleged offense: was it an act or a temptation? And what temptation had ever served as grounds for an indictment?

"The act consisted of putting his thoughts down on paper, in his own hand," said the Attorney General.

This summary, dogmatic judgment would have carried considerable weight in the trial if Monsieur Mornet had connected the draft in question with other documents in the files. Monsieur Mongibeaux's successor as President of the High Court of Justice, Monsieur Louis Noguères, did this later on, and published his conclusions in a disjointed, carelessly written book which could have been a damning indictment if its author had been a writer and not a politician. Monsieur Louis Noguères proved incapable of presenting his case effectively. It is difficult for the reader to keep in step with him, and his train of thought, however logical it may be, remains confused.

In Monsieur Noguères's opinion, the draft of April 1942 is connected with a document entitled "Note for the Press and the Radio." Typewritten and then corrected by both the Marshal and Dr. Ménétrel, this document was based on a message of April 7, 1941, in which the Marshal had already denounced the propaganda of the Gaullists, though without mentioning it by name. Three days later he had clarified the obscure passages of the text:

Deceived by insidious propaganda, [some young Frenchmen] are taking part in subversive action against the German authorities in the Occupied Zone, or are yielding to the promises of the recruiting agents of ex-General de Gaulle. Every day, in fact, boats are trying to leave the coasts of Normandy and Brittany for English ports, and every day our consuls in Spain are taking in young volunteers from the Occupied Zone who come to their offices worn out with hunger and fatigue.

Monsieur Louis Noguères considered the draft message of April 1942 "dangerously clear" in that certain passages would have produced the opposite effect on public opinion from the one intended. What would I have thought if I had heard the message of April 1941 retransmitted by the French North African radio, or if I had read it in the papers? I was so blind that I would probably not have found it particularly striking. The connivance which was so indignantly denied at that time seemed very natural to simple minds like mine. Had we been taken in? Were we complete imbeciles? Or were we to

believe that the old man was at last telling the truth when, at the
beginning of the trial, he declared that he had been working hand in
glove with de Gaulle? Hitler himself had no doubts on that score.

Where was the truth to be found? So far no voice had proclaimed
it. The prosecution had only scolded and grumbled, its witnesses had
thought of little else than protecting themselves, and the defense had
failed as yet to establish the innocence of the old man who, ever since
the beginning of the trial, had kept casting nostalgic glances to his
right, at the flimsy blouse outlining the lovely breasts of Francine
Bonitzer, so close to him and so hostile.

The hearing was adjourned at 5:25. From the washed-out sky that
Saturday, the light fell with heart-rending softness. There was no
muckraking on the quays of the Seine, but only the happiness of
peace rediscovered. Girls walked among the flowers, flowers themselves for the space of a summer's day. In the newspaper printing
houses the presses clattered and groaned, and *Le Figaro* carried an
article in which François Mauriac wrote of the Marshal:

From the depths of that abyss of solitude and old age in which he is
already three parts submerged, why doesn't he tell his judges: "After the
French disaster, when the British Empire was struggling alone against an
omnipotent victor, the fate of the world lay in three cards, but only God
knew which of the three was the winning card. . . . I tried to save France's
prestige in case Hitler should triumph, or in case he should win only a
half victory. Just as another Frenchman remained loyal to our British
ally . . . But of those two Frenchmen, the one who gambled on a German victory always knew that in the event of failure he would be regarded
as a traitor by his contemporaries and perhaps by history. . . . I took that
risk. A nonagenarian Lorenzaccio, I disgraced myself and sacrificed my
honor, so that whatever happened France should survive."

At that point in the trial, nothing was clear. Everyone was asking
how Laval, a Papal count, could have claimed to be working for a
century of peace with Fritz on his back, as Céline put it, and could
have put on a pretense of unselfishness while one hand dipped into

the secret funds and the other clutched the vial of strychnine in his pocket. A brave man, but with one eye on the escape route to South America, he would never have pushed temerity to the point of returning to France, like the Marshal, to justify himself. Muffing everything, even his suicide, because he could never believe he had failed, he succeeded at least in dying bravely in a ditch at Fresnes, a tricolor scarf round his neck, without having time to finish his cry of *"Vive la Fr———."* No man lies at that particular moment.

XV

❦

Monday, August 6, 1945

History was to note that day, but outside the precincts of the First Chamber. On their benches the journalists kept stifling yawns. The heat was oppressive. The glaring light streaming through the high windows shone on foreheads glistening with sweat. President Mongibeaux was relaxing after Laval's deposition. He felt more at ease in front of the minor witnesses, whom the defense had to prod vigorously to stir them into life. The Marshal, whom Madeleine Jacob had nicknamed "the Man with the Wooden Face," only emerged from his slumber to express irritation. Maître Lemaire leaned over toward his colleague Isorni.

"I'm bored," he whispered in his ear.

"Patience," replied the other.

Isorni was waiting for the opportunity to shatter the calm produced by the endless reminiscences being recounted by a brigadier on the Reserve List. General Lacaille, as one might have guessed, had served all his superiors loyally and climbed the hierarchical ladder thanks to his bureaucratic zeal. He had nothing to say that was not a commonplace assertion of the satisfaction to be gained from obedience.

"Isn't the General aware," asked Bâtonnier Payen, "of an attempted *rapprochement* between the Marshal and General Giraud in Algeria?"

In October 1943 General Lacaille had received a visit from a Trappist monk Giraud had sent by way of Spain to ensure unity among the French people when the Allies landed. General Lacaille saw the Marshal, who expressed his high regard for General Giraud. At that time the head of the Provisional Government was not Giraud but de Gaulle, whom the Marshal stubbornly insisted on ignoring. Later on, General Lacaille again offered his services to bring together Admiral Auphan, who had been given full powers by the Marshal, and General Juin, who was General de Gaulle's delegate. Provided that his authority was recognized, Marshal Pétain declared his readiness this time to present General de Gaulle to the country as the head of the government. Just as he had presented Laval.

"Has the accused any comments to make?" asked Monsieur Mongibeaux.

"No," he said, shaking his head.

General Lacaille withdrew, bowing to Pétain as he left.

He was followed by Prince François-Xavier of Bourbon-Parma, a slim, elegant, rather languid figure. In the deportee camps where his participation in the Resistance had taken him, the Prince had never heard any criticism of the Marshal. In his opinion, if it had not been for the Armistice, France would have suffered the same fate as Poland.

"Instead of two hundred thousand deportees, there might well have been two million who would have died in the camps in Germany."

At Vichy the Prince had met the Marshal, who had told him, "I am neither an imperialist nor a royalist. I am trying to save what I can of the French state from a catastrophe." As for the militia, the Prince referred to witnesses who could testify that the Marshal had not wanted that fratricidal army.

After Lacaille came Picquendar, another general on the Reserve List, who was embarrassed and did not know where to look. He had spent his time camouflaging enough material to equip twenty-four divisions and manufacturing armored cars, with the Marshal's "moral support," in underground factories in the Corrèze. The jurors representing the Resistance exploded with indignation. The Maquis had been desperately short of supplies, and RAF crews had risked their lives to drop arms and ammunition by parachute, when there had been vast stocks in hiding places where the Germans had found them when they invaded the Unoccupied Zone.

In a whistling voice Monsieur Noël Pinelli, one of the Paris deputies, who with his weary expression, round head and spectacles looked like Monsieur Vincent Auriol, assured the court that no pressure had been exerted on the National Assembly during its deliberations in July 1940, and that he had been surprised how little opposition there had been. Paris, although an open city, had been terrified of the enemy. The Armistice had given the country a zone over which the national flag had gone on flying. As for the Marshal, he had given the impression of despising all politicians, and had merely tolerated those who had been inflicted on him.

During the adjournment the news of the atom bomb dropped on Hiroshima suddenly spread throughout the Palais de Justice. Nobody knew very much about it, but it was described as a sort of apocalyptic explosion. The Marshal's eyes sparkled when he heard the news. "I must write something about it," he told his jailer Monsieur Simon. "It looks as if it will revolutionize all the principles of strategy."

"This means the end of world war," somebody said.

"And when do you think this trial is going to end?"

When the hearing was resumed, shortly before four o'clock, there was an unexpected scandal. A general on the Active List, Controller of Infantry at the Ministry of War, arrived to give evidence in uniform and clicked his heels in front of the Marshal. This was Major General Lafargue. On his left shoulder he wore the Rhine and Danube patch of the First Army. In a powerful, monotonous voice— a voice very like himself—he embarked on a eulogy of the Marshal. Bald-headed and bespectacled, with a hooked nose and a thick mustache, his leather belt tightly buckled and his face stamped with the serenity common to fools with a sense of mission, he told how he had known both Joffre and Foch. If they had been in power in 1940, he said, everything would have collapsed and France with it.

"The country needed someone who was capable of swallowing not only bitter medicine, but gall and wormwood, and of wearing a crown of thorns."

In his opinion, the Armistice had saved France, Britain, Russia and possibly the United States, and Montoire had been just a trick.

"What did Montoire matter to us? What did we care about collaboration in those circumstances? That was all happening above our heads, and it was necessary as a blind."

What he said made sense, and his reasoning was the product of a noble mind, but his arguments were confused, verbose and grandiloquent. The General enjoyed hearing himself talk, but his audience was bored. He, too, had played at being Pétain and refused to leave his post in France. He naïvely told the court how he had traveled to Vichy to make representations on behalf of his officers, and seemed astonished that some of his remarks should arouse the indignation of both the jury and the Attorney General. He turned pale, threw up his arms, and after a long, futile discussion went off very pleased with himself, standing at attention once more before the Marshal and bowing to him. Madeleine Jacob gave him a final glance and wearily rested her head on her left hand. Jean Schlumberger left the courtroom with the gentle dignity of the Councilor of State he was, to write his report for *Le Figaro*. Standing behind the Marshal, Bâtonnier Payen, in his lawyer's cap, looked like a vicar general waiting on his cardinal.

Yet another bestarred old fogey made his appearance: General Ruby. Pale and white-haired, he remained only five minutes behind the Louis Quinze armchair. As Regional Military Commissioner at Marseille, he had been summoned to Vichy in October 1943, with a dozen other generals in similar posts. The Marshal received them, asked them what progress had been made in the way of underground mobilization, and told them, "You see, I believe the Americans are

going to land, and when they do we shall have to give them our
support."

One last general entered the courtroom: Brigadier Picard, of the
Reserve, who praised the Pétain he had known at Allied Headquarters in 1917. He was asked if he had any more recent information to give the court. He remained silent. The presiding judge
thanked him and gave him permission to go. But before he left, he
threw a final flower to the accused.

"In 1806," he said, "Prussia was beaten more severely than we
were in 1940. She collaborated more thoroughly than any other
country has ever collaborated, since she provided Napoleon with an
army. Yet I have never heard that the Queen of Prussia, or the King
of Prussia, or his ministers were ever troubled on that score later
on."

This remark was greeted with laughter. The hearing was adjourned
at ten to six.

Japan was a long way off. Nobody could imagine the horrors of
the city razed to the ground by the nuclear blast, or the huge number
of victims. Nor did it occur to anyone that Hitler had come within a
few months of beating the United States to the post and hurling that
apocalyptic thunderbolt at London. It had not yet been revealed that
the Allies, lagging behind the enemy in scientific research, had
nipped the secret weapon in the bud by sending hosts of obsolete
bombers to shatter the factories which were making the most terrible
weapon of destruction of all time. Would Hitler have won the war if
he had used the atom bomb first? And in that case, who would have
done the more to serve the interests of the French people and protect
their lives? De Gaulle or Pétain? Laval or Maurice Schumann?

In *L'Ordre*, Julien Benda took up the point made by François
Mauriac. "It would be a fair defense," he wrote, "to say: 'We
believed in a German victory, which was a not unreasonable belief to
hold, and being statesmen, in other words practical men and not
idealists, we acted accordingly.' " Julien Benda recalled the famous

words of the people of southwest France after the Treaty of Brétigny: "We shall accept this peace only with our lips, for our hearts are not in it," and added: "I have always felt that in Pétain's case his heart *was* in it." The author of *The Treason of the Clerks* concluded:

There would have been a certain dignity in declaring: "We acted in the name of a political ideal; we failed, and now you are condemning us in the name of yours. That is quite in order. *Me adsum qui feci.* But mark well that as we face your firing squad we stand by our ideal and utterly reject yours." Anyone speaking like that would have fallen like a Charette or a La Rochejacquelein, taking with them the respect of their adversaries, whereas at present we can feel nothing but contempt.

In *L'Époque* Maurice Clavel came to the defense of a witness who had been told by a member of the jury, "Shut up. . . . The Maquis saved France." Clavel wrote:

In our opinion—and we too have served in the Maquis—we are inclined to think that France was saved by the Anglo-Saxon armies, with the support of the regular French Forces, in conjunction with the Maquis. So that the juror's statement, though probably made with the best of intentions, is simply what we used to call eyewash. . . . Why refuse to admit that there were a few undesirable elements among us? We know perfectly well that that is the case, since we had to suppress them by means of sanctions or full-scale punitive expeditions. Since the whole of France knows that as well as we do, was it wise, by denying their existence, to risk being confused with them in her eyes?

XVI

❧

Tuesday, August 7, 1945

That day France learned that the gentle-faced poet Robert Desnos had died on June 8. He had escaped from a prison camp in Saxony and was walking in a column of specters to meet the Russians when he dropped from exhaustion, like most of his companions. A Czech medical student who spoke French tried in vain to save him. He had some poems on him, written on scraps of paper:

> *I have dreamt of you so much*
> *Written so much, talked so much,*
> *Loved so much the shadow of you*
> *That nothing of you remains.*

The hearing was not resumed as usual at 1:30, and it was learned that one of the jurors, Monsieur Pétrus Faure, was in a Métro train delayed by the suicide of a man who had thrown himself onto the track. The presiding judge sent a car to fetch him.

There were huge headlines across the front pages of the papers. Tokyo had admitted that "a new type of bomb" had caused considerable damage at Hiroshima. A single atom bomb had been dropped from a Flying Fortress, and the entire Allied press had given itself up to an orgy of enthusiasm. Only the leading article in *Combat* reduced the victory to reasonable proportions: "We shall have to choose," wrote Camus,

> between collective suicide and the intelligent use of scientific discoveries. In the meantime it is permissible to think that there is a certain unseemliness about celebrating a discovery which has been placed first of all at the service of the most terrible frenzy of destruction which man has shown for centuries. . . . Faced with the terrifying prospects opening up before mankind, we can see better than ever before that the fight for peace is the only battle worth waging. It is no longer a prayer but an order that must come from the peoples of the world, an order to make a final choice between hell and reason.

There were doubts as to whether the papers were going to be able to continue publication. The permission they had been granted to appear in large format during the trial had not been accompanied by any extra allocation of newsprint. For the past two days, *Combat* had survived only because it had received supplies of newsprint from *France-Soir*.

Like Madame Pierre Laval, Marshal Pétain's wife had protested to the examining magistrate about the charge brought against her husband of dealings with the enemy. It was also learned that General Lafargue, who had given evidence the day before in uniform, had just been relieved of his command. The press, though far from gentle with him, recognized his courage: giving evidence on behalf of the accused when one had everything to lose in one's career was perhaps not particularly intelligent, but it called for respect. The press recalled how Monsieur Léon Noël, in return for his deposition, had been officially admitted to the Institut.

Finally, at two o'clock, the hearing began, and, one by one, Pétain's former ministers were called to give evidence.

The first to appear was Monsieur Marcel Peyrouton. He had been given the post of Minister of the Interior by virtue of his reputation for strength and determination. He gave his place of residence as Fresnes Prison. Bent with worry, his face heavily lined, and with great bags under his eyes, he held a brown felt hat and a pair of kid gloves in his hand. Marshal Pétain pretended not to notice his bow.

It was he who had suggested to the Marshal the idea of having Laval arrested. Apart from that he knew nothing, had done nothing, was responsible for nothing. During the three-quarters of an hour he faced the jury's questions, this man whose energy had been so loudly praised showed nothing but weakness. In a thick, drawling voice, he suggested that it was in a spirit of obedience that he had accepted his high office, and denied having ever given orders for arrests or internments. He knew nothing at all of the camps in southern Algeria where undesirables were imprisoned. Yet I remember photographs of him in a gold-braided uniform, with a ridiculous cord across his chest and an implacable expression on his face, when, on the arrival of the Allies, he succeeded the clownish Châtel as Governor General of Algeria.

"I am simply and solely a government official, and I consider that I owed the government in power the same service that an officer owes France."

Poised above an abyss of emptiness and silence, he remembered nothing. The decrees bearing his signature had been issued without his authority, and the racial law was the work of the Keeper of the Seals. His so-called iron fist was transformed into a timid forefinger raised to ask for the judge's help against the unjust attacks of the jury.

"It is I who am being tried here, Monsieur le Président!"

Bâtonnier Payen tried to get him to talk about the part Pétain had played in the Montoire affair.

"Oh, come now," muttered the Marshal, "he doesn't know anything about that. It was no concern of his."

Angered by yet another "I don't know," one of the jurors exclaimed in place of Monsieur Mongibeaux, "Thank you. The High Court will take note of your answers."

After a last question the presiding judge finally intervened. "You really don't remember?"

Monsieur Peyrouton made no reply. The judge gave him permission to withdraw.

The Marshal looked away contemptuously, although Madeleine Jacob wrote that he gave the witness a conspiratorial wink. The former colonial administrator shot away like a rat.

The next witness, Vice Admiral Fernet, former Secretary General to the Prime Minister, was trembling when he appeared. The public looked at one another in surprise. Where had the poor Marshal dug up all his ministers? Laval was at least somebody. Loustanau-Lacau had alleged that Admiral Fernet had never heard the sound of gunfire, to which the Admiral had objected that he had heard it once—in the Dardanelles.

With surprising firmness for such a little man, the Admiral spoke of the mission of Professor Rougier, who in September 1940 had offered to try to negotiate a secret agreement with the British. The Marshal had given his approval and Professor Rougier had set off for Geneva, Lisbon and London. On his return, just after the Montoire meeting, he was received on November 10 by the Marshal, who also gave his approval to the conclusions of the *modus vivendi:* Britain promised to lift her blockade and not to attack the French colonies, while France agreed to leave de Gaulle with what he had taken and not to hand over her fleet to Germany.

Pale and uneasy, the Admiral answered a few questions.

"Has the Marshal any comments to make on this deposition?"

Monsieur Mongibeaux's use of the words "the Marshal" instead of "the accused" caused a murmur of astonishment. Was the judge's attitude changing?

"No, I have no comments to make."

With his white faunlike goatee attached to a tortured mask, Monsieur Jean-Marie Roussel, Councilor of State, looked like the film star Michel Simon. In his black jacket and striped trousers, he had been president of the commission instructed to review all naturalizations granted since 1927: 250,000 files concerning nearly a million former foreigners, most of them Jews. Thanks to the measures taken to attenuate the effects of the law, only 3 percent of those concerned had been charged.

"I should make it clear," said Maître Isorni, "that we had no ulterior motive in calling Monsieur Roussel, and the Attorney General is too well aware of the profound respect we feel for him to have any doubts on that score."

The journalists stopped writing and nudged one another. The defense did not dare to make the witness say that the vice president of the Commission on Denaturalization had been none other than the Attorney General himself. It was probably to avoid the witness's eyes that Monsieur Mornet kept his head down and went on rummaging among his papers.

Monsieur Roussel had gone to Vichy to answer any questions the Council of Ministers might ask him. No questions were put to him, and he was not granted an audience with the Marshal. He was simply invited to lunch. Before the meal he managed to reassure the Marshal about the care he was taking to trick the Germans and save the Jews. "Well, that's fine, then," said the Marshal. And everyone went into the dining room.

With diabolical malice Maître Isorni tried to get the witness to talk about the other members of the commission who had escaped punishment, and one of whom was leading the prosecution in the present trial. Monsieur Roussel, stiff-collared and tightly buttoned, refused the bait. Far from wishing to do battle, his only thought was to make his escape. As for the Attorney General, huddled in his robes, he remained silent.

A former lawyer and deputy, Monsieur François Martin seemed a little, nondescript character. But as soon as he started speaking, in a voice spiced with a touch of garlic, he gripped everyone's attention. Appointed Prefect of Montauban by the Marshal, he had remained at his post under Pucheu and Laval. He considered that he had followed the "line of conduct" the Marshal had desired, and defended himself skillfully against the charge that he had collaborated. With a rather bombastic southern eloquence he lauded his own merits and those of his chief. He spoke too much of himself, the Marshal's feelings and the Marshal's silences for anyone to believe him. With consider-

able cunning he managed to avoid every trap that was set for him.
The forty minutes of his deposition contributed absolutely nothing.
Like the Admiral he was free to come and go as he pleased, whereas a
guard with a submachine gun slung across his back had escorted
Monsieur Peyrouton and now ushered in Monsieur Jacques Chevalier,
the former Minister of National Education.

A philosopher by profession, allowed out of prison for the occasion, wearing a crumpled suit, Monsieur Chevalier set out, rather
comically, to instruct the court.

"You could say that the Marshal played a double game, because he
played one game with the Germans and another with the British. But
he didn't play a double game in the pejorative sense that he was
secretly doing things he should not have done."

The former dean of the Faculty of Letters at Grenoble had become
a minister by virtue of his friendship with lords and princes. He
claimed that thanks to his friendship with Lord Halifax he had been
able to conclude secret agreements with the British, behind a smoke
screen of hostility, like those which Professor Rougier had arranged
in London. Somewhat pretentious under his natural joviality, he paid
great attention to the journalists, speaking for their benefit and
reading out his documents slowly, in a deep voice. He would have
roused his audience from their apathy if he had revealed to the court
that the Marshal had ignored the information the British Admiralty
had given Vichy about the time schedule and course of a flight
General de Gaulle was to make to Brazzaville. The defense did not
dare to risk eliciting this information.

So *that* was Vichy—that bunch of capons, hens, ducks and pea-
cocks, now trembling in their cages at Fresnes! The old bull who had
reigned over them did at least possess pride and dignity. He still
carried his head high and was still capable of giving a thrust with his
horns, as on the day when, passing an officer in the courtroom who
had not bothered to stand up, he tapped him on the knee with his
kepi. The old man had no liking for cowards, and yet, as a political

novice of eighty-five, he had tolerated all those cowards, together
with the ambitious gang of rogues swarming, waddling and wallow-
ing around him: the manufacturers in search of orders, the spiteful
journalists in search of scandals, the high officials in search of jobs
and honors, the failed politicians in search of petty profits. . . .

"If only the French people knew," his aide-de-camp, Major Bonhomme, used to say. On certain evenings the wife of a famous
explorer used to perform a belly dance half-naked before the
Marshal, or else the once handsome officer gave a secret assignation to
some new mistress enamored of his fame. These were intimate occasions, worthy of a conqueror who seemed to possess eternal youth.
But usually he remained shut up in his hotel room with his silence, in
front of a log fire on which he burned his secret papers. For how
many loyal, trustworthy men could he count among his followers? On
his floor of the hotel the smell of espionage and treason was not as
strong as it was in the anterooms on the ground floor, or in the
corridors where spies and counterspies listened at every keyhole.

What a bunch of rogues they had been at the court of King
Philippe VII! But if the roles had been reversed by a German atom
bomb dropped on London, and the same judges, assisted by another
Attorney General, or perhaps the same one, had had to try de Gaulle,
would the Carlton Gardens gang have shown up in a better light?
And would de Gaulle have deigned to speak?

Yet another man came forward that day to boast with a glib tongue
about the merits of his department and the vigor with which he had
resisted the Germans' demands: ex-Minister Yves Bouthillier. The
franc, he told the court, had remained in a healthy condition throughout the Occupation. Monsieur Mongibeaux found the right phrase to
prick the balloon of his pride.

"A Minister of Finance," he said, "always manages to prove to the
taxpayers that the burden he is imposing on them is extremely light."

Monsieur Bouthillier went off with a sigh of relief. The hearing
was adjourned at six o'clock.

XVII

❖

Wednesday, August 8, 1945

The behavior of the fallen sovereign's courtiers inspired nothing but disgust, and as the exposure of human ignominy is a depressing experience, those who attended the trial did so as a duty. It was the trial of a nation which had given itself to an old man out of despair. Every day the legal correspondents of the national press took their places on the benches with added weariness. Since Laval had come and gone, the edge of Madeleine Jacob's ferocity had grown blunter. Why, after all, should anyone hate the witnesses giving evidence now? These insignificant place-seekers, these petty servants, were obviously terrified. They had served in petty fashion the grandiose error of a grand old man—such was the impression which was beginning to emerge after fifteen days of the trial, conducted in petty fashion too, without either cruelty or genius.

The first witness that day had played a significant part in my life, for it was because, without knowing him, I believed him that I followed the Marshal until November 1942, when he helped me to part company with Pétain. My feelings toward him are compounded of a certain respect and considerable sadness. Nothing in his career marked him out until, with the defeat of France, he became Chief of Air Staff and then Air Minister. His name, Bergeret, could have come out of a novel by Anatole France. Without being a military fireball, he possessed the intelligence of a tax inspector who can deal with any problem, however difficult. Did he come and see us? Did he speak to us? It seems quite likely that he did, but I can't remember, and there is no record of any such visit in my notes. If I ever saw him, he left no mark on my memory. At the time of the trial he was only fifty years old. To be a brigadier at forty-five was no mean achievement.

Tall and gaunt, with a thin, tortured face, and dressed in a worn old suit with no decoration in his buttonhole, he limped stiffly forward and slumped into the witnesses' armchair.

The reader can imagine my feelings as I read his deposition. He spoke in a strong, firm voice, with a conciseness which had something contemptuous about it. He had managed to keep his planes out of the Germans' hands and to store them away after dismantling them. He disguised his flying school as a sports center, camouflaged the airfields in French North Africa, built up a force of fifty-four groups, and organized a secret intelligence service which kept watch on the enemy's movements. Thanks to him, France still had an air force of sorts. Emissaries from Vichy visited us now and then and reassured us. They told us that "the old man was fooling the Germans." We believed them.

One of the jurors reproached General Bergeret for having decorated some air crews in Syria who had fought against the British. The witness was embarrassed and did not dare to say what he should have said. How could he have known what to reply? That sort of thing is not taught in schools of war, but in war itself.

"What of it?" I would have replied in his place. "Didn't the British decorate those of their own men who fought against us? A military decoration is not an indication of the rights or wrongs of a war, but of courage in battle. 'For I . . . am a man set under authority, having under me soldiers, and I say unto one, Go, and he goeth; and to another, Come, and he cometh; and to my servant, Do this, and he doeth it.' Choosing the enemy is a political act. Fighting the enemy is a military act. If all the decorations given for fighting the English had to be thrown away, it would take hundreds of wagons to cart them to the rubbish dump, considering how long France and England have been at war. The officers of the Armistice Army were not expected to judge the orders they were given, but to carry them out, or else resign their commissions. The hazards of war brought them face to face with an enemy who would shoot them down if they didn't shoot him down first. Was he English or German? For a soldier who has to shut his eyes, the aggressor has no nationality. If you want to change that, you must change all the rules of war. I know only one: obey or resign. At the time I obeyed, and I regarded that as my duty. You disobeyed, and you were within your rights. The French Army had to face similar problems of conscience during the Restoration, the Hundred Days and the Commune. If you don't want to face them again in the future, then you must change the Constitution. It is your function not to condemn those who obey, but to make sure that they are obeying a just cause. For my part, I decorated the soldiers who obeyed, and I consider that I did well."

That is what I would have said in General Bergeret's place. I would have added that the blood which had been shed in Syria had been shed in vain, that the Germans had not kept their promises, and that the Air Force units which had fought out there had been disbanded on their return to France. But then, all that was part of the game of war and military stupidity. When you have chosen to make your career in the armed forces, you must be prepared for anything.

Early in November 1942 General Bergeret went to North Africa, for he knew that the Allies were preparing to land there. He suggested to the Marshal that he should take him along so that Pétain should be there when it happened. The Marshal refused; he regarded himself as the guarantor of the million and a half prisoners he was protecting. Once he had arrived in Algiers, General Bergeret had no doubts as to what to do. In his opinion, if the opportunity offered itself, the French had to turn against the Germans.

"For my part," he told the court, "I had to see seventy high-ranking officers of the three services in my room to convince them that, once the Armistice had been broken, all oaths of loyalty taken previously were automatically nullified. And that there was no cause for scruples, no reason to hesitate any longer about what course to adopt . . ."

Finally, by means of the secret naval code, Admiral Auphan sent his famous message to Admiral Darlan: "The Marshal approves of the position you have adopted in Algiers, namely, to end the fighting and resume the struggle; he wishes to express his confidence in you and he places the fate of the Empire in your hands." That message brought the Armistice Army over to the Allies.

Our own feelings were in no doubt. We thought of nothing but taking our revenge on the Germans, and that seemed perfectly compatible with our loyalty to Pétain. In October 1942 I got a printer at Sétif to set up a couple of poems which the Algerian censorship had not allowed my publisher to bring out. One was called "Song for a Time of Trial" and the other "Song for a Day of Vengeance." I had written the latter in July 1942. It called the wrath of heaven down on the enemy's heads. I was ripe for the events which followed.

On November 7 we were in a state of alert. On the morning of the eighth our group captain told us that Algiers had been attacked during the night by Anglo-Saxon vedette boats, that landings had been made in the region of Oran, and that a naval squadron was cruising off the Cap de Fer. Telephone communications with Algiers had been interrupted. We were ordered to get ready to attack. We had practiced dive-bombing for a whole year, and now the time had come to show what we could do: making a short approach in a straight line, diving onto the target at full throttle, taking aim, dropping our bombs and then making a quick getaway. These tactics could take an inexperienced enemy by surprise, but not naval gunners. The Marshal was sending us to our deaths, and we knew it. So much the worse for the fools that we were. We had freely sworn to obey. We loaded our bombs with no joy in our hearts. Our orders were countermanded just as we were about to climb into our cockpits.

Several times during the evening the GOC Constantine ordered us to machine-gun the roads in Kabylia. As it was a dark, filthy night, and we had never been trained to fly in those conditions, we could not obey. The next day I made a reconnaissance flight toward Algiers without seeing a single American vehicle, and nearly killed myself in the mountains in the process. Returning to base at nightfall, I saw a German plane standing near our hangars. Its crew, who had landed on our airfield on hearing that Algiers was in the hands of the Americans, had brought two special envoys from the Fuehrer: Captain Sturtmeyer and Captain von Bertau.

Admiral Esteva, the French Resident General in Tunisia, mentioned the two men that day in a message which reached Vichy at 4:30 in the afternoon of November 9, and warned the government of the harmful effect that German military aid would have on the morale of his troops.

In my book *The Profession of Arms* I have described my strange confrontation with Captain Sturtmeyer and Captain von Bertau. It was the first time I had been able to observe my enemy at close quarters. Without knowing each other, we had already been face to face, and now, all of a sudden, an order from my superiors could impose them on me as comrades in arms. If an old man insisted, I would have to give them help and protection. In my position, and in my ignorance of the conduct of the war, how could I judge what decision my country should make to ensure its salvation? The sound of its suffering scarcely reached my ears, but my natural inclinations made it easy to make a choice. I felt sure that one day Captain Sturtmeyer would lie stretched out on the soil of my country and that the stripe on his trousers would be red with his own blood. Like Achilles I said to him, "There can be no pact between men and lions. We are not allowed to love each other, you and I."

At eight o'clock on November 9, two French planes from Istres landed at our base with Governor General Yves Châtel and his suite. The Governor General rested in a bedroom where the sheets were still warm from Captain Sturtmeyer. He played the braggart with us.

Laval had told him, "It's sheer folly to try to leave." He had replied, "Even if I have to go as far as Tamanrasset, I won't be taken prisoner." In the evening, when the Constantine newspaper, *Dépêche,* reached us, we read the appeal he had issued for our benefit before leaving Vichy: "The fight has started. It is a fight we intend to win." He was not so boastful later on.

German planes were sweeping the coastline between Algiers and Tunis. A rumor suddenly started that General Bergeret was at Sétif. In fact, the person concerned was the Under Secretary of State for Communications, who took off at four o'clock the next morning for Vichy. A second plane, carrying General de la Porte du Theil and the Director of French Railways, slewed around as it was taking off and broke up. General de la Porte du Theil left in a car for Constantine, leaving behind in the plane a greasy green beret, which lay around our offices for a few days like a melancholy trophy, and disappeared in the general upheaval.

On November 10 utter confusion reigned. Fourteen fighter pilots flew in from France, by way of Sardinia and Tunis, under the command of the famous Fleurquin, who for many years had led the French aerobatic team at international meetings. While they were landing we received orders forbidding us to take any part in hostilities within a radius of thirty miles of Algiers. At nine in the evening our Constantine headquarters ordered us not to obstruct the progress of the Americans and to prevent any attempted landings by Axis planes. This unexpected order caused tremendous excitement. Our group captain turned to Fleurquin.

"Well," he said, "all you have to do is obey orders. It's very simple."

"It's not so simple as you think," said Fleurquin. "The Marshal has just declared that he is still in command in French North Africa and orders us to resist."

"That's all a blind."

"So they say every time. Speaking for myself, I believe what I'm told."

A few minutes later, our Constantine headquarters issued fresh orders: "Absolute neutrality. Surrender base to first arrivals." We were completely taken aback.

That day, General Bergeret telephoned from Biskra to confirm the order to oppose the Germans but not to resist the Americans. Not knowing that he had been in North Africa for several days, we thought he too had just arrived from Vichy and must have received these instructions from the Marshal himself. During the evening, an argument with the pilot of the Léo 45 which had crashed at dawn caused me a certain amount of disquiet. He insisted that we owed absolute loyalty to Marshal Pétain and suggested that we should go and machine-gun the Americans at Maison Blanche. I thought he was going too far.

At eleven o'clock on November 11 a dispatch arrived informing us that some Messerschmitt 109's were heading in our direction. Fleurquin ordered his pilots into the air, and we thought he was going to attack. One of his planes crashed during take-off. Fleurquin got the rest together, turned his back on the Messerschmitts and set off for Oujda, where Morocco was still holding out against the Americans. As for us, leaving Sétif to anyone who wanted it, we flew off to Laghouat, where we met more officers who were unsure that they were following the famous path of honor, but were not particularly eager to go over to the dissident Gaullist faction.

On November 14, speaking on Radio Vichy, which some of us could just manage to hear, the Marshal disowned Admiral Darlan and plunged us into fresh perplexity. On the twentieth another message got through to us. We heard the old voice, which seemed to us to be trembling with indignation, calling on us to resist. Was the Marshal just saying that for form's sake and because he knew that, even if we had wanted to, we were no longer capable of resisting? Did it so much as occur to him that he was spreading worry and dissension?

Dr. Ménétrel's notes include this remark made by General Weygand at a meeting of the Council of Ministers: "Our officers are going to think we are mad when we order them to fight at ten o'clock, to stop fighting at noon, and to start again at two o'clock." For our superiors, the problem remained purely theoretical. For us, it affected our very lives and what little honor we had left.

On November 21, after sending off the colors, I got my squadron together and explained the situation to them. We were, in fact, already in a state of dissidence. For my part, I had shilly-shallied long enough. I had finished with the dear old Marshal. Recently I came across the manuscript of a long poem which is full of the anguish I felt at that time. The following lines will give some idea how naïve we were:

> *Loyalty, loyalty! We were only a little army*
> *And we watched each other like hawks. . . .*
> *Sentries with loaded guns guarded our aircraft*
> *From ourselves no less than from strangers.*
> *At times our hearts were distraught. . . .*
> *Our leader has disowned us*
> *But we still carry his picture with us.*
> *Our country has rejected us,*
> *As if we could have betrayed her. . . .*
> *We did not trust those who told us to follow them*
> *And who had deceived so many others before us,*
> *And, hiding our anguish,*
> *We turned our steps to where*
> *We thought we saw the light of dawn.*
>
> *Loyalty, loyalty! Voices kept throwing that word*
> *In our faces, like a curse. . . .*

At the end of the year Marcel Sauvage, whom I had met at Jean Amrouche's home in Tunis, took over a weekly magazine in Algiers and asked me for an article. I explained my position. It was the same as that of a good many officers who had no more committed treason than I had. What cause had I to be ashamed? Why did General Bergeret humiliate himself and twist about in his armchair as if he were on a grill? For having remained for a long time innocent, ingenuous soldiers, loyal to old Pétain? For having been unwilling to destroy the nation's unity? For having been deceived in the name of the most sacred values? Why didn't General Bergeret say all this, on behalf of us all? Why didn't he avenge us?

He didn't dare. After a period in Fresnes Prison he had been transferred to the Val-de-Grâce. His career was finished, and the profession of arms had left him with nothing but a soldier's soul. And yet he impressed the court. Something of the drama we had endured showed through him.

He raised himself laboriously to his feet and went off, leaning on his cane. As he passed in front of the Marshal he saluted him. With the ingratitude of a king Pétain turned his head away.

The next witness was a portly little man, Monsieur Jean Berthelot, a mining engineer, who as a former Under Secretary of State was also behind bars. Petulant, occasionally aggressive and very self-satisfied, he irritated the court by putting forward a series of contradictory arguments. He explained why it had been necessary to keep the trains moving and repair damaged works of art in order to save the country's economy, yet at the same time carry out acts of sabotage in order to harass the Germans. The Marshal agreed. So, for the first time, did the prosecution. Monsieur Berthelot was asked to be brief. Such obvious truths were embarrassing.

The Attorney General muttered, "I must say I place the whole question of dealings with the enemy on a much higher level."

"Monsieur le Président," said Monsieur Berthelot, "I don't know where I had got to."

"That's enough," growled the Marshal.

"The Attorney General and I," said Monsieur Mongibeaux, "are agreed that the French Civil Service did everything in its power to restrain the Germans' demands."

Admiral Bléhaut, who had been in charge of the Navy work camps, came after him and made virtually no impression. Although he was accompanied by a guard, he had had the courage to come in uniform, with two stars on his sleeve. Not knowing which way to face, he hesitated and finally chose an oblique position, just as he had in life. In a soft, barely audible voice he told the court about the Marshal's return to captivity in France.

"It would be interesting to know whether the Marshal came back to France of his own free will," said Bâtonnier Payen.

"Why ask a third party when the Marshal can answer that question himself?" said Monsieur Perney.

"Did the Marshal hear the question the juror has just asked?" inquired the presiding judge. "How did he come back? Was it of his own free will, or was it, on the contrary, under constraint?"

"He has given his reply in writing," said Bâtonnier Payen. "I have read out the letter here in court. Still . . ."

He bent down to speak to the Marshal. There was a sudden silence.

"Did you return to France of your own free will?" he repeated.

The Marshal raised his head slightly.

"You have to consider the departure from Sigmaringen for Switzerland. That is what really mattered."

"For the moment, Monsieur le Maréchal," said Bâtonnier Payen, "these gentlemen have seen fit to ask us only one question: Did you come back to France voluntarily?"

"Yes."

Admiral Bléhaut was honored with a little nod from the accused and the hearing was adjourned.

Pétain had picked a fool as his private secretary for military affairs. The devotion shown by the fool in question had flattered him, and he had not complained about it at the time. He must have smiled at his heel-clicking and his adoring glances and taken him for the idiot he was. But now the idiot had turned up again and was still showing the same ridiculous devotion. For three years, like a faithful dog craving its master's approval, the worthy General Campet had briefed the Marshal every morning on the military situation.

"It wasn't a question of whether the Marshal wanted an Allied victory or a German victory, but of finding out who was going to win the war so that we could side with the victor."

At this terrible gaffe the Marshal stirred angrily in his armchair and started twisting his gloves in his hands. The defense lawyers huddled together on their bench. Nobody could ever tell, with a stupid witness, what blunders he might commit, leaving intelligent men to try to retrieve the situation. The apparatus of a strong French State, founded on the ruins of the Third Republic, was now collapsing in its turn under the blows of misfortune, before the eyes of silent judges and suspicious jurors.

"That's enough!" the accused suddenly exclaimed, waving his hand angrily.

"The Marshal tells me that that's enough. In any case I think I've finished."

The witness insisted on draining the cup to its dregs.

"Then go away!" growled Pétain.

Bâtonnier Payen went over to him as if to place himself between the two men.

"We have been told he could do two things," said the presiding judge. "First, he could stop talking, and second, he could go. Well, he hasn't stopped talking and he hasn't gone."

"I prefer not to answer that," retorted Bâtonnier Payen.

The jury wanted to know what would have happened if the war had worked out differently. Bâtonnier Payen, afraid that the witness might make another gaffe, intervened in spite of the judge's opposition. In his opinion the question was liable to misinterpretation. He suggested that the jury were asking whether the Marshal's sympathies were consistent with his expectation of an Allied victory.

The General agreed. One of the jurors asked if the court could hear the rest of the Marshal's messages. Maître Isorni offered to show the court a film, and this brought a burst of laughter. The presiding judge expressed indignation at the idea of turning the First Chamber into a cinema.

In spite of the rebuke he had received, the General solemnly clicked his heels in front of his old chief before leaving the court-room.

He was followed by another prisoner, a one-armed ex-soldier with a peasant face and a hooked nose. From the huge black mustache with menacing points which concealed his thin lips there emerged a tiny voice which was only just audible.

Major General Debeney, the former commanding officer of the Armistice units at Vichy, spoke of the Marshal's stay at Sigmaringen, his refusal to follow the Germans to the Sudetenland redoubt, and his stubborn insistence on returning to France.

"To defend his honor, so we have been told," the judge broke in. "Will you kindly ask him," he went on, speaking to Bâtonnier Payen and the guard, "how he reconciles that eagerness to defend his honor with his refusal to answer the questions put to him here?"

The guard turned his head stiffly toward the accused, without moving his body, and his smooth cheeks suddenly flushed scarlet.

"Did you hear that, Monsieur le Maréchal?" he asked.

"No, I didn't," growled the old man.

"He has already explained," said the Bâtonnier, throwing up his hands as if he were calling the whole world to witness. "He has told the court why he has not spoken here."

"Let him answer the court if he has something to say," said the judge.

"He has nothing to say."

"Very well," said the judge.

There was an awkward silence. Maître Lemaire came to the Bâtonnier's rescue and asked General Debeney what he thought of the Italian General Roatta, who had been accused of involving the Cagoule in the murder of the Rosselli brothers.

"Wasn't he a member of the Cagoule?" asked Marshal Pétain. There was a roar of laughter. Everyone was tired.

The deposition of the last general to give evidence, sixty-seven-year-old Lieutenant General Martin of the Reserve, was virtually ignored by the press the following day, yet with General Bergeret's deposition it provided the only useful contribution of the day's proceedings.

In June 1940 General Martin had been chief of staff under General Catroux, the Governor General of Indo-China. Catroux's first impulse had been to line up the French Empire with the British. Before taking this irreparable step, the cautious Governor General sent telegrams to General Noguès in Morocco and to General Mittelhauser in Syria. On June 18 Catroux received a Japanese ultimatum calling on him to stop sending supplies to China, which had been at war with Japan for the past two years. The French Ambassador in Tokyo, who passed on the ultimatum, urged General Catroux to comply with it, for he saw no other way of saving Indo-China. Catroux pretended to agree. The French Ambassador in Washington informed General Catroux that the United States Government, without openly saying so, advised him to accept the Japanese ultimatum, while General Noguès reported that without the support of the French fleet he could not hope to defend French North Africa and was therefore giving his allegiance to Vichy. Syria was doing the same. Catroux gave way and closed the Tonkin frontier. Once the Armistice had been signed in France, the Vichy government, which had issued no instructions whatever, reprimanded General Catroux, who replied in a dispatch which the witness read out to the court:

When one is beaten, when one has no submarines and not many planes or antiaircraft guns, one tries to keep what one has without fighting, and one negotiates. That is what I did. . . . My aim is to keep Indo-China without fighting if I can, and by force of arms if that is impossible.

Nobody asked General Martin any questions. Nobody saw any resemblance between Indo-China and France. And nobody seemed to notice that Marshal Pétain had acted in exactly the same way with Germany as Catroux had with Japan. "One tries to keep what one has without fighting." For Bernanos that was the supreme offense, the unforgivable crime: likening France to a small investor ruined in a financial crash who places the rest of his fortune in government stock to make sure of a quiet old age, and henceforth keeps himself to himself. At that moment, like Pétain, Catroux had thought only of his country's material interests.

When the hearing was adjourned at 5:30, people started wondering whether the trial would be over by August 15. Storm clouds were gathering again in the sky and the atmosphere was stifling. The evening papers announced that there was no sign of life left in Hiroshima and that the 350,000 inhabitants of the town had been reduced to ashes. Paris was full of the scent of flowers. The women in their short skirts, with their hair piled high on their heads in fantastic coiffures, personified the joys of peace. Loving couples strolled along the banks of the Seine, while barges went by with washing hanging out on deck instead of flags. At the Théâtre du Châtelet, Jeanne Boitel was playing the title role in *L'Aiglon,* which had been one of Sarah Bernhardt's greatest parts. Edmond Rostand's play was drawing wild applause once more and the people of Paris were glorying in the patriotic emotion of which they had been deprived for five years, not realizing that the atom bomb had reduced the heroism of all the soldiers in the world to dust. Loyal Flambeau could still touch the hearts of an audience. Poor Flambeau! No less stupid than we were, what master would he have served in 1941?

On the other side of the river, in the gloomy office which had been turned into an apartment for his wife and himself, a Marshal of France was changing out of his uniform into a pair of blue pajamas. Sometimes, in the evening while Monsieur Simon was playing bridge with the doctor, the police superintendent and one of the judges, the old man would tap timidly on the door and ask his jailers for permission to stretch his legs in the anteroom.

He remembered how, little over a year before, the same ordinary people who were now weeping over the death of the Duc de Reichstadt at the Châtelet had cheered him and shouted "Long live Pétain!" when he had come to Paris after the English bombing raid on the suburb of La Villette. Cardinal Suhard, who did not dare to give evidence for him now, possibly for fear of compromising an election to the Académie française, had welcomed him outside Notre

Dame in the morning and accompanied him to the throne set up for him in the chancel. A huge crowd had come in behind the procession to hear the Requiem Mass said in memory of the victims. "May God save the world from the ruin toward which it seems to be rushing headlong," the Cardinal had said. "We are grateful to you, Monsieur le Maréchal, for coming to join us in this prayer under the roof of this cathedral."

At lunch the Cardinal had been there again, suavely seated beside Pierre Laval. The news of the Marshal's presence had spread like wildfire and enormous crowds had gathered on the square in front of the town hall, shouting for the Marshal to appear. Despite the cold, Pétain had come out onto the velvet-draped platform without a coat, wearing the same stiff gabardine uniform with the Médaille Militaire over his heart, and carrying his baton like a shepherd's crook. Which in a sense it was. For this man who on certain summer evenings, on the terrace of his country house facing the hills, used to fall asleep in a shepherd's cloak, was a shepherd to his people. When Céline wrote that Pétain had been the last king of France, he was mistaken. Our republics have never rid themselves of a nostalgic regret for the royal fleurs-de-lis. After Philippe VII we have had Charles XI. And after Charles XI?

Who was the greater of the two, Philippe VII or Charles XI? Undoubtedly de Gaulle; but the more beloved and loving of the two, the less ambitious and the closer to the common people, to the workers and shopgirls who make the kings of France, was Pétain. Both hated the gold-braided military men to whom they handed out baubles with amused condescension. Both had an all-consuming passion; they drank in the smell of the crowds, gazed with delight at the human tidal wave of the multitudes, bathed their egos in the torrents of cheers, led the singing of the Marseillaise and uttered the same old commonplaces: "Thanks to you, I can return to my labors with new heart."

Pétain at least made no attempt to conceal his pleasure. Kissing girls was not a tiresome official duty for him. He governed the country lovingly, keeping his rebukes for his intimates, and if he no longer broke plates over his own head as he used to do at mess dinners, he never spread gloom around him. Formerly curt, biting and peremptory, he could still on occasion be icily sarcastic to someone he considered a bore or a nuisance. But now he was always in complete control of his feelings, an Olympian figure who concealed behind a mask of courtesy the distrust of an old peasant who had become a prince through the force of circumstances. He was secrecy itself. He was a king. Coins were struck bearing his francisc, and the stamps of the kingdom bore his portrait. He used the royal plural as one to the manner born, "We, Philippe Pétain . . ." whereas de Gaulle used the first person, "I, General de Gaulle . . ." before speaking of himself as if he were someone else.

"You possess greater power than Louis XIV," Laval told Pétain one day. He was taken aback at first, then agreed that it was true. Accordingly, when dictating correspondence, he did not speak of France but of his people. "My people don't want them," he wrote to Hitler on April 15, 1941, referring to the talks going on with Germany. The French, aged by defeat, recognized themselves in him. Deceived, according to Bernanos, by the men he had taken as his models, he in turn deceived the French people.

How could that old man crowned with golden laurels who received two thousand letters a day have failed to believe in his mission when he saw so many faces raised toward him, so many mouths shouting his name, such a multitude of people massed on the pavements and sitting on the roofs of the Paris buses? "Men and women of France!" his voice thundered from the loudspeakers. The film cameras whirred. The photographers perched on the bronze shoulders of the sea nymphs shot him from every angle. "Never," Bernanos admitted, "has any victorious general, with the possible exception of the young Bonaparte in 1796, enjoyed as much prestige as this handsome old man, with his sententious pronouncements, whose fierce ambition has become a shameful vice with the passing years and has put a lecherous gleam into his dull eyes."

That day, warmed by good wine and the joy of seeing Paris again, he had said, "Friends, it isn't easy for me to get away from my jailers and come to see you, but next time I'll come without them and we'll feel much easier." The crowd roared its appreciation. The German diplomat accompanying him refused to allow the text of his speech to be published in the papers. Afterward, on its way from Bichat Hospital along the Boulevard Saint-Germain and the Champs-Élysées, the Marshal's car had driven over flowers thrown to him by students. Hope was stirring in every breast.

And now he had come back to Paris, his jailers wore a different uniform, and he was held in prison by his own people. What did he think of it all? He shook his hoary head. "Ingrates," he muttered. Nobody heard him.

XVIII

❊

Thursday, August 9, 1945

When Captain Édouard Archambaud of the French Navy came lurching forward with his sailor's gait, the public had the impression that at last a man was entering the courtroom. Tall, thin, bald and clean-shaven, with protruding ears, he spoke fearlessly and calmly, with the self-assurance of a man who knows the truth, but also with a certain refined languor; he was scuttling himself in elegant fashion, with all flags flying.

He had served as private secretary to Admiral Auphan during his chief's seven months as Secretary of State for the Navy. He was a man of shining integrity, who would have resigned if he had had the slightest doubts about the cause he was serving. In the Gaullist camp there would have been a few like him who would have sung the praises of King Charles XI if the Third Reich had won the war. But the court had heard too many old men to be moved by the sincerity of this young officer. They were waiting impatiently for two star performers, Monsieur de Brinon and Darnand, whom the presiding judge had described respectively as "a shady businessman" and a "murderer."

Yet what Captain Archambaud was going to say was of considerable interest: using the private code of the Admiral of the Fleet, he and a friend named Captain Joannin had deciphered three secret telegrams addressed to Admiral Darlan on November 10, 11, and 13, 1942. His deposition made it possible to reconstruct the Vichy drama.

In the evening of November 8 Admiral Auphan attended a Council meeting at which certain ministers called for the help of the German Air Force to repel the Anglo-American invasion. Admiral Auphan, encouraged by the Marshal and supported by Weygand, suggested that they should at least ask the opinion of Admiral Darlan, who was on the spot, and the North African authorities. The telegram sent as a result of this suggestion was, in fact, one of the items of evidence in the trial: "O.K.W. offers support from Sardinia and Sicily. Admiralty asks Admiral of Fleet to indicate where and how he needs that support."

The reply did not reach Vichy until the following morning. It had obviously been drafted with great care. In diplomatic language Admiral Darlan, despite the fact that he himself had signed the agreements in question in 1941, said that foreign assistance in Tunisia was undesirable and that if Germany was none the less determined to lend such assistance, a new formula should be devised to cover the changed situation. During the night, Laval had lost patience and had already granted the Germans use of the French airfields.

On the ninth, naval headquarters at Oran cabled that they were making preparations to sink some cargo ships in the harbor entrance, and that the *Épervier* and the *Typhon* were trying to return to Toulon. Laval left for Munich after insisting that no decision should be taken before his meeting with Hitler. In Algiers Admiral Darlan marked time, confined himself to sending Vichy the text of a draft armistice with the Americans.

On the tenth Laval telephoned from Berchtesgaden. He protested angrily at the idea of an understanding with the Americans, as advocated by the generals in Algiers, Admiral Auphan and Weygand, and hinted that in the event of any such understanding Hitler would take reprisals. Pétain then sent Darlan his first message disowning the

Admiral: "I issued an order to defend North Africa against the aggressor. I hereby confirm that order." Dr. Ménétrel noted in his diary that Weygand exclaimed, "This is a disaster! For my part, I support Darlan." Darlan cunningly announced that he was giving himself up.

"However," Captain Archambaud went on, "the Marshal did not want Admiral Darlan to think that he had really been disowned, and wished to show him that he trusted him. He therefore instructed Admiral Auphan to send him a secret, personal telegram. This is the telegram . . . which I had occasion to encode myself . . .: 'Please understand that that order was necessary for the negotiations now in progress.' "

This clearly implied that the Marshal was in agreement with Darlan and that his messages were issued under constraint. From Morocco General Noguès sent the same officer to Vichy he had sent to Bordeaux on June 17, 1940: Captain Bataille.

At 5:25 the Marshal received a long letter from the Fuehrer ending with the twin zigzag of his cramped signature. Hitler informed him that he felt obliged to send his troops across France to occupy the Mediterranean coast and protect Corsica; as compensation the French Government could install itself at Versailles. Monsieur Louis Noguères notes in his book that the journey of General Noguès's messenger was mentioned both in the preliminary investigation and in Dr. Ménétrel's notebooks.

Arriving at Vichy at 1:30 on November 11, Captain Bataille was allowed to see the Marshal first at seven o'clock and then at five to nine, after which there is no further mention of his name. The letter he had brought from Noguès was extremely respectful in tone but mentioned that the troops in Morocco were obeying orders with great reluctance. The Marshal's reply is not recorded anywhere, and when Captain Bataille got back to Morocco in the late afternoon, General Noguès had just signed a cease-fire agreement with the Americans. A telegram, sent from Vichy at eight in the morning and delayed by events, appointed him the Marshal's delegate for French North

Africa. It was only later that Captain Archambaud encoded another telegram for Darlan: "It is only because it is assumed that you
are a prisoner that you have not been appointed the Marshal's
representative." So the appointment of Noguès did not imply the
repudiation of Darlan, while it expressed approval of a general
known to be changing sides.*

At half past ten it was learned at Vichy that the *Jean-Bart,* which
had escaped from Brest in 1940, had fired on the Americans and had
been half-sunk by them. Field Marshal von Rundstedt was received
by Pétain at 10:40. Every quarter of an hour the radio repeated the
Marshal's message expressing indignation at the violation of the
Armistice and ending with these disillusioned words: "I thought I
had already lived through the darkest days of my life. The situation
today brings back to me the somber memories of 1940. . . . I call
upon the French people at home and in the Empire to trust their
Marshal, whose only thought is for France."

From Algiers Admiral Darlan called on the fleet to leave Toulon
for North Africa. But how could the fleet, with its unquestioning
loyalty to Marshal Pétain, answer that call? When Pétain sent a plane
to Saint-Raphaël to pick up Weygand, the commander of the base
there was so afraid that it might go over to Algiers that he put an
armed escort on board with orders to force the pilot, if necessary, to
fly to Vichy. Admiral Darlan did not possess sufficient prestige to
carry the fleet with him.

Captain Archambaud had also carefully concealed the letter Vice

* General Noguès was tried *in absentia* two years later by the High Court and
sentenced to twenty years' imprisonment. Returning to France in 1954, he gave himself up, was imprisoned at the Val-de-Grâce, then released. His real trial then took
place. When he appeared at the Palais du Luxembourg, Maître de Moro-Giafferi,
the President of the High Court, addressed him in the following terms: "The sentence already passed on you does not deprive you of the eleven decorations you
have won on the field of battle. You may sit down." He was sentenced to civil
degradation, but his sentence was immediately commuted. He was already regarded
as so free of guilt that during the preparation of his trial the Prime Minister called
him in for consultation. Now ninety years old at the time of writing, General
Noguès understandably takes little interest in events. If he had been in General
Catroux's place, he would have acted as Catroux did. It may be doubted whether, in
his place, Catroux, in his wisdom and prudence, would have acted differently from
General Noguès.

Admiral Auphan, Secretary of State for the Navy, sent to Grand
Admiral Raeder in repudiation of Darlan:

> I do not have the honor of knowing you personally, but both of us are
> fighting men and sailors, which is a sufficient introduction. You are at the
> head of the German Navy just as I am now at the head of the French
> Navy, under the orders of Marshal Pétain, the head of state. As a patriot
> like myself, you will understand the emotion which grips the French Navy
> as it fights fiercely and unflinchingly against its aggressors, who were your
> enemies, but for whom—I refer to the Americans—it felt no hatred.

In return Admiral Auphan asked the Germans to respect the isolation
of the French Navy in Toulon. Admiral Platon was not the only
French sailor who was a disgrace to France. This problem of conscience could probably have been solved as easily as ours in the Air
Force, and the French fleet would have found glory in some other way
than scuttling itself, if the Navy had not been so eager, a century and
a half after Trafalgar, to take its revenge on Nelson.

On November 13 Captain Archambaud encoded a third telegram which General Bergeret had mentioned, but which was not the
same one: "Marshal and President in close agreement, but before
answering you we must consult Occupation authorities." Officers
came from as far away as Dakar to study this message at the Admiralty in Algiers, to see whether it released them from the oath
which the old king was loudly insisting should be observed in spite of
everything. That same day, indeed, Marshal Pétain issued a fresh
appeal to the Army: "In the present confusion some are asking where
the path of honor lies. . . . The only course to follow is to gather
round me. You have taken an oath of loyalty to me. Keep your
word."

What use were secret messages, Captain? The Captain obeyed his
Vice Admiral, the Vice Admiral obeyed the Marshal, and the Admiral of the Fleet started negotiations with the Americans while at
the same time shouting, "Long live the Marshal!" A few thousand
soldiers, sailors and airmen died at the hands of the British and
Americans to convince the Germans that France was observing the

conditions of the 1940 Armistice and the 1941 Berlin agreement, while their officers scratched at their consciences as if they were suffering from a spiritual itch. Captain Archambaud had still not recovered from it, and I cannot say for certain that we had either. A member of the jury, Monsieur Pierre-Bloch, asked the witness what personal message from the Marshal Captain Bataille had brought back for General Noguès. The witness did not know, and the presiding judge did not consider it necessary to send for Captain Bataille. Nobody pressed the point—the defense for fear of damaging their client's chances, and the prosecution for fear of clearing the accused. In any case it would have done no good. The Marshal had said nothing to Captain Bataille. That man of silence let events decide matters for him.

With Pierre Laval's return from Berchtesgaden, events took a new turn. The issue ceased to be a matter for havering admirals. Those who felt tempted to abandon the Germans, like Admiral Auphan, had to resign their commands. Weygand was arrested, and as for the Marshal . . . the Marshal was up in the clouds. At eighty-five Pétain's mind had begun to wander. A few days later the French fleet blew up during the night at Toulon. Captain Archambaud could not bring himself to talk about that. The memory still hurt. Perhaps he had read what Bernanos had written about what he called "the Toulon bluff": "In the harbor where Bonaparte once saw his youthful glory born, ships with illustrious names died in the place of men."

"Has the accused anything to say?" the presiding judge asked maliciously.

What could he have said? Without a single glance for the faithful sailor, he sat motionless in his armchair, gazing idly at the public and at the brooch which beautiful Francine Bonitzer of L'Aurore had pinned on her blouse that day.

The next witness was the former Secretary General for Industrial Production, Monsieur René Norguet, a marine engineer in the prime of life, with delicate hands, a rosette in his buttonhole, and the complexion of a Mexican playboy. His deposition did not advance matters to any great degree. Speaking in a hurried voice, he told the court that the country's accounts had been faked and stocks of raw materials hidden away. One of the Resistance jurors congratulated him. The engineer reported that the government had given him their support and that one day the Marshal had told Monsieur Darquier de Pellepoix: "Torturer-in-Chief, I keep on hearing too much about you."

"That's correct," said the Marshal.

Good men are a bore, while traitors have always drawn full houses. Everyone turned round to see Monsieur de Brinon come through the witnesses' door. The accused, too, turned to the right.

Those who had seen Ambassador de Brinon in his days of glory, sitting beside the head of state or in a Mercedes, found it hard to recognize this shifty-eyed skeleton in his gray striped suit. He limped over to the armchair and slumped into it, shot from every angle by the photographers, only to hear Monsieur Mongibeaux address him, as he had Laval, in ignominious terms.

"I shall not ask you for your name and occupation. Nor shall I ask you to take the oath."

Was he implying that in a court of law doubt was the prerogative of honor? Monsieur Paul Reynaud, and Monsieur Édouard Herriot, though both well known to the court, had been asked to give their names. So had the accused. Had the dogs Laval and Brinon lost their pedigrees? The oath too, for a man who was a traitor and in prison, could have restored a little of the dignity he had lost. The former head of the French Delegation in the Occupied Zone glanced wearily at the judges and the jury. There was a handkerchief in the breast pocket of his jacket, and the rosette of an officer of the Legion of Honor in his buttonhole. "An old sea gull battered by the storm" was how Philippe Bourdel later described him, while Maurice Clavel compared him to a crow which had lost its feathers. He sat there like a hunted bird on a rock, bald-headed and stiff-legged, his plumage bristling, his broken beak alternately raised toward the coffered ceiling and pointing to the ground.

"I always reported to the Marshal everything I did. Every time he asked me about what was happening in the Occupied Zone I always replied, I think, with complete truthfulness."

His eyes lowered, he spoke in a dull, rasping, irritating voice, and disguised his trembling by thrusting one hand in his pocket and toying with his cane with the other. For half an hour he recounted once more the conversation at Montoire and Laval's arrest.

"On his return from Berchtesgaden, Admiral Darlan made a statement, the gist of which was: 'France has a choice between recovery and destruction. I have chosen recovery.' "

It was a point of view. In any case it was the point of view of Monsieur de Brinon, who like Laval had always advocated a reconciliation with Germany, which has since become a fact. Why, then, was that man there, and why did he later have to die before a French firing squad, shouting, *"Vive la France!"* so bravely that the new President of the High Court, Monsieur Louis Noguères, paid tribute to his courage as he stood over his corpse?

The answer was a question of circumstances, which goes by the name of ethics. Captain Archambaud remained loyal to his chief, who wrote complimentary letters to Grand Admiral Raeder, while we were prepared to bomb the Americans—though when I found myself face to face with Captain Sturtmeyer, I knew perfectly well, from the way my heart was pounding in my chest, that for the time being we could not fight side by side. Monsieur de Brinon's great friend was Herr Abetz, the German Ambassador. On his desk in the Place Beauvau there were two photographs, one of Pétain and the other of Goering. ("There's one too many," Pétain said when he saw them.) Monsieur Pierre Laval paid homage to Adolf Hitler and did his best to please him. But they believed in a German victory or hoped for one. And what would have happened if Hitler had won in 1941? Everyone knows that we would have obeyed orders. Three-quarters of France sang the song, "Marshal, here we are." Girls offered Pétain bouquets of flowers. Monsieur Pierre Laval would have been acclaimed for restoring French power and prestige. Admiral Darlan would have sent the fleet into action to avenge Trafalgar, and we in the Air Force would have flown Stukas and Heinkels with easy consciences, until the day we discovered that it was better to go hungry than to get our rations from the Kommandantur, and that a certain Jesus, who died for having given hope to the world, would have worn a yellow star in our times, and died with poets in an extermination camp.

With his left hand cupped crablike around his ear, the accused listened calmly to his former Ambassador talking in a Quai d'Orsay drawl about the congratulatory telegram to Hitler after the failure of the Dieppe landing. "Another blunder by that shit de Brinon," he had said at the time to one of his prefects. A pygmy caught at the same time as the big game, it was natural for Monsieur de Brinon to take refuge under the old bull's horns.

"Monsieur le Président," said the witness, "might I ask for a glass of water?"

He was brought one. It was Vichy water again. He drank it greedily. His deposition lasted an hour. The public found it disappointing. Both prosecution and defense remained silent. The presiding judge did not know what judicial term to use to describe this man who no longer had any name or occupation. He solved the problem by adjourning the hearing. Monsieur de Brinon bowed to the Marshal, who said a few words to him that no one heard, and went off with his tail between his legs. After he had disappeared in complete silence through the witnesses' door, the court rose.

When the hearing was resumed, half an hour later, Darnand lumbered in, wearing tight-fitting militiaman's trousers and a windbreaker under a double-breasted gray jacket, with the rosette of the Legion of Honor in his buttonhole. Square-headed, with his eyes half closed, his forehead framed in close-cropped white hair, and his rugged jaw bristling with dark stubble, he looked like a broad-shouldered farm laborer in his Sunday best.

"How long have you known the Marshal?"

"The first time I saw the Marshal was on the eighteenth of July, 1918. . . ."

A thin, piping voice came out of that burly brute's mouth. Was it in that eunuch's squeak that he had sworn loyalty to Hitler and ordered men to be murdered? And was he regarded as a man of importance? What hidden taint did he suffer from? What revenge did he need to take on life and men? What appetites or urges were concealed behind that rugged face of a peasant caught poaching on the squire's land? Was he too a scoundrel and a villain? The next day Monsieur Lavagne, the former assistant director of the Marshal's civilian staff, would describe him as "a fool and a brute." At the moment he was not even that. He was nothing any more, and showed himself humble, docile, almost servile. He explained how he had served the Marshal as head of the militia, how the Marshal had thanked him for remaining loyal to him, and how he had become Secretary General for the Maintenance of Order with access to the Council of Ministers.

"And the Marshal never seemed surprised to see you?"

"Certainly not."

The Marshal had criticized him only once, on April 6, 1944, when the Americans were at Rennes.

"Let me reply about Montoire," the Marshal said to his lawyers.

Bâtonnier Payen intervened and begged him to be quiet. He slumped back in his armchair, sulky and disappointed.

"Guards, you can take him away," said the presiding judge, jerking his goatee in the direction of the witness.

"Take him away?" Once again the judge did not know what term to use. Neither the prosecution nor the defense had accepted Darnand as a witness, and this was not his trial. He was just a mad dog to be put down with a bullet in the back of his red neck. He went out grim-faced. The hero whom General Pétain had decorated with the Médaille Militaire in July 1918, because the victory of Champagne had been partly due to information he had brought back from a reconnaissance sortie, died bravely too. When the Attorney General came with the lawyers and clerks to wake him, they found him on his

knees. He had spent the night praying with Father Bruckberger.
"You'll allow me to have my breakfast?" he said. The former leader
of the militia was a crusader after his fashion. But he had chosen the
wrong cross.

The Abbé Rodhain did not stay longer than ten minutes. To the
accompaniment of ecclesiastical gestures the former Chaplain General
to the prisons sang the praises of the Marshal who had supported him
in his ministry.

"Who was the only person at Vichy to whom I could describe all
our clandestine work in the deportee camps and who urged me to
continue? The Marshal. That is the truth, I tell you."

The next witness, the former prefect, Charles Donati, annoyed the
jury and worried the defense with his clumsy aggressiveness. Gaunt
and balding, with a florid complexion and the left sleeve of his jacket
hanging empty, he started the row he had been hoping for.

"Without anger or hatred I deplore, for France's sake and the
Marshal's, the fact that so many Frenchmen should have hearts and
minds incapable of feeling or understanding how sublime and heroic
his attitude was."

"And what about our dead?" cried the juror in a squadron leader's
uniform, Monsieur Lévêque.

"Millions and millions of Frenchmen think that this trial is a
colossal political blunder which risks ending in—"

An angry murmur came from the public.

"Since we were liberated a year ago," the former prefect continued.

"It is obvious," said the Attorney General, "that you have taken
the chair at a lot of public meetings."

Monsieur Donati glared at the Attorney General.

"I beg permission to express publicly a sentiment which fills the
hearts of the French people and which, during the year since we
allegedly regained our freedom, nobody has been able to express in
public."

"I demand the enforcement of Article 270!" cried a member of the jury, referring to the rule that the presiding judge must prevent any undue prolongation of a trial.

"If a witness had said anything like that during the Occupation, the Marshal would have had him sentenced on the spot to two years' imprisonment."

"We are more tolerant," said the judge. "I call upon the usher to take the witness away."

There were shouts of "To Fresnes! To Fresnes!"

Bâtonnier Payen pretended to be absorbed in contemplation of the Marshal, who was twisting his gloves in his hands.

Beak-nosed Captain Jean Tracou, one of the Marshal's former departmental secretaries, defended his chief skillfully. He read out the letter Ribbentrop sent Pétain in November 1943 through the diplomat who spied on him at Vichy, Renthe-Finck:

If one examines Franco-German relations during the past three years, it becomes obvious that the measures you have taken as head of the French State have all too often had the effect of obstructing collaboration. On the other hand, this constant fight against any attempt at reconstruction has, through your persistent opposition, made it impossible to appoint to the most important posts in the French Government and administration men whose loyalty would have allowed the pursuance of a policy of consolidation. . . .

Why should anyone doubt the truth of what Captain Tracou said? For two months Pétain refused to read the message of April 28, 1944, inspired by Renthe-Finck before reluctantly agreeing, and in contradiction to what Darnand had just said, Monsieur Tracou assured the court that the Marshal had never sat at the same table as the leader of the militia.

"I myself often asked the Marshal, especially after that message of April 1944, 'Why don't you leave?' He always replied, 'You don't know what those people are capable of doing.' I said, 'Can we sink any lower? We have had Oradour,* the deportations, more and more

* A reference to the German massacre of the entire population of the French village of Oradour-sur-Glane (634 people) on June 10, 1944.

horrors every day. Do you think if you left it would be any worse? I don't think so.' That was what I said to him. But now I realize I was wrong. In July 1944 Germany was strong enough to suppress a French revolt with a wholesale blood bath. We would have seen Oradour repeated a hundredfold. That is the fate from which the Marshal's presence saved us. . . ."

After answering a few questions the witness withdrew. He had convinced nobody. Later on he wrote a brave, loyal book about the Marshal: the Gospel according to Saint Jean Tracou.

The next witness, an official of the Ministry of Labor in the Unoccupied Zone, was neither impressive nor convincing. It was very hot. Joseph Kessel put his head in his hands and gazed dreamily at the light striking the gilded spire of the Sainte-Chapelle.

The hearing was adjourned.

XIX

❧

Friday, August 10, 1945

The morning papers had come out with huge headlines: "Japan offers to surrender," leaving only a few inches' space for the trial. Judges and lawyers seemed to be sunk in boredom. Like the witnesses for the prosecution, the defense witnesses were contributing nothing decisive. No cry came from the depths of the soul to move the court. When the judge ordered General Juin's evidence to be read out, Bâtonnier Payen's face looked like a bare, wind-swept promontory.

The chief clerk started reading. The Bâtonnier had put three questions to General Juin. In answer to the first—"What was the position of the African army before the Allied landing in November 1942?"—General Juin stated that the army in question had played a cautious game at the time, giving no support to the Axis powers and making no secret of its anti-German feelings. "It regarded the word *collaboration* as meaningless, but on the whole it saw the victor of Verdun as a leader whose prestige was unquestionable and who it hoped would one day give the signal to take up arms again. It was said to be Gaullist and eager for revenge." That was true.

In answer to the second question—"Did Marshal Pétain's secret telegram have any influence on the decisions taken at that time?"—General Juin replied: "I can assure the court that Admiral Auphan's two telegrams were a great help to us. They enabled us to ease a great many consciences tormented by the oath of loyalty and still undecided."

In answer to the third question—"Was Marshal Pétain's name useful in maintaining peace and unity in North Africa?"—General Juin replied that the Marshal enjoyed great prestige in the eyes of the Moslems.

General Juin had not been given permission to come to the Palais de Justice in person; de Gaulle wanted to protect his glory from the mud being thrown about in the trial and from a comparison with the Marshal. Someone might have asked whether Juin was a traitor because he had accompanied Darlan to Berlin and negotiated or signed military agreements which could have committed him to fighting side by side with Field Marshal Rommel. The defense lawyers were advised not to remind the court about this. Otherwise what would the Army have thought?

An ordinary black chair had taken the place of the Louis Quinze armchair. Everyone was bored with hearing the same old refrain. Joseph Kessel, his mane of hair flowing over his shoulders, turned a weary gaze on the first five witnesses that day—worthy, decent men who saluted the Marshal, indulged in a dig at "poor Admiral Darlan," and hurried out, very dignified, to the cafés on the Place Saint-Michel where their wives were waiting anxiously for them with glasses of beer.

Since the previous day American troops had been marching and driving through the streets in the rain, with their colors flying and girls perched on the wings of their jeeps, in celebration of the Allied victory over Japan. Paris was hungry and had slept off her patriotic wine. Her heart was no longer in it.

At this distance from the trial, I keep reading and rereading the headline *Le Canard enchaîné* carried that week: "After the Reich's victory, Charles de Gaulle is tried by the High Court." He would have been convicted of treason against King Lear and executed.

Was Pétain an ambitious man ruined by his own ambition or a

martyr? In any case he was no more the villain described by the
prosecution witnesses than Juin, nor an abominable scoundrel who
sacrificed his country, like a fair maiden, to the wicked Adolf. But
the jurors who were about to pass judgment on him had suffered.
They had only just emerged from a long night of shipwreck. They
could not enjoy the light of summer as a victory, because they missed
the comrades who had disappeared forever. They regarded it as their
duty to avenge them, and considered that forgetting them would be a
monstrous betrayal. And the responsibility for the blood that had
been spilt they placed on that tired old man whose sleepy eyes occasionally lit up with a gleam of cunning.

When the court wearily reassembled after the adjournment, the
clerk read out a report by General Catroux on the Franco-Japanese
crisis of June 1940. It might have been in Chinese for all that anyone
understood.

"Tomorrow, what new idol shall we be asked to destroy?" asked
another witness. "I can understand the attitude of people who want
justice at any price. . . .   If the French people had been consulted
in July, August and September 1940, I imagine a good many of those
who have come here to give evidence would have been shot in
accordance with the will of the French people."

That was true. Paul Reynaud, Daladier, Léon Blum and Herriot
would undoubtedly have been shot by the people and the Army, who
in their anger and stupefaction believed that they were responsible for
the defeat of France. Marshal Pétain did not thank any of the witnesses. He was fast asleep, lulled by the soft murmur of praise.

During the course of the trial Maître Isorni had received a visit
from a little old man who claimed to be both one of the first Gaullists and indignant at the accusations leveled at the Marshal. His very
name added to the comical impression he made: he was called
General Éon, like the chevalier famed for his courage, his eccentrici-
ties and his dubious sex. He came into the courtroom like a dancer
who had lost his way. Not knowing whom to greet first, he gave a

ceremonious bow to the shorthand writers, whom he took for the
judges, then to the judges and jury, walked around the witnesses'
chair, and, in a piping voice, launched into a strategic and sentimental
discourse of the most frenzied lyricism. He had given his age as sixty-
five, but looked a hundred.

"General, we had you subpoenaed—" began a dismayed Maître
Isorni.

"We are both thinking the same thing," interrupted Monsieur
Mongibeaux. "We would like the witness to confine himself to the
points on which he has been questioned."

Maître Isorni tried in vain to get General Éon to keep to the facts.
At one point the General suddenly exclaimed that General
de Gaulle's appeal of June 18, 1940, was "very French," and, he
added after a pirouette, "very pretty." The last word set off a roar of
laughter which spread across the courtroom to the defense bench and
even to the Marshal. Maître Lemaire was howling with laughter, his
face buried in his hands, and there were tears in Isorni's eyes. Only
Bâtonnier Payen was shaking his head in distress.

"You don't insist on General Éon's deposition continuing?"

Convulsed with laughter, his self-control finally shattered by the
comic side of the situation, Maître Isorni found it hard to bring out
the answer: "No." General Éon started to leave, then turned back.

"May I say one last word?" he asked.

Without waiting for a reply, he hopped and skipped out of the
courtroom.

The pastoral letter, as Monsieur Mongibeaux called it, from Cardinal Liénart, the Bishop of Lille, restored dignity to the hearing. It
breathed a spirit of peace. "When a man has had to govern in such
tragic circumstances, to judge him fairly you must set against the list
of evils he could not spare France the list of even worse evils from
which he succeeded in saving her. . . ."

In a voice which he tried to keep steady, Bâtonnier Payen read out
another letter from a sublieutenant in the Navy who had been a

companion of Henriette Psichari's son, and in a few words evoked the drama of those families whose sons served different causes under the same flag. It was as pure and terrible as a tragedy, and the next witness, whom the usher guided toward the chair because he was blind, seemed to come straight out of Sophocles.

Holding his white cane in his left hand, he took the oath with the dignity of a King Oedipus, as if he had put out his own eyes for a crime he had committed unwittingly. Moving about as he spoke, so that he had to be led back to his place, and constantly raising his hand to ward off the light which hurt him yet attracted him, General de Lannurien wanted to save the jury from committing the same crime by convicting Marshal Pétain, his former pupil and friend.

At dinner one evening in November 1942, in the Hôtel du Parc at Vichy, someone had urged him to leave, saying, "Monsieur le Maréchal, the Germans will take you away by force, and the Gaullists will bring you to trial." As he left the table, Pétain placed one hand on General de Lannurien's shoulder and whispered, "The Germans can take me away by force if they want to, the French can put me on trial if they wish, but as long as I am free I shall not leave."

"If, by some misfortune . . ."

The blind old man was panting for breath, and his quiet voice broke. He was addressing the living and the dead, in a darkness that would never end for him. Everyone listened open-mouthed. Bâtonnier Payen stood taut-faced watching him. All of a sudden Francine Bonitzer, with her elaborate coiffure, got up and hurried out with some other reporters to file her copy.

"If, by some misfortune," the witness repeated, "this man is degraded, in that theatrical setting which some people will dream about once the obscene comedy has been enacted, and he passes before the ranks, bent with age, pale with affronted dignity, but with his head held high, then far from being humiliated, he will be exalted."

"It's Darnand's fault, Darnand's fault!" shouted a member of the public, who was promptly removed from the courtroom.

The Marshal turned toward his lawyers, seized with what looked like rage.

"Why?" he stammered.

"Take care," the blind man went on, "lest one day, by our fault, the blood and alleged shame of this man fall on the whole of France, on ourselves and on our children."

Applause started at the back of the courtroom, moved toward the front benches like an approaching shower of hail and overwhelmed the court.

"No demonstrations!" shouted the presiding judge. "This is a scandal!"

Monsieur Germinal, one of the deputy jurors representing the Resistance, stood up. He was a young man with rugged features and a beetling brow. He sat behind bearded Monsieur Perney and on the right of Monsieur Lévêque in his squadron leader's uniform. Suddenly he dominated the courtroom with his massive build and sturdy shoulders. A lock of his hair fell over his right temple. His eyes were sunken, his lips pitiless, his jaw set. He took a piece of paper out of his pocket. The applause grew louder as if to prevent him from intervening.

"Oh, yes," said Monsieur Germinal, standing firm, "I insist on speaking."

Calm was suddenly restored, and he read out a passage from a letter in which the same General de Lannurien asked Marshal Pétain to take personal action to suppress "the terrorists," and praised the good work of Darnand and Philippe Henriot. A terrible silence fell over the courtroom.

The Marshal stood up, ghastly pale, and, pushing aside his lawyers as they tried to intervene, walked slowly toward the witness.

"I ask permission to speak," he said. "I wish to speak for once to say that I am in no way responsible for General de Lannurien's presence here. . . . I was not consulted."

"No questions, gentlemen?" asked the presiding judge, putting on his cap. "You may withdraw," he added hurriedly.

Going back to his seat, Pétain shook hands with the General, saying a few words to him which in the hubbub nobody heard.

Maître Isorni flew into a temper. What was the Marshal up to?

Why had he made that idiotic statement? Why did he insist on spreading confusion and thwarting the efforts of his best friends? If he had wanted to show that he disapproved of an attitude adopted by General de Lannurien which risked alienating the Resistance, how could he have failed to understand that at the same time he was nullifying the emotion which had momentarily swept away all accusations and doubts? Did he think he was still the sovereign, protected from his enemies by the love of his people? Did he imagine that he was going to emerge victorious from this trial and return through cheering crowds to his house on the hills of Antibes?

"I don't want that sort of testimony," the Marshal said sulkily.

XX

❦

Saturday, August 11, 1945

Over twenty years later, Monsieur Mornet's closing speech for the prosecution has a different effect on the reader than it had on those who heard it. Monsieur Mornet is now crumbling in his grave, and his hoarse voice, which was to weaken under the strain that day, has fallen silent forever. What the old Attorney General wrote with the pen of a defender of the state is not lacking in grandeur. There is a saying in the Palais de Justice that the pen is a slave—a saying which recognizes that a public prosecutor lacks certain liberties which a defense lawyer has the right to use and sometimes a duty to abuse. Attorney General Mornet had been famous for his passionate fervor ever since he had displayed it in the Bolo-Pacha case and directed it against Mata Hari. Quick-tempered and authoritarian, he was a man easily stirred to indignation, who nursed a secret love for trees and animals. This vegetarian who had little taste for the pleasures of the table could suddenly become, out of patriotism, pitiless and bloodthirsty.

These twenty pages of the *Journal officiel,* yellowed by time, have to be placed in the context of that stifling afternoon. The showers the previous day had made the air softer. The sky was dark with clouds, and now and then the windows were obscured by a flurry of warm rain. The solemn heads of drowsy judges or jurors nodded and then dropped onto their shoulders. The guests crowding the hard benches in the gallery, as if the trial were a reception ceremony at the Académie française, kept yawning. Monsieur Mornet's endless quotations merged together in a monotonous barking to which the ear gradually became accustomed, so that in the end nobody heard anything. The crowded courtroom of the First Chamber sank into a torpor. Sweat formed on the judges' foreheads and streamed down their bodies under the ermine trimmings.

Before the hearing had been resumed, everyone had been wondering whether the Attorney General might not have received a directive from the Rue Saint-Dominique urging moderation. For three weeks he had uttered threats, endured humiliations and hammered his fist on his heavy bundle of papers, repeating, "My brief, my brief . . ."

When he stood up, a small, gaunt figure in his red robes, his hair tousled and his face bristling with yellowish stubble, pushing back his fur hood encircled with the broad cravat of the Legion of Honor, he showed right from the start that he was going to keep all his promises. With his pointed beak and his deep-set eyes, snatching up each sheet of his speech with his clawlike hand, and flanked by a massive pile of documents crowned with a blotter, he circled like a bird of prey above the chaos of the trial.

The Marshal, his nostrils pinched, his hands occasionally stroking his triple-wreathed kepi with his gloves, seemed to be in a state of collapse. But this time he was not dozing beside his guard. His curious trapezoidal head padded with tufts of white hair at the temples and at the base of the neck, his cheeks sunken, his chin tucked into the lapels of his tunic, he was listening to the harsh voice coming from his left, the side of his good ear.

"What will Mornet be like?" he had asked Isorni before the hearing.

"Monsieur Mornet will ask for your head with the greatest possible courtesy," the lawyer had replied with a smile.

Ensconced in a stubborn dignity, his blue eyes scarcely watering, his mustache covering his colorless lips, the central figure of an occasion now approaching its close like a stormy sunset, he sat there splashed by the spray from a tempest which would go on raging for a whole day. It was not so long since Claudel . . . Would his lawyers think of reading out the lines Claudel had written in December 1940?

Marshal, here is France in your arms, with no one in the world but you, and slowly reviving with a whisper. . . .

Admittedly in the meantime Claudel had composed another ode to de Gaulle.

They have all asked for my body, so will you ask for my soul? And the General replies:
"Woman, be silent, and ask only for what I am capable of giving you."

Pétain had been shown this ode. He had read it and then pushed it away; it was very bad.

Bent with age, spitting and spluttering, using his last reserves of strength to throw his voice, the Attorney General brought out the word which was going to decide everything.

"For four years—what am I saying?—even now, France is the victim of an ambiguity, the most confusing of all ambiguities, the one which by means of a famous name serves as a screen for treason. . . ."

Treason? "What is a traitor?" asked Rossel, who was executed by a firing squad in 1871, and answered: "A man who acts contrary to what he believes is right." Rossel knew what he was talking about.

"The motives influencing the author," said the Attorney General, "paralyze his patriotic reflex and rob him of the understanding of certain shameful things which no nation can forgive those who inflict them on it. And what no nation can forgive its representatives is condemning it to accept complete defeat . . . humiliating it in the eyes of the world, placing it in bondage to its victor . . . using the cover of a hypocritical neutrality to wage a secret war against its

erstwhile companions-in-arms in defiance of its pledges to them, and
to give barely concealed aid to the common enemy. No nation, in fact,
can forgive actions which bring it into disgrace. . . ."

Facing the court and prancing from one end of his desk to another,
Monsieur Mornet muttered his accusations, brandishing a pair of
pince-nez which he kept taking off and immediately putting back on.
Between showers, the August light streamed over his bent back, and
lit up his head.

"A vain desire for power for power's sake, combined with an
authoritarian instinct which seems to develop with age, as well as
hatred for the preceding regime . . ."

The Attorney General was talking too fast, and the Marshal's
mind did not have time to grasp what he was saying. The old man
kept catching at a random word and turning it over and over. His
features contracted and his hands clutched the arms of his chair or the
buckle of his belt. Was the Attorney General actually going to talk
about the Cagoule?

"The Pétain affair began as an attempt to overthrow the Republic. . . ."

Twenty years later, the five columns of close print in the *Journal
officiel* devoted to the plot against the Republic can only raise a smile.
Pétain's criticism of the system could be found almost word for word,
together with criticisms of the Third and Fourth Republics, on the
lips of another man, although that man was elected by the French
people to the highest office in the state:

During the three-quarters of a century preceding the war, the political
regime to which the French people were submitted was based on the
cultivation of discontent. . . . It is a strong state that we wish to found
on the ruins of the state which collapsed more under the weight of its
errors and defeats than under the blows of the enemy. . . . Already this
new regime has given the measure of its strength by accomplishing in a
few weeks tasks which the governments of the Third Republic had not
dared to face. The history of social legislation in that period makes pitiful
reading. . . . Our defeat was really nothing but a military reflection of

the taints and weaknesses of the former political regime. . . . All France's troubles derive from the policy by which the Chambers decide the fate of the government.

Twenty years later, who would be ready to swear that these words were not written by de Gaulle? Twenty years later, who would dare to condemn the Marshal for believing and repeating that he personified France? Who would dream of criticizing him for asking the French people to follow him? And whom did de Gaulle take as his model in war, character, doctrine and style? "The essence of prestige," de Gaulle once wrote,

is the impression given by a leader that he is endowed with an extraordinary character, that his person possesses a mysterious, indefinable quality which is peculiar to him. Those leaders whose prestige has gone down to history did in fact share the ability to remain in some way inscrutable to their subordinates, and thus to keep them morally on tenterhooks so that they enjoyed a reputation for unpredictability. . . . This is because they possessed the art of isolating themselves morally, keeping part of themselves secret and mysterious, whereas the vast majority of men conceal nothing but their self-interest. It is because they have studied their every gesture to make the strongest possible impression, whereas the common herd do not observe themselves.

Such was the portrait which de Gaulle painted in 1927, on three separate occasions, at weekly intervals, in the presence of Pétain himself, before the professors of the École de Guerre.

Alexander would not have conquered Asia nor Caesar Gaul, Galileo would not have proved the movement of the earth, Columbus would not have discovered America, Richelieu would not have restored the authority of the throne, Boileau would not have laid down the rules of classical taste, Carnot would not have organized the victory of the revolutionary armies, Napoleon would not have founded the Empire, Lesseps would not have cut through the Isthmus, Bismarck would not have achieved German unity, Pétain would not have reorganized the French Army in the midst of war, and Clemenceau would not have saved his country if they had heeded the counsels of base prudence or the suggestions of cowardly humility.

That series of lectures had ended in the office of General Héring, the Director of the École de Guerre, with the exclamation: "De Gaulle is Pétain plagiarized!" Six years later it became a book with a dedication to Pétain worthy of Bossuet. Pétain was the younger man's acknowledged spiritual master. Shunned by the bigots after his second marriage to a divorced woman, he had even agreed to be godfather to Philippe de Gaulle, the son of a disciple who imitated his gruff silences, interspersed with sudden sallies, and his haughty way of summoning his wife and solemnly addressing her as "Madame."

Then, little by little, the personality of the prize pupil, whom Pétain called "an impossible, unbearable character," eaten up with pride and contemptuously known in the Army as "the journalist" because he wrote so many articles, had hardened. He had drawn away from his master until they had finally been parted by a trivial quarrel, born of an author's sensitivity. "I shall have taught everyone that there are times when a loyal, disciplined soldier must disobey orders, and can disobey orders without debasing himself." What Rossel wrote on the eve of his execution de Gaulle could apply to himself. To justify himself he possessed what most enhances a man in the eyes of his fellows: courage in adversity.

After a flying start, the final speech for the prosecution started flagging now and then, and descended into boredom. Bâtonnier Payen took notes. Maître Isorni listened with one hand resting against his cheek. Maître Lemaire put on a show of profound concentration which was a mask for sleep. The first hour of Monsieur Mornet's speech tired his listeners. It was hard to imagine Pétain hatching a plot while he was Ambassador in Madrid and then refusing to join the Daladier Cabinet. It was difficult, too, to believe that Pétain and Weygand had concluded an armistice to discredit the Republic and substitute a military government. Had the Army been defeated? Could French North Africa have resisted? Monsieur Mornet gave no answer to these questions, just as he did not explain why no one had thought of ordering the Toulon fleet to leave port. One can only just make out his intention of showing that there had been a masochistic military plot to destroy the country in order to overthrow the regime.

Nobody now can possibly believe that anything but military defeat pushed the country into the abyss, and that the Armistice did not go some way toward attenuating the national disaster. With the country's institutions in decay, neither Clemenceau nor de Gaulle could have done any better with a broken weapon in their hands. We can now compare the atmosphere at Vichy in July 1940 with the atmosphere in Paris in May 1958. Fear and the clatter of tanks always haunt the nights of a dying republic. Who protested at the time what was a parody of legality? What voices could be raised in defense of a wounded whore in whom no one was willing to recognize a mother? Pétain's offense lay elsewhere. The Armistice was not an acceptance of defeat but a pause pending a change of fortune.

Monsieur Mornet did not succeed in drawing from his dry heart the accents which would have damned the accused. The court did not hear his blows strike home. But they are there nonetheless in the record of the hearing—blows such as this quotation from an appeal by the Marshal: "Certain Frenchmen, harking back to the worst days of our history, and spurning authority, are carrying out acts of sabotage and spreading real terror by means of unspeakable crimes." The implication was that the French people should remain obedient and submissive, walking in orderly ranks behind their schoolmaster as he scolded the rowdy boys, or, as Bernanos put it, climb onto the knees of the weeping Marshal, shutting their eyes, to drink from the military feeding bottle of shame. And yet, when the Marshal's sycophants criticized the Gaullists in his presence, thinking that this would please him, he used to growl, "Bad Frenchmen, you call them? How do you know? Let's wait and see."

"And now," the Attorney General went on, shaking his robes, "to come to those lies which the Marshal condemned so roundly and which he said caused us so much harm—who was deceived? When was he telling the truth? When was he lying? For, after all, the

people of France knew only what they were told; the troops, when
they were ordered to fire on the invader . . . knew nothing but that
order; I imagine that the junior officers, NCO's and men of the North
African forces never knew of the existence of Admiral Auphan's
despatch . . . or of those more or less secret telegrams in more or
less ambiguous language. They knew only what was said openly and
broadcast openly."

Monsieur Mornet was mistaken. The French people were not taken
in by the Marshal's lofty messages any more than we were. The lies
which were used on us and which we used ourselves acquired a
special merit from the fact that they were intended to deceive the
Germans. We lived by hidden meanings. Everyone knew the answers
to whatever questions might be asked. The deceit did not lie there.

When the Attorney General asked who had been fooled, I asked
myself the same question, for we had certainly been deceived. Not by
a message of congratulation to Hitler after the failure of the Dieppe
landing, which Pétain could have signed without upsetting us too
much. That trick was part of the game, and the preliminary investigation before the Pétain trial failed to reveal any evidence to the
contrary. Laval, too, used Pétain's prestige to declare that he hoped
for a German victory. As for de Gaulle's references on the London
radio to "Old Man Defeat," we were unmoved by such blasphemy. If
our indifference now strikes me, in retrospect, as an aberration, it
must have been a collective aberration, for I cannot remember that de
Gaulle's insults stirred our consciences to any significant degree.

"There have even been allegations that he was hand in glove with
de Gaulle," exclaimed Monsieur Mornet with an indignation which
may actually have been sincere.

When we considered some of our attempts to break our bonds, we
sometimes told ourselves that they would serve no useful purpose
because by changing sides we would confuse the issue. That complicity in a patriotism which could not be denied to one side or the
other was so obvious that if it had not existed it would have had to be
invented. Sentenced first of all to four years' imprisonment in July

1940, de Gaulle was sentenced to death on August 2 by a jury of seven generals. Just for form's sake. The walls of Troy heard the same sort of verbal warfare centuries before.

"That, I hope, gentlemen, will put an end to the allegations of concerted action between Marshal de Gaulle and General Pétain," cried Monsieur Mornet, getting his stars mixed up.

The accused smiled at the mistake.

How, in all honesty, could the Attorney General cite denials by the British Government in support of his case? Was there anyone left who still believed statements of that sort? Being a statesman or a diplomat means knowing how to use subterfuge to conceal a fact or cloak a silence. For ordinary folk in China and for the great and powerful in other lands, the language of diplomacy is a means of disguising falsehood. If Monsieur Jacques Chevalier had admitted that the British had once given Vichy details of a journey General de Gaulle was going to make, he would have drawn an angry denial from London. Conduct of that sort was incompatible with the honor of His Majesty's Government.

But honor is a word which governments do not hesitate to employ for reasons of state, whenever it can be used to cover up some particularly shameful act. The British had wanted to rid themselves of their Cross of Lorraine and its troublesome Christ, and they had not lacked a Caiaphas in the intelligence service to hand him over in chains to Pétain. On that occasion, Pétain had overlooked the resentment he felt toward the onetime disciple who had insulted him. In the presence of witnesses the shameful information had been thrown into the fire, but de Gaulle had not shown the slightest gratitude. Now the old man simply smiled and shook his head over the whole incident. By the time the hearing was adjourned, at 3:45, Monsieur Mornet had failed to make any impression on the jury.

The defense lawyers split up to test the general opinion. They resumed their seats looking reassured. The Attorney General was not in the best of form. His voice occasionally dropped to a dull growl which was barely audible. Was he more affected than he wished to reveal by the threatening letters he kept receiving at the Palais de Justice, and which he left his secretary or his clerk to open? Was he performing his task as a dismal duty, or even botching it? Or was his age telling on him? Perhaps this hour of glory, the dream of every ambitious lawyer, struck him as too heavy with servitude and unworthy of a man of honor. After all his threats, everyone expected a savage brilliance from him which he had not shown. The gloomy Attorney General had overwhelmed his audience with boredom.

In the galleries paved with black and white marble, where the lawyers' robes brushed against the submachine guns of the guards, voices buzzed in conversation. The sunlight moved around until it fell on the flying buttresses of the Sainte-Chapelle. After an adjournment lasting over three-quarters of an hour the accused was brought back and the court returned. This time the Attorney General turned to face the jurors opposite him. He had changed his jacket during the adjournment and was full of a new vigor.

He continued with his list of accusations, condemning Pétain's submissiveness and the Montoire meeting, and recalling the imprisonment and destruction of the fleet at Toulon. As far away as the West Indies orders had been given to sink ships and gold reserves and destroy aircraft rather than hand them over to the Allies. In his opinion this frenzied insistence on destroying everything was the mark of a childish senility, that deplorable senility which presided over France in her misfortune.

To show the extent of France's humiliation, Monsieur Mornet hit on a brilliant device. He read out a quotation from the philosopher Fichte's *Speech to the German Nation:*

We have been defeated. Do we also want to be despised? Do we want to add the loss of honor to all our other losses? Let us take care not to excite our victors' scorn. The surest way of earning their contempt would be to give up our way of life and try to resemble them by adopting theirs.

That, said Monsieur Mornet, was what Pétain had done by remaining in office and collaborating with the enemy. In a piece of bravura which impressed his audience, the Attorney General defended the judiciary which had cheated to save lives during the Occupation, and particularly the Riom Court of which he had nearly been a member.

He came back to the Marshal's letters to Hitler, solemn declarations inspired by fear and hatred of Bolshevism, and to his proposal that France should man one of the battlements of the Atlantic Wall. This list of cowardly actions, great and small, accumulated day by day, proved that King Philippe VII, reigning over a kingdom of ruins, had lost his sense of reality and even his sense of that honor which he mentioned in all his speeches.

Despite twenty years of indulgence and forgetfulness, no one can read pages 332 and 333 of the *Journal officiel* without being affected by the Attorney General's painstaking collection of the saddest texts of that period. The shame which during the three weeks of the trial had been masked beneath pleas *pro domo,* faltering accusations and ingenuous excuses is gathered together in those six columns of close print and blown into the reader's face. Try as he may to protect himself, he cannot help being contaminated. Monsieur Mornet was no orator. But like the chairman of a parliamentary committee reading out an important report, he had accumulated in his dark-stained hands explosive charges which, when they went off, covered a whole nation with disgrace. As he listened to the scornful old voice, the Marshal picked up his gloves, squeezed them between his fingers, put them down in front of him, shifted his little table, pushed his kepi away. The emotion boiling up inside him alternately brought a flush to his cheeks or drained them of blood.

As I recall the naïveté I showed in those days, my lips form once again the words of the song: "Marshal, here we are." The fact is that we believed in him. We had pinned up in front of us a picture of that venerable old leader, crowned with laurels. That innocent rosy face, those clear blue eyes, belonged to a king who had won the most terrible battle in history. His simple style captivated us. As the knights of a humiliated army, eager to devote ourselves to a great cause under the leadership of a great man, why should we have been

sparing of our love? Others better equipped than ourselves to criticize
had been deceived. In 1942 Paul Valéry, who was no fool, added a
fresh portico to the temple raised in Pétain's honor by gratitude and
admiration. To a new Plutarch writing the lives of illustrious men,
the life of Pétain offered remarkable scope. What reason could we
have advanced for spurning him or doubting him—we who were
unworthy to untie his shoelaces?

There was only one: an instinctive rejection of defeat, the feeling
that an injustice was being done, over our heads, against us and in
spite of us, and the conviction that we had to say no. Bernanos, who
had left France after Munich to recover from his shame in Brazil,
covered sheets of paper with his long angular handwriting, letting
out an angry roar now and then. If his prophetic voice had reached
our ears, it might have drowned the voices of the courtiers and
academicians. Pressed to the proud old breast of King Philippe VII,
we could hear nothing but the beating of a funeral drum.

It was a question of latitude. From Rio de Janeiro a man could
judge France better than from Algiers, because he saw her from a
greater distance. If the fortunes of war had taken me to Beirut, I
would probably have spurned slavery disguised as piety, once the army
of the Levant had been deprived of its illustrious leader, that princely
bastard obsessed with questions of dignity and precedence.

Twenty years later, I find myself in agreement with the Attorney
General: we were deceived. In the name of our country we were
forced to accept disasters caused by the negligence of the governments
of the Third Republic. We believed for a while that those misfortunes were due to the union of Jews and Freemasons, that the coming
to power of a Marshal of France would save the situation, and that all
we had to do was be patient for a time. Saint-Exupéry, as far away as
New York, allowed himself to be deceived, and Bernanos himself
admitted, "Who knows if I might not have been tempted to yield
to that abject spell?"

We had our excuses. The most significant of them was there before
the jury's eyes, in a khaki gabardine uniform, with his black-

ribboned, gold-braided kepi resting on a little table which had perhaps once contained a chamber pot. Now the sunlight had left the august forehead and shone only on the top of the oak paneling above the public entrance at the back of the courtroom.

Oddly enough, it is not a feeling of anger which has succeeded my shame, but one of immense pity. Why didn't that venerable octogenarian of Villeneuve-Loubet stay on the heights of Antibes, where he could look out on his vines and the sea, cultivating his vineyards between visits to Paris for the dictionary sessions of the Académie française? Why hadn't he used his much-vaunted common sense and thrown out the messengers who came to him from all sides during that period of political skulduggery to announce that his hour was at hand? Didn't he know that miracles happen only once? But when you have begun your career at fifty-eight, and fame has fallen on your shoulders in your sixties, what a temptation it must be, at eighty-four, to tell yourself that fate has chosen you to marry a beautiful orphan and famous heiress, who has fallen in love with your glory and wishes to warm your old bones at night in her bed!

Poor dear old Marshal! The memory of his early successes had encouraged him to give his arm to a young bride who could have been his granddaughter. After all, Victor Hugo, another member of the Académie française, had deflowered virgins and finished his *Legend of the Centuries* at the same age. An old man full of youthful ardor, intoxicated by the flattery which his overweening pride attracted, and surrounded by other old men greedy for honors and places, or reciting solemn formulas, he mounted the ramshackle throne hurriedly set up for him in a staid hotel in a spa. He was not even King of Bourges, but simply King of Vichy, where his despicable courtiers helped him to trick us. A large section of the French intelligentsia were gathered there, enjoying the warmth of the heated drawing rooms, admiring the admirals' caps hanging in the cloakrooms, and basking in the reassuring aura of bourgeois order. Apart from old Esteva, who could possibly have suspected the admirals of naïveté? And who could have guessed that the Grand Admiral of the Fleet had sold the Toulon squadron for a mess of pottage, together with the young officers who were going to die after an abortive attempt at revolt?

The Attorney General cleared his throat, picked up a fresh sheet from his pile of papers, and almost bent double over his desk. He had come to the Syrian affair of 1941.

"This is what Marshal Pétain cabled to the High Commissioner:

The Admiral of the Fleet has wired you about the Franco-German negotiations. I wish to stress personally the great importance of these negotiations and my determination to pursue, without any ulterior motive, the policy which will proceed from them. . . . The reference to Syria will give you confirmation of our intention to defend, by all the means in our power, the territory under your authority; to ensure as at Dakar the freedom of its skies; and to give there in what I know to be difficult political and military circumstances the measure of our desire to collaborate with the New Order."

Pétain had never repudiated that terrible tribute to Adolf Hitler's New Order, which with a little less luck might have become a reality for us. At Saint Jean d'Acre two thousand soldiers, one-tenth of the total force, and a few dozen officers, left the Vichy Army to join the forces of General de Gaulle. The same number lay in the cemeteries of Syria, killed by French and British bullets. If I had been there, which way would I have turned in the name of loyalty? A year later, the Allies landed on the shores of North Africa with an armada which made the earth tremble, and the old man started uttering his threats: "France and her honor are at stake. We are being attacked and we shall defend ourselves. That is the order I give you." The bounds of stupidity and trickery had been exceeded. A few days later I bade you farewell, Monsieur le Maréchal.

At Vichy the old man was being besieged. His chief of staff at Verdun, parliamentary deputies, Weygand, ministers and aides-de-camp were all begging him to leave for Algiers. The plane, a Glenn

Martin, was standing by, its engines warming up. The pilot, a Colonel Gorostarzu who had been his Air Attaché in Madrid, had promised he would stay below five thousand feet so as not to place any strain on his passenger's tired old heart. But to all these pleas the Marshal curtly answered no. As the witnesses told the story, he seemed once again to be choosing the hardest path, preparing to share the fate of the French people rather than that of the liberators. He told Weygand, "I shall not leave, even if my glory should perish as a result." The words emerging from the august mustache were as deceptive as ever. The old joker was staying at Vichy, his buttocks clinging to the meager stuffing of his throne, simply and solely because he was afraid of flying. He was terrified of crashing in flames during take-off, or of hitting an air pocket, and he disguised this fear under solemn excuses which very nearly took me in once more.

He ought to have been put aboard the plane without suspecting anything, much as Loustanau-Lacau and Squadron Leader Faye, who died in a deportee camp, planned to kidnap him in 1941 and fly him to London, where they intended to present their poisoned gift to de Gaulle. If there had been a single breath of youth left in his body, would he have hesitated a moment? Did he really think that he could still serve as a shield to a France which the Wehrmacht was about to occupy from Dunkirk to Toulon, or that he could save the Jews from a wholesale massacre? What new misfortunes could befall the country and what reprisals could be carried out when resistance was hardening and the Reich, badly mauled in Russia, had to deploy its armies to defend the Mediterranean front? On the other hand, what surpassing glory he would have won if he had gathered together the North African armies and returned with them to France two years later, instead of moldering away at Sigmaringen with his militia, his new writing paper and his crates of Chambertin! But old men dislike changing their habits. He refused to budge. The excuse he offered is not lacking in grandeur. It is consistent with honor and even faith. It is also the excuse of an old man, washed up like a dead dog on a shore bright with the morning sun.

One evening in June 1947, Colonel Rémy was talking bitterly about Marshal Pétain when de Gaulle, in an indulgent mood for once, stopped him.

"Rémy," he said, "remember that France must always have two strings to her bow. In 1940 she needed the Pétain string as well as the de Gaulle string. I shall never understand why the Marshal didn't go to Algiers in November 1942. The French in Algeria would have cheered him, the Americans would have embraced him, the English would have followed him, and as for us, my dear Rémy, we wouldn't have counted for very much. The Marshal would have made a triumphant return to Paris on his white charger."

Rémy was completely taken aback. He didn't sleep all night. Everything had to be thought out again if Pétain wasn't a traitor. One of the first soldiers to join de Gaulle in 1940, this highly intelligent man, with the face of a centurion masked by the general appearance of a country lawyer, had organized one of the most powerful intelligence networks of the war. For nearly three years he remained silent, bearing this burden of doubt by himself. Then, after a minute study of the transcript of Pétain's trial, he decided to publish the remark made by the President of the RPF in a propaganda booklet entitled *De Gaulle the Unknown.* De Gaulle was shown the manuscript and struck out the revealing comment with his own hand. Yet Rémy had not been dreaming: de Gaulle had said that. And since he had said it, why conceal it? Why add to the disunity of the French people? In 1950 Rémy finally published de Gaulle's comment in an article in *Carrefour* entitled "Justice and Disgrace." He expected a denial, but was simply treated to a display of ill-humor.

After that, Colonel Rémy put de Gaulle and Marshal Pétain on the same footing, and loved them both, while I tried to forget them. Both won great glory, and both conquered in turn the hearts of the French people, who in their wisdom understood that they needed both a shield and a sword.

Why did Pétain wait until he was imprisoned on the Île d'Yeu before writing down in a lucid moment this comment which sum-

marizes the whole French drama: "De Gaulle: We must continue the
fight in North Africa and organize resistance there. Pétain: You can
only fight if you are alive"? And why did the victorious sword
condemn the shield? "It is the cause, and not our will, which asks
such actions from our hands: we'll wash away all stains in Freedom's
fountain!" So speaks one of the Venetian conspirators in Byron's
Marino Faliero.

In November 1942, the Marshal, in his senile cunning, thought
that Providence had done well in sending his Admiral of the Fleet
to Algiers and that his Dauphin would keep his place warm in North
Africa. Providence was indeed at work: young Bony de la Chapelle,
to whom no one, oddly enough, has set up a monument, killed
Darlan with a few revolver shots. If it had not been for him, French
unity would have been built on an armistice and not on a revolt, and
the pontiffs of collaboration would have ousted the London rebel and
thwarted the grand designs of history. The Marshal had missed the
bus—or martyrdom in Darlan's place.

In 1944, under pressure from his German jailers, he wrote and
broadcast a new message: "People of France, this alleged liberation is
the most deceptive of all the mirages to which you might be tempted
to yield. . . . Any one of you, whether soldier, official, or ordinary
citizen, who joins one of the resistance groups, is compromising the
future of our country." At that time we were bombing the Ruhr with
the RAF. We carried the Cross of Lorraine on our Halifaxes, and yet
there were some of us who in their heart of hearts still believed in the
Marshal. I was not one of them. But if I admired his disciple de
Gaulle, as one admires a man who takes enormous risks, I disliked
his way of taking revenge on his old master. How innocent military
men can be, and what magic lies in the words *discipline* and *loyalty*
when they are sown in the hearts of simple men at arms!

This time the Attorney General had convinced me. It was too much
for me, this string of tearful exhortations which were simply appeals
for renunciation. Couldn't the dear old man see that the Allies were

going to win? How could the victor of Verdun, who told his private
secretary never to forget that Germany had lost the First World War,
allow himself to become a collaborator? How could he endure the
proximity of a Darnand, just because he had decorated him in 1918?
How could he recommend him to Laval for his energy and courage?
How could he shake hands with French officers, doubtless including
idiots like myself, but wearing German uniforms, and decorated with
the Iron Cross? How could he let so many stupid and shameful acts
be committed in his name?

Monsieur Mornet paused for a moment, rested his hands on his
desk and took off his pince-nez. A sudden, dreadful silence fell upon
the courtroom. He had finished. He had just quoted Juvenal: "The
worst catastrophe is, out of fear of losing a wretched existence, to lose
the only reason for living: honor." If nothing else, the Marshal had
understood that. He had explained his feelings on the subject more
than once. When he had chosen to remain with the French people
under the pretext of saving them from the fate of Poland, he had
accepted the loss of the appearance of honor. He had taken upon
himself the stigma of cowardice and ignominy. Colonel Rémy admired him all the more for this and compared him to Charles de
Foucauld.

The Attorney General's voice became hoarser and seemed to be
struggling through a mist.

"The law of France, gentlemen, contains no article allowing the
substitution, on grounds of age, for the supreme penalty, of an
equivalent penalty comprising the same degradation. Taking my
stand on the law, braving the threats which have been made against
my life, and also the insults of a minority still blinded by its hatred or
its faith, thinking of all the harm done to France by a name and the
man who bears it with all the glory once attached to it, and speaking
without hatred or passion, I ask the High Court to pronounce
sentence of death on the man who was once Marshal Pétain."

And he sat down, putting his papers together, while time halted its
course in quivering suspense. Everyone looked at the Marshal. His

eyes fixed on the Attorney General, he was nervously fingering his Médaille Militaire, his hand going up to the silver pin fastening the ribbon to his tunic.

"Before the hearing is adjourned . . ." said Monsieur Mongibeaux, in a clear, calm voice, putting on his spectacles.

He went on to read out a letter which Monsieur Rochat, the former Secretary General for Foreign Affairs, had sent him from Switzerland. Monsieur Rochat had enjoyed the trust of both the Marshal and Laval. His loyalty had made him one of the most important men in Vichy. Gaullists and collaborators had listened to him with respect. He had been present at the discussion between Pétain and Laval of the notorious statement, "I hope for a German victory." The Marshal, he informed the court, had told Laval, "If I were in your place, I would at least omit the words *I believe in.*" "I told the Marshal," wrote Monsieur Rochat,

that such an alteration was inadequate. I repeated that what was left of the sentence was equally unacceptable, and that the whole passage ought to be struck out. In the meantime Pierre Laval altered his text in accordance with the Marshal's suggestion . . . and he read it out. . . . The Marshal made no comment.

"Will you kindly pass on this letter, Bâtonnier?" said the judge.

The hearing was adjourned at a quarter to seven, to the accompaniment of a sinister rumble of thunder. The defense lawyers silently accompanied the accused to his room. In the Cour de Mai the paving stones were gleaming.

XXI

Monday, August 13, 1945

Sunday morning was showery. To the actors in the drama it seemed that the heat was more oppressive than ever. Yet it was only 80 degrees in the shade that day. The defense lawyers met together and then called on Marshal Pétain, who was bitterly brooding over the closing speech for the prosecution.

"It's incredible," he kept saying, shaking his head.

Had he forgotten what Monsieur François Valentin, the Director General of the French Legion of Combatants, prompted by the Marshal's orderly officer, had said to him at the time when, under German pressure, he had been getting ready to relieve Weygand of his command in North Africa? "Watch out, Monsieur le Maréchal!" he had said. "Watch out for yourself! Have a care, or one day the French people will spit on your stars!"

Major Bonhomme, who died in an accident in 1943, had warned Monsieur Valentin that if he merely reminded the Marshal of Verdun, his exhortations would be in vain. "He won't even hear you," Bonhomme had told him. "Look at Laval; he had the right idea. He called Pétain an old fool to his face. Don't be afraid. You must bang your fist on the table, shout at him and yell, 'Monsieur le Maréchal, they'll hang you! They'll spit in your face! They'll burn

down your fine house at Villeneuve-Loubet!' Then he'll start pricking
up his ears." Well, now that time had come!

In *Combat* Bernanos wrote:

> France is disgusted with the Pétain trial; the country finds it nauseating.
> As a demonstration of civic justice the Marshal's trial is worth exactly
> what the grotesque and disastrous Toulon episode was worth as a demon-
> stration of military heroism. The people who crowd into the First Chamber
> every day are clearly no more eager to participate in a real act of justice than
> Admiral Laborde and his officers were to go down with their ships. . . .
> It's all a farce.

Monday morning was sunny. About midday, some fine-weather
clouds appeared in the sky, driven by a light westerly breeze. The
presiding judge asked the defense in what order their representatives
wished to speak.

"I shall be speaking first," said the Bâtonnier.

"Leave me alone!" exclaimed Marshal Pétain, who was being
pestered by the photographers.

The press, which was indignant at the failure to grant it the
supplementary allowance of newsprint promised for the duration of
the trial, and which suspected some dark design on the part of the
government, was threatening to boycott the trial the following day. It
had praised the vigor and spirit of the old Attorney General, who at
other times had seemed brutal and clumsy. Bâtonnier Payen decided
that it was essential to avoid fighting him on his own ground, and
that the defense had to dispose the jurors to indulgence by showing
them what Marshal Pétain had been and what prestige France still
enjoyed, thanks to him, at home and abroad.

The leader of the defense set about this task in his own way.
Attack was not his forte; he was neither the fire that kills nor the fire
that spreads; he erected ramparts around his client, built a series of
towers and installed culverins and archers in them. There was no
infernal machine hidden in the folds of his robes. With considerable
economy of gesture he began his speech in a dull voice which was
barely audible, even close up. He recalled what the heads of state and

generals thought of Pétain at the end of the First World War, his victories in the Riff, and tributes to his humility and loyalty. What he said was solid, well argued and boring. The accused, who had looked nervous at the beginning of the hearing, relaxed.

Suddenly the Bâtonnier had a burst of eloquence which moved his audience.

"If you want his head," he cried, "take it. We give it to you. There will be no appeal for mercy, no petition for a reprieve. If you pronounce sentence of death, that sentence will be carried out. He has said this, he has written it, and I now repeat it in his name: he is not defending his life. . . . It is his honor that he is defending. It is also the honor, the liberty and the lives of those who followed him."

Then once again the Bâtonnier returned to his lament. The papers seized at Vichy and in Paris had not all been examined. Important witnesses, in prison, abroad or in the service of the state, had not dared to give evidence. Nobody could believe that at his age the Marshal could have wanted to betray his country.

Turning his back on the Attorney General, the Bâtonnier addressed the jurors representing the Resistance. Then he suddenly turned farther to the right, to face the clerk who had read out the indictment.

"What, in fact, do we find in your indictment? It is intriguing to note, gentlemen, that the whole thing is written in the conditional: 'The Marshal is alleged to have said . . .'"

Monsieur Jean Lot, the chief clerk, pretended to be absorbed in his correspondence.

One by one, the Bâtonnier went through the charges in the indictment. Then he reproached the witnesses for the prosecution with having used the trial to plead their own causes and with having shifted their own responsibilities onto the Marshal's shoulders. He went back to 1939 when Pétain was Ambassador in Madrid and recalled the praises lavished on him by Monsieur Daladier when he offered him a place in his Cabinet. How could anyone see any trace of ambition in the Marshal's refusal? A few weeks before, Pétain had declined an offer to stand for the Presidency of the Republic on the

ground of age. Then Monsieur Paul Reynaud sent a general to
Madrid to beg the victor of Verdun to return, and announced to the
country in lyrical terms that the Marshal was going to join his
Cabinet.

The idea of an Armistice had already been raised on May 25,
1940, at a meeting of the War Council. In June, continuing the
struggle would have brought utter catastrophe. Everyone considered it
essential to bring hostilities to an end. Capitulation would have
placed France in the enemy's power; the Armistice saved the Army
and the nation. Resistance in French North Africa was regarded as
out of the question. As for the fleet, Monsieur Paul Reynaud had told
the court that it could not have sailed to England because Italy would
have attacked Tunisia, while Monsieur Albert Lebrun had testified
that Britain had been satisfied with the knowledge that the French
fleet was not under German control.

Here the Bâtonnier was quoting the sort of nonsense that Bernanos
had denounced. Monsieur Albert Lebrun, recalling the meeting on
June 19, 1940, between the commanders in chief of the British and
French navies, had gone so far as to say: "The British left the
meeting extremely satisfied." To lessen Pétain's guilt for having shut
up the French fleet in Toulon, Bâtonnier Payen tried to show that the
Marshal had done no worse than the sinister little men who had
preceded him.

His face lit with a smile which he tried in vain to make contagious,
he painted a reassuring portrait of a fatherly King Pétain. He
represented the Marshal's refusal to leave Vichy as a martyrdom and
his reign as a pontificate, and he quoted comments from the foreign
press describing the Armistice as a stroke of good luck for France. He
even called in de Gaulle to help him.

"I don't know what you think about all this," he said, in a gloomy,
staccato voice to which he tried to lend a familiar tone. "You almost
certainly have a ready-made opinion on the subject, but I can assure
you, from what I have seen and heard, that the Armistice was greeted
everywhere with an immense relief which may not have been born of

heroism but was definitely born of satisfaction. To put it bluntly and crudely, the state of mind of the vast majority of the French people at that moment was: 'Let's get it over with. We're sick and tired of the whole business.' "

The Bâtonnier had finished. He had been speaking for two hours. The hearing was adjourned. The Marshal, who had been dozing like some members of the jury, woke up. The Bâtonnier's speech had not been an example of great oratory; it was a careful historical compilation, badly arranged and read out in a flat voice, but Pierre Scize for one described it as talented and moving. The Bâtonnier had exhausted himself summoning up inadequate reserves of physical strength. His sharp, handsome features, twitching with emotion, were not warmed by any flame. Like the melancholy ferryman who paddled across the dark waters of the Styx, he was obviously taking his client's boat toward the underworld.

During the adjournment it was learned that all the members of the High Court had received an anonymous letter threatening them with death if Pétain was not acquitted.

When the hearing was resumed at four o'clock, Maître Lemaire began speaking.

A huge broad forehead and full cheeks gave this sturdy, imposing figure a jovial, debonair appearance. He immediately launched into an attack on the Attorney General, and, for want of arguments against the prosecution, set about demolishing the prosecutor. Maître Lemaire spoke in a loud, firm voice with occasional tremolos, frowning, toying with his sleeves, leaning over the bar, juggling with his files, and interspersing his comments with pregnant pauses.

The Attorney General fell into the trap. He stood up, bristling with indignation, and barked, "You are making a personal attack on me, Maître Lemaire. I regret having to interrupt you, but I cannot tolerate such conduct."

Bâtonnier Payen tugged at his colleague's robes to stop him, but Maître Lemaire asked him to let him go on. The Bâtonnier sat down again, looking uneasy. The altercation continued, in spite of an intervention by the presiding judge, and took on the appearance of a personal quarrel. The Attorney General put up a lame defense against the accusation of having been entrusted with leading the anti-Communist drive on behalf of the Vichy Ministry of Justice. With his sad moon face turned toward the ceiling and a bitter twist to his mouth, Maître Lemaire kept his arms raised during the Attorney General's interruptions and went on speaking. He annoyed and irritated his audience by turns. His attacks on the indictment were more skillful, but were so violent that they became monotonous. The simplest statements, as he boomed them out, took on a solemnity which robbed them of their force.

Reading Maître Lemaire's speech does not satisfy the mind. The polemicist's qualities have vanished, and the carefully balanced phrases, the abundant commonplaces and the oratorical devices don't succeed in setting off the lawyer's best arguments. Today one reads his speech without admiration, and his audience listened to it without conviction. On the other hand, Maître Lemaire possessed the knack of capturing the court's attention as soon as he concentrated his fire on the Attorney General perched in his eyrie. Trying to rebut the accusation that Pétain had plotted against the Republic, based on his three days incognito in Paris and his remark to Monsieur de Monzie in January 1940, "They'll need me in the second fortnight in May," Maître Lemaire didn't attempt to dispel the court's suspicions; he merely made fun of them.

"This is serious, you say, Attorney General. But has it occurred to you that if we followed this argument of yours to its logical conclusion, we would find Monsieur Paul Reynaud guilty, for after all, who was it, in the second fortnight in May, who sent for Marshal Pétain?"

Huddled in his furs, Monsieur Mornet, who had turned his back on Maître Lemaire, raised his eyes to heaven in exasperation.

The defense lawyer had better luck quoting the statements in which the former ministers of the Third Republic recognized the legality of the powers which had been granted Pétain. He concluded in simpler fashion, by also quoting Fichte:

" 'Treason is the real rallying cry for a riot, the cry which gives wings to the mob, which brings brave men and cowards together, and which gives a single heart to a hundred thousand men.' Well, gentlemen, don't listen to that cry of panic. You must not return your verdict under the influence of the anxiety gripping the country. No, there was no crime against the Republic and the nation, and I call upon you to clear the Marshal's honor of that accusation."

Glancing at his watch, the presiding judge asked his assessors whether it might not be best to adjourn the hearing.

Thinking he had been asked a question, Marshal Pétain turned toward Maître Lemaire, his face radiant with joy, and mumbled, "I can only give my approval to what my defense counsel has said."

Bâtonnier Payen would have preferred the speeches for the defense to continue into the evening.

"Shall I be obliged to come?" asked Pétain.

The hearing was adjourned to the following morning. When the defense lawyers accompanied the accused back to his room, he gave vent to a childish gaiety.

"Lemaire was terrific," he told his wife, without a single word for the Bâtonnier, whom he had found boring. "Mornet really caught it."

Maître Isorni joined the jurors.

"If we sentence him to death," Monsieur Lecompte-Boinet told him, "we shall be called murderers and General de Gaulle will get the credit for granting him a reprieve. And if we don't sentence him to death, we shall be called cowards."

And Monsieur Gabriel Delattre told him, "There's still hope. It all depends on you. You can still save him."

XXII

❋

Tuesday, August 14, 1945

Storms had broken out in the southwest and center of the country; the sun rose in a cloudy sky. Shortly before nine o'clock it started raining hard, and the cyclists in the streets took shelter in the carriage gateways.

Jacques Isorni heaved a sigh of relief. An insane hope filled his heart. The atmosphere in the First Chamber would be less stifling and perhaps he had a better chance of convincing the court. Through the Comte Marchand, first valet to Napoleon, through his maternal great-grandmother who had looked after the King of Rome in his childhood, and through his mother, a passionate supporter of Dreyfus of the kind that existed in a few conservative families, he belonged to what is called the Right, but his father had been a poor foreigner who loathed the bourgeoisie and believed in the virtue of making one's own way in the world.

A member of the Resistance throughout the Occupation, Jacques Isorni had not come into contact with the collaborators until 1945, when his profession had taken him into the prisons. There he had become friendly with Brasillach, and he was deeply grieved by his failure to save him from execution. Now strong ties of affection bound him to the tired, hunted old man whom he had visited in his distress, at the Fort of Montrouge. So great a degree of misfortune aroused in Isorni a generosity which adversity had never managed to stifle in him. He discovered in his heart an affection for King Philippe VII which became a sort of filial complicity. No, Marshal Pétain couldn't be a traitor, and it was Isorni's duty to save him. To do that, he had to shake him out of his torpor and prevent him from giving in. Isorni was determined to ask for justice, not pity, for the Marshal, and if he was to convince the jury, he needed to possess the sort of faith that moves mountains.

From his study windows he could just make out the river between lines of poplars, beyond the trees in the Jardin des Plantes. Not for anything in the world would Isorni have exchanged his black robes for the regal mantle of the presiding judge or the crimson toga of the Attorney General. The man who had asked for Robert Brasillach's head still lived in the same building, on the same floor as himself; every night the telephone rang in the apartment next door and an anonymous voice called for revenge for the poet's death. The Attorney General could not sleep any more and was getting ready to move. If Isorni failed, at least he would not have blood on his hands, while if he succeeded . . .

He knew his brief thoroughly, and above all he knew Pétain the man. He had accumulated pages of notes. Occasionally the speech which he was incapable of writing out and learning by heart unfolded in his imagination, harmonious, sonorous, heart-rending. Now, all of a sudden, he felt empty, dejected. If, on the night of a premiere, an actor gets stage fright, he can always turn for help to his memory and to gestures he has rehearsed hundreds of times. Isorni suddenly had the impression that his intellectual faculties were paralyzed. He was seized with panic. Would he be able to utter the cries he had felt rising to his lips ever since the trial had begun? Dry-mouthed and heavy of heart, he cycled toward the Île de la Cité. The rain had stopped, but the sky was still cloudy. Squads of policemen were guarding all the approaches. The Minister of the Interior was afraid

of a commando attack intended to cut off the Prefecture of Police
from the Palais de Justice.

Once again the hearing began with a speech by Bâtonnier Payen. In
that grim, crowded courtroom he found it hard to control his
emotion. This time the Marshal's fate would be known before another
day dawned. The nervousness which could be read in the features of
the accused was revealed in the Bâtonnier by jerky movements of the
chin which turned his face to the right, toward the Resistance jurors
who had to be won over at all costs. His voice, as flat as ever, tried
now and then to vibrate and failed. The Bâtonnier shone in cases of
civil law, for he knew how to take advantage of every clause and
comma, but he lacked the gift of melting hearts and drawing tears. In
any case, that was not his purpose; in his opinion Marshal Pétain was
not responsible for his actions. His voice was lost under the lofty
ceiling and he could not manage to make himself heard. His starchy,
conventional style was capable of influencing a board of directors, but
not a body of men who were going to pronounce on the honor of a
king.

Nonetheless, reading his second speech twenty years later, I find it
impressive. Better constructed than his first, it rests on a solid
foundation.

First of all he summarized the point of view held by Laval and his
colleagues. In 1940 it seemed that Great Britain was bound to suffer
the same fate as France in a very short time, and that Germany was
going to dominate Europe; in order to escape destruction, it was
essential to come to an understanding with the victor. And yet Pétain
believed in a British victory, and he had given too many proofs of
his hatred for Germany for anyone to believe that he had changed. So
he hedged. For the time being, there could be no question of resisting
the occupying power, as even de Gaulle admitted in London. The
Marshal therefore urged the people of France to avoid giving
grounds for reprisals, and confined himself to not giving the Germans what they asked for.

Was this a double game? A famous writer—for some reason Bâtonnier Payen didn't say it was François Mauriac—had written: "If the Marshal had played the Nazi card to counterbalance de Gaulle, who was playing the British card . . . it would have been excusable." The Marshal had never played the Nazi card. He had used the classic tactics of the weak man confronting the strong man. He had employed cunning like Scharnhorst in 1806—"Our system will consist exclusively of hedging, of avoiding any engagement and of flattering"—or like Thiers in 1871, who offered Field Marshal Manteuffel the hospitality of his own home.

He had refused to give Germany the bases she demanded in North Africa and at Dakar, refused to go to Berlin, refused to approve the Darlan memorandum, and refused to declare war on England. The guarantees which were extracted from him were worthless. And then old age had taken its toll. A colonel in the Medical Corps had recorded a remark made by Laval: "Oh, you know, he's all right for three or four hours a day, especially in the morning, when he's rested, because he's well looked after and waited on hand and foot. But when he's tired, especially in the evening, you can get him to sign anything you like and he doesn't know a thing." The discussion of Laval's notorious statement that he hoped for a German victory had taken place late one afternoon.

Maître Lemaire leaned across to Maître Isorni.

"This is going to be horrible," he whispered.

The Marshal stirred in his armchair and made angry gestures of denial. As usual he was furious at being regarded as senile. The Bâtonnier did not press the point. Marshal Pétain, he explained, had given way because that was the lesser of two evils. He had written a reassuring letter to Hitler to get him to swallow the dismissal of Laval, and had employed a great many other tricks and stratagems. If he had remained silent, who would have borne the consequences of his silence? Monsieur Léon Noël had criticized the Marshal for not putting up more of a resistance, but when the British had invaded Syria, even General de Gaulle had made only a verbal protest.

Prudent, patient and cunning, Pétain had won every battle after his

own fashion. Every time he could, he disowned his official pronouncements in private conversation. When, under considerable pressure by the German authorities, he broadcast his terrible message of
June 1944, he summoned the central committee of the French Legion
of Combatants the same evening to say that he retracted every word
and wished that to be clearly understood. The only congratulations he
had sent in connection with the failure of the Dieppe landing had
been to the local population on the dignity of its endurance. The
notorious telegram was a forgery.

"I know whom I'm talking to," said Bâtonnier Payen. "I'm
talking to intelligent men, conscientious men; consequently it isn't by
shouting or screaming that I'm likely to convince them."

In a good-natured tone of voice, and speaking as if this were
merely a case of embezzlement that was being tried, the Bâtonnier
went on with his argument. Marshal Pétain had camouflaged stocks of
arms, built up an army capable of fighting behind the German lines,
stood firm in the face of enemy propaganda, sent the Americans the
blueprints of France's tanks, obtained the liberation of prisoners of
war in exchange for a handshake, dispatched messengers to London,
and reassured Churchill by appointing a Minister of National Education who boasted of his friendship with Lord Halifax. With regard
to de Gaulle, the Marshal had written in his own hand the following
comment on the death sentence passed upon him: "It goes without
saying that that sentence passed in the absence of the accused could
only be theoretical. It was never my intention to have it carried out."
As for the Syrian affair, could he conceivably have acted any differently?

Unfortunately the Bâtonnier's audience was bored. The accused
was asleep and his features seemed to be marked with a sadness not
far removed from despair. The jurors kept stifling yawns. One of
them opened a newspaper and immersed himself in a report of the
Socialist Congress. His neighbors had to nudge him to persuade him
to put the paper back in his pocket.

Bâtonnier Payen went stubbornly on, taking advantage of his
client's drowsiness to produce evidence of his lack of responsibility.

He quoted a letter from one of the Marshal's advisers: "Right from the start I often maintained that the poor Marshal was the victim of a positive conspiracy. Those around him kept the truth from him, under the pretext of humoring him, or else openly deceived him, or else shilly-shallied with him indefinitely."

Stung by these insulting allegations, the Marshal opened his eyes, flushed scarlet and stirred in his seat. At a quarter past three the hearing was adjourned.

"He's pleaded senility," the Marshal said angrily to Isorni.

And imitating a boxer, he added, "Just let him put on the gloves with me!"

"Oh, if only it had been Moro!" people were saying. Maître de Moro-Giafferi, who had been seen in the refreshment room, had not even come near the First Chamber. If he had been in Bâtonnier Payen's place, he would have thumped his papers, uttered roars of anger, drawn laughter and tears from his audience, shown the futility of the prosecution's case, and triumphantly proved his client's innocence.

Isorni's mouth was parched. For a moment he wondered whether he had been wrong to take the pills which the ferocious Madeleine Jacob, touched by his plight, had offered him during the adjournment. Had anyone ever seen a supporter give a member of the opposing team the means to put up a better fight? But the journalists had gradually come to feel a genuine regard for this lawyer, and recognized that the defense depended on his zeal and conviction. After the goal scored by the Attorney General, in a difficult and often mediocre match, the defense could still force a draw, and perhaps even win the day. Without daring to say so, the press almost hoped it would. Isorni was a more likable figure than Monsieur Mornet. "Slumped in a velvet chair," Maître Isorni wrote later, "I must have looked rather green about the gills. To revive me, Madame Pétain simply offered me some Vittel water in the Marshal's glass." When the hearing was resumed after an adjournment lasting fifty minutes, the lawyer had some difficulty getting back to his bench.

"Maître Iscrni, I call upon you to speak," said Monsieur Mongibeaux.

The microphone which had just been installed on the presiding
judge's table relayed these words through the loudspeaker in the press
room.

Isorni stood up, rigid with fear, a mist swimming in front of his
eyes.

"Gentlemen of the High Court, day after day I have heard the
words *Armistice, Montoire, Syria, National Assembly.* And now and
then I have had the feeling . . ."

The brassy voice carried well. Little by little it gained assurance.
The public quivered with pleasure as a breath of youth swept through
the courtroom and a mysterious bond of sympathy was established
between the lawyer and those listening to him. Isorni had only to
appear for his cause to be half won, just as at the theater an actor can
produce the miracle of belief in what he is saying by his mere
presence, and carry the audience with him. Nothing mattered any
more but the tragedy drawing to its close. Isorni had finally abolished
the boredom, heat and anguish of the last hearing. Defended by him,
the accused was no longer a tired old man, but King Philippe VII
come home to his people to justify himself.

"The moral concessions which were likely to reflect on the leader's
honor were borne by the leader alone. But the material advantages
were for whom? They were for the French people."

Without causing any offense to the Attorney General, Isorni
cleverly turned to his own advantage the argument the prosecution
had used in favor of the judges who had continued to hear cases
during the Occupation. "What would have happened without us?"
the Attorney General had asked. It was easy to conclude that Marshal
Pétain had rendered the same service to the country. Little by little,
as Isorni went on speaking, another picture emerged of the old
monarch of Vichy bravely and cautiously setting the weight of his
inertia and his glory against the Germans.

"The question was whether the French were going to sentence
fewer men themselves to prevent the Germans from sentencing

more. . . . There was no crime, gentlemen. There was the most tragic problem of conscience which has ever faced a government caught between two horrors. He believed that he had chosen the lesser of the two."

Every time an appeal for mercy had been submitted to him, the Marshal had granted a reprieve.

"He is a man who may have sacrificed legal principles, and who, once again, may have made moral concessions, but a man who had only one aim and purpose, namely, to save human lives."

The Germans had obliged him, against his will and against his feelings, to make statements which hurt him far more than those who heard them. Could anyone seriously maintain that if it had not been for him there would have been no French workers in Germany? The Germans had asked for over two million workers. They had received six hundred thousand. They had demanded women. Not a single Frenchwoman had gone to Germany.

"He promulgated a law forbidding a certain number of Jews to carry out their normal activities. . . . But it was he who, at a meeting of the Council of Ministers, insisted on a decree making exceptions in the case of war veterans and their families. It was he who prevented the wearing of the yellow star in the Unoccupied Zone. It was he, and he alone, who prevented the promulgation of the law to deprive all Jews naturalized since 1927 of their citizenship. Beyond you, I address all those Jews who have suffered and who today accuse Marshal Pétain. I ask them this question: 'If you had to live through it all again, would you prefer not to have an Unoccupied Zone where you could find temporary shelter, even though it was under Marshal Pétain's authority?' Out of five and a half million Jews living in Poland in 1939, three million four hundred thousand were murdered by the Nazis. In Warsaw only five thousand out of four hundred thousand survived."

His features tense, his high forehead gleaming in the sunlight, and brandishing the innocence of his King before his audience, Isorni was tearing his heart out. His warm voice, growing louder and louder to become a prophetic thunder, swept away one by one the accusations made by the Attorney General, who sat huddled in his seat with his hunched back settled deep in his stall.

"Gentlemen of the Resistance . . ."

Isorni left his bench and walked out into the center of the courtroom, in front of the accused and a little behind the place where the witnesses had given their evidence.

". . . I turn particularly to you."

The seven columns of the *Journal officiel* which contain the rest of Isorni's speech will long be treasured as a model of legal eloquence. A breath of life passed through the feverish, crowded courtroom like a wind that blows up suddenly and makes the earth groan. "Isorni looked like an archangel," Madeleine Jacob wrote in admiration. For half an hour everyone believed that Pétain was in truth the saint and martyr described by the lawyer, the leader of the French Resistance admired by men of integrity and lauded by the greatest poet in the Académie française: "Sir, at Verdun you undertook, planned, personified that immortal resistance." None of the atrocities perpetrated by the police or the militia had been given his approval. Crimes had sometimes been committed in his name of which he knew nothing, and if Darnand had become a minister . . .

"Gentlemen, a murderer was not appointed a minister; a minister was appointed who became a murderer. The distinction is important."

When he had learned of the horrors that were being perpetrated, the Marshal wrote to Pierre Laval, admittedly rather late in the day:

It is important that Monsieur Darnand, Secretary General of the Militia and Secretary of State for the Interior, should take urgent measures to prevent the drama which is looming up; otherwise, when France is liberated one day, she will see her territory transformed into a vast battlefield for the settling of scores, and the French people will once again have to pay the price for this new fratricidal struggle.

Now, said Isorni, the whole country was suffering from the scourge of banditry. Men were claiming to be members of the Resistance simply in order to kill with impunity. It was said that since the Liberation one hundred thousand Frenchmen, a third of the number handed over to the Germans, had died.

Isorni looked straight at the two jurors who had caused him the most trouble during the trial. They were sitting together, the inscrutable Lévêque, his arms folded across his Air Force tunic, and Germinal, the man with the revolutionary name, tight-lipped and hard-eyed. He could feel them wavering.

"I can still hear, gentlemen," he went on, "a cry which came from this side of the High Court. One of the jurors exclaimed, 'What about our dead?' Believe me, we mourn those dead together. But other Frenchmen have also died at the hands of the Germans, Frenchmen who died shouting, 'Long live the Marshal!' You have cited the depositions of the dead. You have let us hear the evidence of the persecuted. You have revived the memory of the captives. Well, let me in my turn call to the bar those who are alive, those who have been set free, those who have been protected. You have heard the voices of the men who went away; let me hear the voices of the women who stayed behind. Let them all come today to stand by the Marshal and let them in their turn protect him who protected them. . . ."

No one could resist Isorni's lyricism. He seemed to be possessed by a divine force as he stretched out imploring arms. The faith consuming him spread like a fire stoked by the wind. The accused, deeply moved, sat hunched in the depths of his armchair. Everyone was holding his breath. Tears were beginning to roll down people's cheeks. "It seems to me," wrote Madeleine Jacob, "that when, in years to come, people talk about the Pétain trial, it is the name of Maître Isorni that will dominate the whole story." Even today, there are men who, although they were not present at the trial, quote passages from Isorni's speech by heart, twenty years later, so moved were they by the extracts published in the press at that time.

Now Isorni, panting for breath, was agreeing to accompany Marshal Pétain to his death if sentence of death was passed upon him, but warning the judges that they would be present, wherever they might be, at the execution.

"You will all be there! And in the depths of your horror-stricken souls you will see how this Marshal of France you have condemned to death accepts that death. And that noble, ashen face will never leave you as long as you live. . . . Since when have our people set Genevieve, the protector of the city, against Joan, who freed the land? Since when have they been at daggers drawn, irreconcilable foes? Since when have French hands stubbornly refused to take other French hands stretched out beseechingly? O my country, victorious but torn asunder! When will there be an end to the shedding of blood, blood all the more precious now that we know that only our brothers are left to shed it? When will our nation cease to be divided? Gentlemen, at this very moment, when peace has at last come to the whole world, when the sound of battle has ceased and mothers have begun to breathe again, let peace, our peace, save our holy land from further torment! Judges of the High Court, listen to me, hear my plea. You are only judges. You are only judging a man. But you hold in your hands the destiny of France."

Silence fell abruptly, unexpectedly, as when a storm which has been raging all night suddenly ceases. Maître Isorni walked slowly back to his seat. Monsieur Mongibeaux, speaking almost in a whisper, declared the hearing adjourned. At once there arose a noise such as you hear in the woods when the wind falls upon the trees to ravage them. The Attorney General pushed his way through the crowd and clasped Isorni to his ermine-covered breast.

"Ah," he said, "you have expressed so well all my own feelings."

"It's disgraceful!" Bâtonnier Payen kept saying, shocked that any lawyer should have used such arguments in order to convince a jury.

In his room, Marshal Pétain embraced Isorni.

"I have never seen him so moved before," Madame Pétain said of her husband. "He regards you as his son."

When the hearing was resumed, it was a quarter past six. The light was no longer slanting through the windows, almost as if because Maître Isorni had passed by like a comet. Never before had Bâtonnier Payen's eloquence seemed so insipid. Never have I felt so puzzled about the choice of that sad, timid, uneasy lawyer to lead the defense. As I read his closing speech, even the merits I recognized in his arguments the day before vanished. Possibly because he began with a monumental blunder.

To demolish the accusation of collaboration, he recalled the impromptu speech the Marshal made in January 1942, during a visit to the National Council. "Gentlemen," he had said, "when you go back to your departments you may well be asked certain questions, notably this one: What does the Marshal think about collaboration? My reply, which I authorize you and indeed ask you to make known, is quite clear. I consider that collaboration is possible between two peoples only if those two peoples are on an equal footing."

The obvious implication was that if Germany had returned all her French prisoners, stimulated the recovery of the French economy, and recognized French authority over the Unoccupied Zone, the Marshal would have turned Franco-German friendship into a Franco-German alliance. How could Bâtonnier Payen have failed to understand that by pressing this point he was once again raising the doubts that Maître Isorni had swept away?

In the long, well-meaning speech which the Bâtonnier took nearly three hours to deliver, one looks in vain for anything which might have helped the accused. Bâtonnier Payen would have been well advised to cut his speech short, as the presiding judge suggested he might. But his touchy, sensitive vanity made it impossible for him to believe that Isorni had won the day by himself. He even went so far in his scrupulous folly as to produce further documents in support of the points Isorni had raised. Unfortunately, on Bâtonnier Payen's lips everything became petty and commonplace once more, and his repeated insistence that the jury had to believe him only increased their suspicions. As for his style, it was mediocrity itself.

Besides, how could Bâtonnier Payen have imagined that the jury were going to believe the stories he told them? The story of the Marshal giving secret orders to welcome the Americans to North Africa in November 1942? Or the story of the Marshal slapping the

American chargé d'affaires on the back and humming the Marseillaise as he handed over his protest at Roosevelt's message and at the North African landings? This trial of an old man, which a young man had almost won, was in danger of being lost by another old man.

Luckily for the accused, his defense counsel was so boring that nobody listened to him. The light was gradually fading, and judges and jury found the encroaching shadows tempting. They had only to abandon themselves to them to fall asleep. Only the Marshal seemed to be excited by the approaching end of the trial. He was seized with a sort of impatience which led him to comment by word or gesture on his counsel's speech.

"That's ancient history," he said when the Bâtonnier quoted Ribbentrop's letter once more.

Alas, Bâtonnier Payen spared the audience nothing. They waited for him to start praising de Gaulle, recalling Louis XVI and quoting Michelet. The walls looked as if they were hung with pink-gray tapestry. Finally the long peroration drew to a reluctant close. A last burst of passion shook the Bâtonnier's dull voice and brought out a hiccup like the bark of a dog.

"Yes, I feel confident. I was about to say, 'whatever your decision might be,' but I refuse to entertain any doubts as to your decision. There remain three words to be added, which must be the last words to echo round this courtroom. I utter those words, I shout them out with all my heart, in my name, in his name, and I trust in the names of all those present: *Vive la France!"*

The lawyer's arms fell to his sides, and suddenly it was seen that he was crying. There was a short burst of applause at the back of the courtroom.

"Accused," said the presiding judge, "have you anything to add in your defense?"

"Yes, I would like to speak."

He stood up. His face, which had suddenly turned crimson, was hidden by the stifling gloom. Holding himself very erect, speaking in a loud, panting voice, and without the aid of his spectacles, he read out, as on the first day of the trial, a statement which his lawyers had hurriedly prepared.

"In the course of this trial I have deliberately remained silent, after explaining to the people of France the reasons for my attitude. My only thought was to remain on French soil, in accordance with my promise, in an attempt to protect them and alleviate their sufferings. Come what may, they will not forget. They know that I defended them as I defended Verdun. Gentlemen of the High Court, my life and liberty are in your hands, but my honor I entrust to my country. Deal with me according to your consciences. My conscience is clear, for on the threshold of death I can say that during my long life I have never had any other ambition than to serve France."

He lowered his hands and fell silent.

"The hearing is closed," said the presiding judge. "The court will now retire to deliberate."

It was five past nine.

Everyone hurried along the dark, echoing corridors toward the refreshment room. Darkness had fallen, and the arms and helmets of the guards gleamed in the faint glow of the lights. Policemen were sitting at the foot of the Sainte-Chapelle with handkerchiefs spread on their knees, eating snacks. At the fork in the Seine, above the arches of the Pont Neuf and the roofs of the Louvre which hid the city from sight, the sky was turning crimson.

XXIII

❧

The Night of August 14–15, 1945

The Palais de Justice suddenly emptied. In the deserted First Chamber, where the air still smelt of sweat and tears, of the women's perfume and the gendarmes' leather, a man calmly sat down on the witnesses' bench, as if he were beginning a vigil. It was Dr. Paul, the police surgeon. The twenty-four jurors were invited to the President's chambers where a buffet loaded with cold hake and mayonnaise, cheese and fruit, hurriedly bought by the judicial authorities, had been set up under blazing lights as if for a banquet. The malaise felt by the simpler-minded jurors swiftly gave way to joy at the prospect of satisfying hunger and thirst. They ogled the rows of bottles of wine and mineral water. There were no waiters because of the need for complete secrecy.

"Help yourselves, gentlemen."

The jurors suddenly looked at the man who had just issued this invitation, and who was standing beneath the full-length portrait of the bewigged and red-robed Guillaume de Lamoignon, the President of the Court of Appeal in 1677. To their surprise they recognized Monsieur Mongibeaux. Without his robes or his hood, and dressed in an ordinary suit, he looked like a provincial poet, with his little goatee and his bow tie. His two assessors, Monsieur Donat-Guigue and Monsieur Picard, likewise stripped of their pomp, said nothing.

235

So *that* was what they looked like in private, those judges endowed by their official apparel with the dignity of high priests!

Glasses were filled and emptied. The small company was separated from the city and its noise by curtains hiding the starless night and by armed guards standing at the doors. The oppressive languor which had bent the jurors' shoulders had given place to a solemn tranquillity: each juror was trying to rid himself of feelings of hatred or indulgence in order to listen only to his conscience. The company ate heartily, standing up.

Once the fruit had been finished, the presiding judge opened the door of the jury room.

"Gentlemen," he said in a debonair voice with a hint of a Périgord accent, "if you will be so kind as to come in and sit down, we can begin our discussion."

The jurors followed him. On the dark paneled walls hung the portraits of all the former Presidents of the Court of Appeal, intimidating figures with their pale faces fringed with beards or side whiskers, and their crimson robes loaded with ermine and decorations, old-fashioned symbols of a justice which authority had made grandiose and liturgical so that men should believe in it.

The jurors sat down under the chandelier which lit up two narrow tables placed together and covered with a tasseled green cloth. Over a big black marble mantelpiece an anonymous bust was set in a medallion. Nobody dared to ask to whom the grim, bearded face belonged, and even today scarcely anyone knows. Some of the ushers think it is Henri IV, to whom it bears a certain resemblance. It is, in fact, Achille I de Harlay, Counselor and then President of the Court of Appeal in the sixteenth century, who stood up to the Duc de Guise.

Although the windows were shut, everyone suddenly heard the sound of a pile of arms falling to the ground outside, followed by shouts from the guards.

"Gentlemen of the jury, my assessors and I wish to ask you whether you would agree to a sentence of five years' exile."

Everyone leaned forward to look at Monsieur Mongibeaux. Had

they heard him correctly? Voices were raised in protest. The jurors were annoyed at Monsieur Mongibeaux's casual assumption that an acquittal was a matter of course and that it could be agreed on within a few minutes.

Monsieur Picard sensed their disquiet and spoke first. He was sitting on the left of Monsieur Mongibeaux, as in the courtroom. Grave-faced, he slowly read out his observations. He did not believe in either the plot against the Republic or Pétain's guilt. He held forth at length on the meaning of the verb "to betray," *"tradere"* in Latin, and expressed the opinion that the Marshal had acted out of political ambition. In his view everything could be explained by senility. He gave his audience to understand that he would not vote in favor of the death sentence. Some of the jurors picked their teeth as they listened to him.

Monsieur Donat-Guigue in turn slowly expounded his conviction that treason had not been proved, and then asked the leader of the parliamentary jurors, Monsieur Gabriel Delattre, who was sitting opposite Monsieur Mongibeaux, to give his opinion.

This slight, bespectacled, gentle-faced man, a former trial lawyer himself, had taken little part in the trial. For three-quarters of an hour he spoke of Vichy, Laval, Hitler, Pétain, and the repercussions the verdict would have at home and abroad.

After him the former Minister Pierre-Bloch launched into a fierce harangue. Grim-faced, and speaking clearly and incisively, he said that the gravity of the occasion was such that nobody should beat about the bush. If there were some jurors who wanted the death sentence and others who wanted hard labor or acquittal, they should speak their minds clearly.

"I would be grateful," he added firmly, "if Monsieur Donat-Guigue would tell us what sentences are entailed by Article 80 of the Penal Code on the one hand and Articles 75 and 87 on the other."

"Well," answered Monsieur Donat-Guigue, "Article 80 entails a sentence of hard labor for life, but the law states that this penalty does not exist for persons aged over seventy. On the other hand, Articles 75 and 87 entail the death sentence."

Monsieur Pierre-Bloch asked for a vote to be taken on a show of hands before there was any further discussion. This was agreed to, except that a majority of the jurors called for a secret ballot. Each voting paper was to carry the figure 75, for death, or the figure 80, for hard labor. The smoke from the jurors' cigarettes floated in front of their expressionless faces, and then went straight up toward the chandelier before disappearing in the shadows beneath the ornate plaster ceiling. The ballot box was passed around the table in the midst of an uneasy silence.

Monsieur Mongibeaux solemnly turned it upside down and unfolded the voting papers one by one, arranging them on the table in front of him, the 75's for death on the left and the 80's for hard labor on the right.

"It must be clearly understood, gentlemen, that the result of the vote which we have just taken simply gives us an idea of your opinions and is in no way binding on you for the final vote which will be taken later."

Everyone agreed. From the courtyard of the Palais de Justice came the sound of men's laughter. At first the votes were evenly distributed, but suddenly the 75's piled up and crushed the 80's. By eighteen votes to eight* the jurors and assessors had voted for the death sentence. Provisionally.

The Marshal dined in his room with his wife, then stretched out on his bed. The chaplain was due to come at midnight to say Mass. In spite of the heat, the Marshal had only taken off his belt. He was breathing gently, almost indifferent to the drama being enacted a few paces from him. He missed Isorni's company; he would have liked to have him with him. For the first time he was unable to control his nerves completely, as he had done in all the crises in which he had been faced with a choice. He was not cut out for the role of accused, and several times during the trial he had been unable to refrain from showing his annoyance.

* The presiding judge did not cast his vote until later (see p. 244).

Suddenly his features relaxed into something resembling a smile. To the great relief of the politicians, he had become in turn a military leader, a prince, and then a king by the will of the people. And he had always had to resist blandishments and pressure. Now everyone had forgotten how badly they had needed him. The only mistake he admitted making was his failure to demand a referendum ratifying his accession to power in 1940; by an overwhelming majority the French people would have confirmed his title of head of state and approved of that Armistice which the Gaullists regarded as a crime.

Had he been misled by the enthusiasm that accompanied him everywhere? Borne aloft on a wave of cheering as on a triumphal shield every time he had visited the Occupied Zone, had he been ingenuous enough to let his popularity go to his head? As late as 1944, here in Paris itself, his car had been almost submerged by the crowds. But de Gaulle had had the same reception when he walked down the Champs Élysées three months later. A bitter line creased the old man's cheeks.

The crowds were the same who now shouted, "Long live de Gaulle!" And not a word, not a sign had come from the ambitious young man whom he had defended against the pontiffs of the École de Guerre, who had already tried to rob him of his literary fame before robbing him of his military glory, and who would not hesitate to use his dead body as a steppingstone to supreme power. De Gaulle had remained deaf to every offer to present him with a legitimate succession to the throne, and Pétain was sure that he would not make a single conciliatory gesture. The proud rebel wanted a victory due only to himself and his insubordination.

Yet it would have taken so little, in 1940, to bring de Gaulle into Pétain's Cabinet. In giving way to Weygand, who didn't want a young puppy who had treated him to some cutting comments to be put in command of five-star generals, the old man had shown a lack of flair for the first time in his life. When General Colson, the Minister of War, suggested de Gaulle as Under Secretary of State, General Weygand, the Minister of National Defense, replied, "You've no idea what trouble you're asking for!" Pétain saw a chance of taking his revenge for the way his ideas had been used in *France and Her Army*, and smilingly acquiesced. He ought to have overruled Weygand. When de Gaulle had come to greet him at his table in the sinister Hôtel Splendide at Bordeaux on June 15, 1940, a single word from Pétain would have done the trick. Since then he had often amused himself thinking of what he might have said. "My dear de Gaulle, here is our country once again at grips with tragic events. Forget, as I shall forget, all that has separated us, and think only of what unites us. Help me to save our country. I need you by my side."

He gave a brief chuckle at the idea. What would de Gaulle have done if he had joined his Cabinet? He would have helped to conclude the Armistice. And how would he have fought the occupying power? With cunning. Pétain would have pushed irony to the extent of sending him to sign the Berlin agreements in place of General Juin. De Gaulle's rebellion had been just a question of pique. But if he had stayed, who would have wielded the sword?

The Marshal did not have time to answer that question. The door opened. Was it midnight already? Canon Pottevin, whom the police had smuggled into the Palais de Justice by way of the gloomy underground passages, came in, bowed, and took his vestments, the chalice and the silver-plated paten out of his bag. He was a little man with powerful jaws and a rather prominent nose. The Marshal liked him because he had a kindly face whereas so many ecclesiastics looked like renegades. The nuns arranged a cloth, candlesticks and tiny altar cruets on the black marble mantelpiece under its big mirror, and held out the chasuble and the white silk stole. At the Pontifical Mass at Notre Dame, that morning of the Assumption of Our Lady to which Louis XIII had dedicated the Kingdom of France in 1638, the archbishop and his clergy would be bent under the heavy gold-embroidered vestments which had not been used since the solemn prayers which Paul Reynaud and his government had attended on May 19, 1940.

"*Introibo ad altare Dei*," said the canon, making the sign of the cross.

The nuns' voices chanted the response. *"Ad Deum qui laetificat juventutem meam. . . ."*

The Marshal remained standing until the Offertory, then sat down. Would they be celebrating his own assumption in a few hours' time? Two days before, he had said to one of the nuns, "We shall soon know. I should like you to pray for me." In the liturgy that morning, everything was redolent of joy.

The canon wondered whether this jubilation of the Church, at the very moment when the jury were deliberating, might not be a sign of hope. He intentionally picked out the passage from the Forty-fifth Psalm which served as an introduction to the Gospel: *"Propter veritatem et mansuetudinem et justitiam. . . ."* Wasn't it also for the cause of truth, mercy and justice that the Marshal, whom he could hear breathing behind him, had fought all his life? He included his name in the Prayers for the Living. But how long would he remain among the living?

The old man was having trouble following the prayers. What did that matter? He had felt at peace ever since he had made his confession and taken Communion—in secret, to avoid public comment. He recalled the day when the clergy and the military and civil authorities had been waiting for him outside the porch of the Cathedral of Trèves where a Verdun anniversary was being celebrated. To the astonishment of his staff, he had ordered his driver to draw up at one of the side doors, through which he had entered the Cathedral in his sky-blue cape with his baton in his hand, forcing the procession to do a spectacular about-turn to join him. That day de Gaulle had said admiringly, "The Marshal is an artist and the greatest actor of our times." Everywhere bishops and cardinals in *capa magna* had waited for him with processions of canons and seminarists to conduct him to his throne in the chancel, to the thunder of Bach chorales from the organ. The deacon used to come and cense him.

Now chaplains crept through the darkness to hurry through Low Masses in courtroom buildings and fortresses, and soon perhaps . . .

Isorni had tried to convince the Marshal that the death sentence which he regarded as inevitable would enhance his fame. Isorni had a peculiar sense of humor. And he could be wrong.

In the refreshment room the din of voices was growing louder. Wine and beer were flowing like water. At some tables people were drinking brandy and liqueurs. Journalists and lawyers kept coming up to the defense attorneys, who were still in their robes, to offer their congratulations. The *choucroute* served by the overworked waiters had done something to stave off hunger. People were crowded together on the benches and in front of the bar. Through the open windows they could see the gates opening and more police vans lining up in the yard beside the radio truck entangled in its cables. It was one o'clock in the morning. Press correspondents were telephoning to their papers, which had at last received their extra supplies of newsprint and were getting ready to rush out special editions. Every now and then someone went off to look at the silent night, coming back a little later. There was no light filtering out of the jury room, but a bell had rung once or twice to summon a secretary or a clerk.

As it was forbidden to leave the Palais de Justice before the verdict had been read out, some of the journalists went back to the First Chamber, where a few bulbs were shedding a funereal light, settled down in the jurors' armchairs and dropped off to sleep. In the public section of the courtroom spectators were standing about, whispering among themselves.

The discussion in the jury room was dragging on. The eighteen votes for the death sentence in the preliminary ballot seemed to have upset the jurors. Monsieur Delattre continued his argument against the supreme penalty.

"Who knows," he said, "whether in a few years Pétain may not be regarded as innocent and our sons may not suffer for having as fathers the men who killed him?"

Then he described the execution: a former Marshal of France dragged into the ditches of a fortress and shot like a traitor, his blood staining the earth. . . . René Bénard supported him.

Monsieur Lévy-Alphandéry, the Radical-Socialist Deputy for the Marne, a man of ninety like Pétain, who out of prudence had abstained from the famous vote in the National Assembly in July 1940, expounded the moral problem confronting him. As a patriot from an old Alsatian family he condemned Pétain, but as a Jew he could not help feeling grateful to him for having protected his coreligionists.

Monsieur Pierre-Bloch spoke up again to make a sharp reply. He was a Jew too, but he felt no inhibitions either as a juror or as a man. In his view there could be no doubt that Pétain had committed treason. He read out again Pétain's letter to Hitler of December 11, 1943, in reply to attacks by Ribbentrop: "I recalled Monsieur Laval to power in 1942 because I thought he was capable of getting the people of France to understand and accept the policy which had led me to ask for the Armistice. . . ." In his opinion the last words of the sentence provided a key to the Marshal's ideas, which had already been formulated in the same terms on January 11, 1942. Pierre-Bloch believed that it was out of hatred of the Republican regime, and not in order to trick the enemy, that the French head of state had thought of concluding an alliance with Hitler. Pétain had turned a deaf ear to the appeals of King George VI and President Roosevelt. As for what posterity might decide, Pierre-Bloch preferred to think of the widows of his comrades who had been shot by the Germans during Pétain's reign.

Several jurors voiced their approval of what he had said. Pierre Stibbe, Jean Seignon, Lecompte-Boinet, General Mangin's son-in-law, and the Christian Trade-Unionist Maurice Guérin. Pierre-Bloch added that he could understand people feeling qualms about having an old man shot, but that he was there to judge a trial for treason and nothing else, and that nobody would understand if subordinates were sentenced to death and not their leader. On the other hand, de Gaulle could order a reprieve for reasons of state. Pierre-Bloch had no objection to the jury's making a recommendation of mercy.

A confused discussion followed, which Monsieur Mongibeaux failed to control. It recalled the dialogue in Byron's play after Doge Marino Faliero has been sentenced to death:

"He hath been guilty, but there may be mercy."
"Not in this case with justice."
"Alas! Signor, he who is only just is cruel; who upon the earth would live were all judged justly?"
"His punishment is safety to the state."
"He was a subject, and hath served the state; he was your general, and hath served the state; he is your sovereign, and hath ruled the state."
"He is a traitor, and betrayed the state."

About one o'clock in the morning some of the jurors called for a vote. In a silence even more oppressive than the first time, the ballot box was passed around the table. As the President counted the votes the verdict remained in doubt for a long time. In turn the advocates of mercy and the partisans of firmness thought they had won the day. Finally, by fourteen votes to thirteen, Marshal Pétain was sentenced to death. Nine of the Resistance jurors had probably voted for the supreme penalty. The other five votes for the death sentence could only have come from the parliamentary jurors. These included Monsieur Louis Prot, the Deputy for the Somme, to whom the defense had raised no objection, not realizing that he was a Communist, and six Socialists. This meant that at the last moment two Socialists had changed their mind. The Communist decided the issue. Another possibility is that the scales were tipped by General Mangin's son-in-law, who had been won over by Monsieur Pierre-Bloch.

With no sign of emotion, Monsieur Mongibeaux took some papers out of his pocket, and after putting on one side those he had prepared for Pétain's acquittal, read out the grounds for the death sentence. A committee of five jurors under the chairmanship of Pierre-Bloch started working out a final version, giving treason precedence over the plot against the Republic.

About half past two in the morning, the new text was read out to the full assembly. Immediately afterward Pierre Stibbe asked for military degradation to be added to the dishonor of the death sentence. Pierre-Bloch opposed this suggestion, much to the relief of the presiding judge and his assessors, and asked Monsieur Mongibeaux to read out the text referring to the penalty of national indignity. The jury then discovered that anyone sentenced to national indignity lost his rank, his decorations and even his property, and Pierre-Bloch suggested that this was the penalty they should inflict. Another vote was taken. By eighteen votes to four, with five abstentions, the penalty of national indignity was adopted. The presiding judge sent for a secretary to type out the court's judgment. A recommendaton of mercy was immediately circulated among the jurors, and collected seventeen signatures.

The rumor went around the refreshment room that the end was drawing near. The defense lawyers went to see the accused. He was resting again on his bed, with his hands on the buckle of his belt as if he were dying. As they stood at his bedside, they lowered their voices.

It was after four o'clock in the morning when the bell rang to mark the resumption of the hearing. The Palais de Justice suddenly came to life. Lights lit up. Orders were barked out. In the dark, under the threatening sky, squads of police took up their positions. Two police vans, an ambulance, cars and motorcyclists lined up in the courtyards. People who had been sleeping on the benches in the halls and corridors rushed toward the First Chamber, which was packed to the doors within a few moments. Oddly enough, the usher forgot to light the big chandeliers, and a mournful half-light filled the courtroom.

The judges and jurors slowly went to their places, their faces pale. The seats of the six deputy jurors, who had not taken part in the deliberations, remained empty. Monsieur Mongibeaux ordered the accused to be brought in. He appeared looking very pale, tugging at his tunic, and walking with a tired, mechanical gait, as if the spring driving him had almost worn out. He went over to his armchair and sat down. Attorney General Mornet, looking more hunchbacked than ever, settled into his seat, wrapped in his furs.

Monsieur Mongibeaux turned on the light on the table in front of him. The silence was so profound that everyone could hear the click of the switch. A wan light streamed out from under the green shade, illuminating the center of the courtroom and making the walls look darker. Anyone would have sworn that they had changed color. The blue-gray tint with which they had shone for twenty afternoons seemed to be swallowed up in the shadows. A few journalists thought that in the emotion of the moment Monsieur Mongibeaux had forgotten to remove his cap. It was not forgetfulness. Entrusted with the task of delivering the judgment of the court, and speaking in the name of the French people, he kept his mortarboard on his head to show, like those princes who enjoyed the privilege of remaining covered in the royal presence, that he bowed to no one.

"In the case which has just been heard," said Monsieur Mongibeaux, correcting the position of the microphone which was carrying his voice to the radio transmitter and to the loudspeaker near the press telephones, "whereas the High Court is not empowered to take into account alleged deeds and words preceding its constitution and of which it has not had direct cognizance; whereas it is irrelevant to . . ."

The preliminary observations took a long time. As Minister of War in the Doumergue Cabinet, where he met Pierre Laval, Pétain had imagined he could play a leading part in the nation's affairs. He had done nothing to discourage the press campaigns in his favor, remained in touch with the shady individuals who were trying to overthrow the regime, and announced in March 1940 that the country would soon have need of him. Appointed Prime Minister, he had asked for the Armistice, prevented the government from leaving France, and obtained supreme control of the state.

The accused cocked his head to one side, twisted his gloves in his hands, touched his kepi and then his lips under his mustache, and turned now and then to look at his lawyers standing stiffly in front of their bench. Bâtonnier Payen blew his nose, pressed his handkerchief to his lips, then stuffed it feverishly back in his pocket.

". . . after assuming power in those circumstances Pétain soon went on to abolish the Republican institutions. . . ."

Without conviction, and indeed with a certain awkwardness, the judge's voice recalled Laval's actions in the government, the meeting at Montoire, the concessions made to the Germans, the military moves in the Middle East, the Legion against Bolshevism, the policy of collaboration with Germany, the resistance to the Allied landings in North Africa, the appointment of Philippe Henriot as Minister of Propaganda and of Darnand as Secretary General for the Maintenance of Order, the European crusade of workers employed in Germany, the arrests and executions, and the acceptance of Hitler's violation of the Armistice.

". . . whereas during the hearings of the High Court, Pétain has systematically remained silent . . ."

By now the accused had fallen into a doze. Nobody ever discovered whether he had been overcome by fatigue or whether he had decided to go to sleep. In the corridors the journalists were standing near the loudspeakers, listening.

". . . whereas it is impossible to accept such a line of defense, and it is hard to understand how support for the Allies could take the form of help for the Germans; whereas, moreover . . ."

At twenty-one minutes past four Monsieur Mongibeaux finally paused, then raised his voice and went on reading. His only moment of grandeur was due to his resemblance to Benintende, Chief of the Council of Ten, announcing his sentence to the Doge: "Marino Faliero, Doge of Venice, Count of Val di Marino, Senator, and some time General of the Fleet and Army, noble Venetian, many times and oft intrusted by the state with high employments, even to the highest, listen to the sentence." The faces of the defense lawyers tightened. Bâtonnier Payen jerked his chin to one side. Isorni looked paler than ever. Monsieur Donat-Guigue seemed to sink back into the depths of his chair, as if he wanted to escape.

"Whereas in conclusion there is no doubt that he had dealings with Germany, a power at war with France, in order to cooperate with the enemy, crimes punishable under Articles 75 and 87 of the Penal Code, on these grounds the High Court of Justice sentences Pétain to the death penalty, national indignity, and the confiscation of his property. In view of the great age of the accused, the High Court of Justice recommends that the death sentence be not carried out."

In France, where the portraits of the country's kings are not displayed in line of succession, the place of King Philippe VII, unlike that of Marino Faliero in Venice, would not be covered with a black veil.

"Dealings with the enemy?" Twenty years later there is still no proof. The documents produced at subsequent trials, including the Nuremberg Tribunal, are not conclusive one way or the other. The most serious accusation against Pétain was made in the course of the Benoist-Méchin trial: it was said that on January 11, 1942, at a meeting of the Council of Ministers, Marshal Pétain decided to declare war on the Allies and side with Hitler. The accusation was based on Monsieur Benoist-Méchin's reports to Admiral Darlan after his conversations with Otto Abetz, the Reich's Ambassador to France, and a telegram from Otto Abetz to his Minister, Ribbentrop. In fact, it was not a question of a general or partial mobilization against the Allies, but of local operations which actually took place, and of the illusion cherished by Ambassador Abetz that he had succeeded in involving France in the war.

As for the meeting of the Council of Ministers on January 11, 1942, Pétain, questioned on the Île d'Yeu on January 15, 1947, denied that it had ever taken place, and nobody ever found any record of it. It is true that Ambassador Abetz stated in his telegram: "The persons who were present at this meeting all undertook to maintain absolute secrecy. Marshal Pétain authorized Benoist-Méchin to inform me about it." Did the meeting really take place, and if it did, how are we ever to discover the truth if it was in the interest of all the Council members to conceal it, both during their lives and after their deaths?

"What on earth shall I be able to say to him?" Marshal Pétain asked Laval when the latter told him of his imminent meeting with Hitler at Montoire.

Laval reassured him: Hitler talked all the time, and all one had to do was listen to him. But a report from Abetz dated October 8, 1940, recommended a meeting between the Chancellor and Pétain which he had been asked to arrange on the Marshal's behalf. Who was lying here? It seems to have been Pétain. But what were his motives? And who can say for certain that his intention was not to trick the enemy?

In 1945 the officers I was serving with exchanged only vague comments on the trial. Among my friends there were still a few who believed in Marshal Pétain. What did I think of Pétain being sentenced to death and reprieved at the same time? I would not have recommended a reprieve if I had voted for the death penalty. For age is no excuse, and treason, if you believe in it, must be paid for. In fact, I have only just learned now why I didn't know what to think then.

The fact is that there was neither innocence nor guilt, but simply a man confronted with political events and tried by politicians. Pétain was neither the Trojan horse of treason nor the savior of France, but simply an old man who tried to ward off the enemy's blows. When he heard the accused cry out, in the twilight of the First Chamber, "I defended you as I defended Verdun," Maurice Clavel, who was reporting the trial for *L'Époque,* wrote with tears in his eyes: "What if he were telling the truth?" Why, yes, that *was* the truth! Otherwise why should Pétain have taken the trouble to justify himself?

Throughout the Occupation, like a garrulous, debonair schoolmaster, he had insisted on lecturing his pupils, forever explaining to the French people the reasons for his attitude and theirs. A year before, almost to the day, on the point of leaving for Sigmaringen, he had written: "Everything I have accepted, agreed to, endured, whether willingly or not, was for your protection." He had not written any memoirs or adjusted events to suit his attitude. As thrifty with French blood as anyone could be, the man whom Renthe-Finck called "the old fox" or "Marshal *Immer Nein*" had done everything he could to trick the Germans, and had even managed to pay them in paper instead of gold to the extent of finally unloading assignats on them which did not even bear the stamp of the Banque de France.

Bernanos expressed indignation that defeat should have cost us less than victory. What a tragedy! France needed a Prince de Condé, and all she got was a liquidator! "My honor consists of staying at this post, facing danger without an army, without a fleet, in the midst of an unhappy population." An old man's honor, capable of arousing indignation and expressed in a dry little voice, but honor all the same. It was the honor of Marino Faliero, as expressed by Lord Byron:

> I have fought and bled; commanded, ay, and conquered;
> Have made and marred peace oft in embassies,
> As it might chance to be our country's vantage. . . .
> But would you know why I have done all this?
> Ask of the bleeding pelican why she
> Hath ripped her bosom? Had the bird a voice,
> She'd tell thee 'twas for *all* her little ones.

The High Priest of French renunciation, as Bernanos called him, loved to remain silent but never stopped talking. He used to ask his colleagues—one of whom is now a member of the Académie française—to write his speeches for him, like a schoolmaster assigning his class an essay. Then he took a word from one draft, a phrase from another, and after breaking everything up, he planned, filed and polished the fragments, which he fitted together, dictionary in hand, for days on end, trying out his effects on visitors until he arrived at the desired conciseness. Perhaps it intoxicated him to hear his own voice on the radio.

He hated traitors, yet he was on good terms with Philippe Henriot. He had created a petty France afraid of suffering, had chosen temporary submission for her in preference to rebellion, and had dragged us with him into obedience to misfortune behind a whole gang of milksops, shady politicians and scuttle-happy admirals who all loathed one another. Myth, illusion, traces of bygone glory, were all there, and even a touch of Gallic lechery as maids and countesses had their bottoms pinched on the way to the dinner table. With old age raised to the dignity of a system and a religion, Pétain was not so much a shield as an eiderdown, though admittedly an eiderdown so well stuffed with feathers that it took all the force out of the enemy's blows.

Why had he told Anatole de Monzie in March 1940 that the country would need him in May? "Old men and comets," wrote Jonathan Swift, "have been reverenced for the same reason: their long beards, and pretences to foretell events." Was Pétain's remark a whimsical sally, a premonition or an indication of a plot? Like every officer who suffered taunts and jeers in buses at that time, he was, wittingly or unwittingly, a supporter of the Cagoule. During the battle of Verdun he is alleged to have said to Poincaré, "The Constitution? I don't give a damn about it." What French officer hasn't said the same thing? If, in January 1958, de Gaulle had announced his return to power in May, would that have made him a traitor, and did you have to be a sorcerer to foresee it?

In that world of deceit in which few observers could see their way and Presidents of the Republic admitted that treaties were worthless once national security was at stake, Pétain had been called to power to ward off an unprecedented disaster, and his glory had been exalted to godlike proportions to make the country's shame a little more bearable. From then on, the old man, who had taken over the government at eighty-five after commanding a brigade at the age of retirement, had adopted the attitude of all old men: he had decided not to budge. Whatever misfortunes might occur, he would not leave the soil of France. Even in November 1942 he stayed at Vichy and, with a

dignity which never left him and attained the grandeur of self-sacrifice, transformed a political error into an act of nobility.
There is no Pétain mystery; with his common sense, prudence and self-control, the man possesses such glaring transparency that it is almost purity. He preferred dishonor to a snow-white charger, and he was innocent in his cunning. He believed that he was the personification of France, but so does de Gaulle, with even greater conviction and greater touchiness. Pétain imposed a maudlin, stay-at-home, vegetarian dictatorship on France, de Gaulle an absolute monarchy.

Too proud to be a plotter, too strong to be a mediocrity, too ambitious to be an *arriviste,* he nurtured in his solitude a passion for power which was strengthened over the years by his awareness of his own merits, by the obstacles he encountered, and by his contempt for others. Glory had once lavished her bitter caresses upon him. But she had not satisfied him, for want of loving him alone. And now, all of a sudden . . . events offered his pride and his gifts the long-awaited opportunity to spread their wings.

Is this de Gaulle portrayed by d'Astier or Pétain described by Mauriac?
The two characters bear an uncanny resemblance to each other, and one may reasonably wonder, twenty years later, whether drawing this sketch of his master in his memoirs, de Gaulle might not have been executing a self-portrait. Both in fact were born to reign, and, rivals in ambition, they were separated only by a defeat, accepted by one and rejected by the other. Both loved crowds and exhortations, and a grandiose military style mingled in private with racy expressions; both were prodigal of compliments for the common people and sparing with favors for their courtiers. One preoccupied in the winter of his life with weakness and the other with rebuffs, both were determined in their different ways to bring the kingdom to safety, Pétain shaking hands with Hitler and de Gaulle flirting with Marxism-Leninism. "If we deserved Pétain," wrote François Mauriac in *Le Figaro* of July 26, 1945,

we also, thank God, deserved de Gaulle: the spirit of surrender and the spirit of resistance found themselves personified in two Frenchmen, and measured swords in a duel to the death. But each of those two men represented far more than himself, and since the humblest of us shares the glory of the leader of the French Resistance, let us not forget that part of ourselves may at times have been guilty of complicity with that broken old man.

And Camus wrote on almost the same day: "We shall never know what he spared us; we shall never know what France would have been without Vichy."

Pétain allowed Darnand to torture and hand over patriots, but he saved the lives of other patriots; he despised the militia, but he tolerated it; he allowed the racial laws to be promulgated, but a gauleiter would have exterminated the Jews. There are Jews among his most ardent supporters as well as among his most implacable accusers, and all are right. If the Unoccupied Zone had enabled Bernanos to escape from Hitler to the Brazilian forests, he might perhaps have found extenuating circumstances in Pétain's case.

What I now know is that Pétain was not a traitor, and that none of us who loved and served him was a traitor. True, we felt very small and almost guilty beside our Free French comrades and the heroes of Bir Hakeim, who looked down at us with scorn. A perjurer had released us from our oaths of loyalty, but at the same time we had lost all faith in mankind and in our leaders. I found it impossible ever to attach myself to them again, rather as a child who has lost his father grudges his mother's new husband his affection.

If I had been there, I would have wiped away the spittle he was receiving full in the face, and I would have said to the condemned man: "Monsieur le Maréchal, I no longer love you because you did not give us back the pride we needed so badly, and because when you sacrificed your honor you also sacrificed ours. We were hungry for danger, glory and love. You gave us gall and wormwood. On the day he died, Charles de Foucauld wrote these words to a friend—words which Colonel Rémy finds deeply moving: 'Let us leave honor to anyone who wants it.' It is all very well to preach that between red clay walls in the middle of a desert when you are a saint. But if soldiers have no honor, they waste away and die. Honor will always be their daily bread, and woe to him who deprives them of it. It was because de Gaulle later chose justice in preference to honor that they rebelled against him in Algeria, eaten up with honor and taking new oaths no one had asked them to swear. I might well have committed the same folly if I had still been in the services and if my mother had been alive.

"Perhaps you, too, were a saint, Monsieur le Maréchal. But in 1940 your disciple de Gaulle chose rebellion. He risked what awaited you five years later: prison walls, barred windows, solitude, parcels opened and ransacked, a visit from your wife once a week in the presence of a third person, and no furniture save a camp bed, a pitcher and bowl, a sagging armchair, and a mess tin on a bare table. Who would have felt any pity for him? You perhaps, and you would have set him free, for you were more generous than he. Besides, if it hadn't been for us, there would have been no drama. If, in order to obey you, we hadn't been obliged to scuttle our ships or fire on our brothers-in-arms when they rebelled against you, there would have been no problems of conscience. So many boys born at that period were called Philippe after you. So much the worse for us! Like certain second lieutenants I have known, I might have died in your service. So much the worse for you! And I would have shed a tear for you and for the young men we had been, who had believed in you and now no longer believed in anyone, in the harsh light of a victory half swallowed up in that vast shipwreck."

"Guards," said Monsieur Mongibeaux, "take the prisoner away."

"What, is it all over?" asked the Marshal.

Deathly pale, Maître Isorni stretched out his broad sleeve in a protective gesture.

"Come," he said.

There were a few timid shouts of *"Vive la France!"* and "Swine!"

An Army captain was expelled. The Attorney General barked, "Silence! This is disgraceful!"

Bâtonnier Payen and his colleagues helped the Marshal to stand up. In the light of the photographers' flashbulbs, he drew himself up, pale and haggard. With his gloves in his left hand and his kepi in his right, looking curiously discomposed, the flesh of his face hanging down below his chin, his eyes half-closed, he seemed to stagger slightly.

Bâtonnier Payen told him that the death sentence would not be carried out.

"That's kind of them," he said. And he thought to himself: "I had de Gaulle sentenced to death; now he has had me sentenced. We are quits." Then, feeling suddenly stronger, King Philippe VII turned around, very erect, and walked away bare-headed, with sovereign dignity, between the gendarmes. The last picture we have of him that day shows him from behind. The light from the flashbulbs is gleaming on the snowy hair, on the seven stars on his right arm, on the triple gold wreath around his kepi, on his silk belt, and on the leather shoulder belts of the guards.

He was hustled out of the Palais de Justice so quickly that while he was changing his clothes he forgot his eyeglasses and his heavy silver watch, with its engraving of a lion crowned with the Gallic francisc and two ears of corn. To trick the reporters, a convoy of two police vans with a motorcycle escort was sent off along the road to the Fort of Montrouge. Ten minutes later, an ambulance took Marshal Pétain to the airfield at Villa Coublay, where General de Gaulle's personal Dakota—a princely gesture or a cruel refinement?—was waiting for him, decorated with the Cross of Lorraine. At dawn it took off for Pau with the condemned man, while the police escorted the Attorney General and the judges to their homes.

At a quarter to eleven, he entered the fortress of Le Portalet and was locked in cell No. 5, in which Mandel had once been imprisoned on his orders. The fortress was perched on a rocky crest three thousand feet up, in a gap in the mountains between two walls of granite.

In Paris, when the special editions of the papers came out, it was raining. Big posters announced peace all over the world, together with the verdict of the trial. The sky cleared about midday, but in the evening it rained again. It was a fitting setting for the shade of King Philippe VII, sentenced to death by judges who had sworn loyalty to him, and wandering among his people on the frontiers of love and hate, deceived and dishonored, before coming to rest at last among the bones of his soldiers, in the grim glory of battle.

Index

About the Author

Jules Roy, born in Algeria in 1907, was an officer in the French Army, and then the Air Force, from 1927 to 1953. As bomber commander in the RAF, he received the Distinguished Flying Cross for thirty-seven missions over Germany. In 1953 he resigned from the Army in Indo-China "in order not to participate in a war which he considered unjust and idiotic."

His book *The Battle of Dienbienphu* was described by the *New York Times* as "a classic of its kind, authoritative, eloquent and agonized, and it reads like a Greek tragedy." He has written plays, essays, and novels, and has been a reporter for the Paris weekly *L'Express*.